ART GALLERY OF NEW SOUTH WALES

HANDBOOK

ART
GALLERY
NSW

ART GALLERY OF NEW SOUTH WALES
HANDBOOK

Works of art selected by
Edmund Capon, Director

Descriptive texts written by
Bruce James
with the curatorial staff of the Gallery

National Library of Australia Cataloguing-in-publication data:

Art Gallery of New South Wales.
Art Gallery of New South Wales.

New ed.
Includes index.
ISBN 0 7313 8948 4.

1. Art Gallery of New South Wales – Catalogues. 2. Art – New South
Wales – Sydney – Catalogues. I. Capon, Edmund. II. James, Bruce.
III. Title.

708.99441

Writer Bruce James

Director Edmund Capon

Curators
Anthony Bond, Head Curator, International Art
Victoria Lynn, Curator Contemporary Art
Judy Annear, Senior Curator Photography
Richard Beresford, Senior Curator European Art, pre-1900
Barry Pearce, Head Curator, Australian Art
Hetti Perkins, Curator Aboriginal and Torres Strait Islander Art
Deborah Edwards, Curator Australian Art
Hendrik Kolenberg, Senior Curator Australian Prints and Drawings
Jackie Menzies, Head Curator, Asian Art
Chiaki Ajioka, Curator Japanese Art
Yang Liu, Curator Chinese Art

Word Processing Leanne Primmer

Copy Editor Suzannah Biernoff

Cataloguing and documentation Jesmond Calleja

Photography Jenni Carter, Christopher Snee, Ray Woodbury

Design Mark Boxshall

Film Digital Pre-press Imaging Ltd, Sydney

Printer Samhwa Printing Co., Ltd., Seoul

Distribution Art Gallery of New South Wales, Art Gallery Road,
The Domain NSW 2000 Australia. Telephone: +61 2 9225 1733.

Dimensions are given in centimetres (height x width x depth).
Works of art featured here may not all be on display at any given time.

Cover: Pablo Picasso, *Nude in a rocking chair* 1956.

PRESIDENT'S FOREWORD

The President's Council was established by the Gallery in 1995 under the auspices of the Board of Trustees to offer companies and partnerships, through their chief executives, a personal association with the Art Gallery of New South Wales, one of Australia's leading art institutions.

The President's Council furthers the tradition of corporate partnership and patronage of the Gallery. Its aim is to create a corporate network which attracts and retains for the Gallery the continuing interest and financial support of the business community who offer the Gallery their considerable expertise in marketing, business and financial areas. In the current economic climate, institutions such as the Gallery require continued support from the private sector. For Council members the opportunity to be part of the cultural experience and to introduce their clients, partners and staff to art is an important aspect of the partnership with the Art Gallery of New South Wales.

Funds raised through membership of the President's Council are devoted exclusively to the sponsorship of exhibitions and public programmes, an area for which the Gallery has no financial support other than that raised directly by it through the corporate sector, augmented by exhibition entry fees for a select number of exhibitions. Major exhibitions sponsored by the President's Council include Masterpieces of the Twentieth Century: The Beyeler Collection; Dancing to the Flute; and, most recently, Classic Cézanne.

Each year the Gallery produces some twelve major publications which are distributed nationally and internationally. The *Art Gallery of New South Wales Handbook* is the first major Gallery publication sponsored by the President's Council, a sponsorship which has enabled the Gallery to update important information on the permanent collections for all visitors to the Gallery in the lead-up to the year 2000.

David Gonski
President

INTRODUCTION

The imposing classical façade of the Art Gallery of New South Wales conceals a surprisingly contemporary and varied building with similarly rich and rewarding collections of art from around the world. Many a first-time visitor to the Gallery is struck, after passing through its porticoed entrance and the elegant classical oval foyer, by the immediate confrontation of the clarity of space and travertine of an unashamedly late twentieth-century museum building. It is a bold statement which characterises the happy but uncompromising blend of old and new that is such a feature of this Gallery.

The Art Gallery of New South Wales was formally established in 1874 out of the New South Wales Academy of Art. In that same year five trustees were appointed to administer a vote of 500 pounds annually from the New South Wales Government 'towards the formation of a Gallery of Art'. This grant came from the Education Department of the government and the trustees continued to be responsible to that department until 1971, when it became responsible to the Department of Culture and then, in 1980, to the newly established Ministry for the Arts. When that first Board of Trustees was charged with the duty of purchasing works of art they appointed a Committee of Selection in London but, fortunately, they did have the 'liberty to invest some portion of the money in the colony should it be deemed advisable'. However, those terms evolved into the certainty of attitude and for the first fifty years of its formal existence the Gallery's purchasing of works of art was virtually totally confined to London and Sydney.

This of course did have its rewards. In London the Committee of Selection, among many purchases of dubious distinction, bought a number of quite outstanding works that have become absolute icons in the Gallery's collections: for example, Ford Madox Brown's epic *Chaucer at the Court of Edward III*, the study for which is in the Tate Gallery in London; Poynter's majestic *The visit of the Queen of Sheba to King Solomon*; Alphonse de Neuville's epic *The defence of Rorke's Drift* that was painted in 1880, acquired by the Gallery in 1882 and remains to this day one of our most popular and talked about pictures; and even more obscurely the committee purchased in 1886 the deeply melancholy *The sons of Clovis II*, painted by Evariste Luminais in 1880 and shown to great acclaim at the Paris Salon that same year.

There is no doubt that the most unlikely pictures can attain a special and often bewildering status in museum collections, which reflects more on the taste and attitude of the community than it does on the significance of

the painting as a work of art: *The sons of Clovis II* is an example; so too is Margetson's *The sea hath its pearls* of 1897, a sentimental example of Victorian classicism, acquired in the year it was painted, and which to this day remains a Gallery favourite.

At the same time, in Sydney, the Gallery acquired works, virtually from the easel, that have subsequently become indelible icons in the annals of Australian art. Among them are Streeton's *Fire's on*, painted in 1891 and purchased two years later; McCubbin's *On the wallaby track*, painted in 1896 and acquired the following year; and Roberts' *Shearing at Newstead (The Golden Fleece)*, painted in 1894 and purchased the same year. It could justly be said that the Art Gallery of New South Wales and its early history and collecting policies were a very true reflection of local community attitude and sentiment of the time.

Having begun with a certain flourish in its collecting the Gallery, from the outset of the twentieth century, entered into some decades of hesitant acquisitions activity. There were in those fallow decades up to the end of the Second World War some outstanding Australian acquisitions, with iconic works such as Tom Roberts' *Bailed up*, bought in 1933, Hugh Ramsay's richly priggish *The sisters*, bought in 1921, and the unashamedly Europhile Rupert Bunny's magnificent and wholly indulgent *A summer morning*, painted in 1910 and purchased in 1911; but these were all retrospective purchases and the activity seemed to lack that imagination and risk which entertained the idea of buying works of the day. With the Committee of Selection in London having ceased, even fewer non-Australian works were acquired. Among the few that were made are Fantin-Latour's elegant but unsurprising *Flowers and fruit* of 1866 and, of much greater significance, Pissarro's *Peasants' house, Eragny* of 1887, which demonstrates just how dynamic and lively Pissarro's pointillism could be. Bearing in mind the degree of conservatism in the acquisitions activities of the Gallery when it was acquired in 1935, it must have been a painting that caused some surprises, but no doubt delighted Australian modernists such as Roland Wakelin and Grace Cossington Smith.

There was, without doubt, a much greater sense of purpose to the Gallery's collecting ambitions after the Second World War. In the first two decades of the post-war era pictures as diverse as Bernardo Strozzi's superb

The release of St. Peter, Monet's *Port-Goulphar, Belle Île*, Matthew Smith's *La chemise jaune*, Lambert's wonderfully insouciant portrait of Miss Thea Proctor, Phillips Fox's impressionistic *The ferry*, Grace Cossington Smith's influential *The sock knitter* and Drysdale's *Walls of China* were among the more significant paintings acquired. However, it must be admitted that, for an art museum with aspirations and the broad responsibilities of a state art museum, the pace of acquisitions was still slow and relatively narrow. The idea of buying contemporary art was only reluctantly entertained and largely confined to Australian works, but through the initiative of the then assistant director, Tony Tuckson, and a patron, Dr Stuart Scougall, a strong and positive start on the collection of Aboriginal art was made in the late 1950s and early 1960s.

With the opening of the Captain Cook extensions in 1972, which provided not only much-needed new permanent and temporary display space but also space that had modern facilities and a contemporary attitude, the Gallery assumed a more gregarious role. Not only was the exhibition programme enlivened but so too were the acquisitions. In the 1970s works such as Bonnard's *Self-portrait*, Stella's huge *Khurasan gate variation II* and Bacon's *Study for self-portrait* entered the non-Australian collections and were clear indications of the Gallery stretching its horizons and its aspirations. Since that time the development of the collections has been guided by determined objectives, a more gregarious vision, and the ambition to establish the permanent collections, and indeed the Gallery – through its scholarship, exhibitions and programmes – as an institution of world renown.

In the early 1980s two events combined to contribute greatly towards the growth of the collections: firstly, the creation of formal curatorial departments for Australian, European, Contemporary, Asian art and Photography; and secondly, the establishment of the Art Gallery of New South Wales Foundation. With initial support from the New South Wales Government the Foundation has over the years raised a capital fund, the income from which is directed solely towards the purchase of significant works of art. Its very first purchase, Ernst Ludwig Kirchner's *Three bathers*, set a standard that was followed with the subsequent acquisition of works as varied as Philip Guston's *East Tenth*, Beccafumi's *Madonna and child with the infant*

John the Baptist, Bronzino's glistening portrait of *Duke Cosimo I de'Medici in armour*, as well as outstanding acquisitions for the Asian collections, of which the most recent has been a monumental, sixth-century Chinese figure of the Buddha.

The Foundation was one of the Gallery's first serious initiatives to raise funds for acquisitions from the private sector. Its impact was felt immediately and effectively, and not only in enhancing the Gallery's acquisitions budget. In the cause of fund-raising, the objectives must be clarified and the necessities impressed, all of which helps to more firmly position the Gallery, its role and indeed its value, in the public mind. Thus, in the wake of the establishment of the Foundation, private patronage, particularly in respect of acquisitions, has played a very much more significant part in the Gallery's activities.

In recent years the European collections have been enormously enriched through gifts such as the James Fairfax collection of Old Masters which has, thus far, included major paintings by Jacob van Ruisdael, François Boucher, Peter Paul Rubens, Claude Lorrain and Canaletto; the Art Gallery Society's purchase of Prospero Fontana's imposing altarpiece depicting the Deposition; and William Bowmore's gift of Nattier's elegant *Portrait of Madame de la Porte*. The Contemporary collections have been similarly expanded through the Mervyn Horton Bequest, which has funded the purchase of major works by, among others, Kiefer, Kounellis, Clemente, Auerbach and Kapoor; while the development of the Asian collections has in recent years been similarly dependent upon private benefaction, particularly the Sternberg funds, Ken and Yasuko Myer, and the distinguished Sydney collector of Chinese Imperial porcelain, Hepburn Myrtle. The establishment of collection benefactor programmes for specific aspects has provided the means for individual expressions of interest and has been especially helpful to the development of the Contemporary Australian and the Photography collections. Not surprisingly, the Australian collections are supported through a wide range of gifts from local patrons and collectors, and the Art Gallery Society. This Gallery may lay justifiable claim to the best and most broadly representative collection of Australian art – historical, contemporary and Aboriginal; it is a claim to pre-eminence that we seek to retain.

Collecting policies must, like the collections they enshrine, change and evolve. Attitude, sentiment, opportunity, availability, curatorial expertise, public interest, funding – all are considerations that have, or might have, an impact upon a museum's collecting activities. With such effective foundations this Gallery is now enhancing, above all, its contemporary and its Asian representations as areas of special concern which reflect the attitudes and interests that are very much characteristics of modern Australia and Sydney in particular.

The pace and scope of acquisitions activity have, in recent years, been enhanced. It is a reflection of the current condition of this Gallery as, with the advent of major exhibitions and an exhibition programme of some thirty-five events a year, an enhanced and wide-ranging series of public support programmes, increased financial self-reliance and an increased expectation to fulfil a broader public role, circumstances have imposed new demands upon us. No longer can we hide behind our curatorial and scholarly veils in the pretence that research and learning are our only interests: our audiences are an absolutely fundamental part of the dynamic of this institution. A visit to an art museum these days involves much more than an engagement with the work of art: it means definitive and informing interpretation, a visit to the shop, a visit to the restaurant, probably at least one special exhibition and, perhaps, a return in the evening to a lecture, film, concert or some other special event. All these things have combined to redefine the image of the traditional art museum, but such public services and responsibilities, and the lure of the 'event', must not divert from the care and development of the collections.

It is the collections that *are* the museum. This *Handbook*, selective though it must be, introduces those collections, illustrates many of their highlights and, happily, many of their unexpected, even eccentric, moments.

Edmund Capon
Director

Western Collection

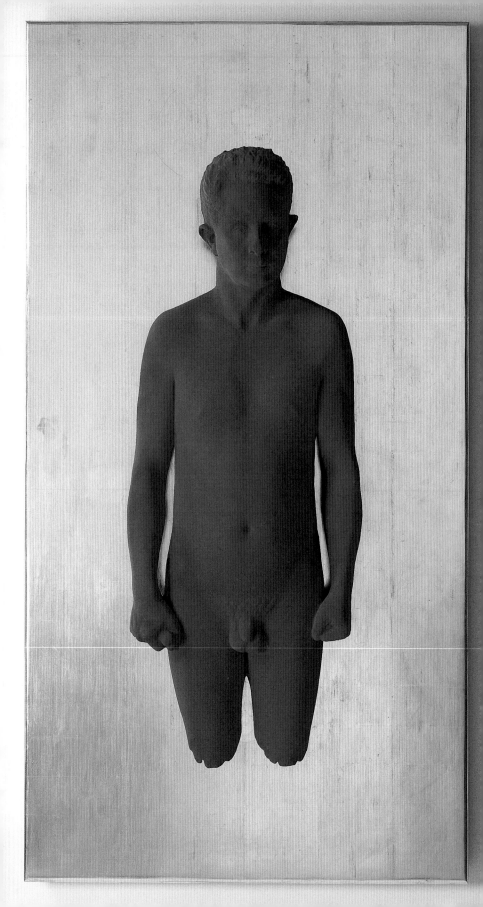

Western Collection

The Western Department was formed in 1995 by bringing together the European collection of pre-1900, as well as nineteenth- and twentieth-century masters, with the Contemporary Department and the Photography Department. The assimilation of these created a department that is broadly international in its scope.

In the early years the emphasis of the European collection was on British Academic and French Salon painters, and it was not until well into the twentieth century that major nineteenth-century modern artists were acquired. The Gallery's Old Master collection has in recent years benefited greatly from the generosity of James Fairfax, who began to donate works of Dutch, French and Italian painters from the seventeenth and eighteenth centuries. To these have been added a small but impressive group of Italian Mannerist paintings by Bronzino, Beccafumi and dell'Abate. All these works hang in the splendid Old Courts.

Twentieth-century British art occupies a significant place in the collection, and the representation of Modernist traditions has now been extended to include major European figures such as Bonnard, Braque, Picasso, Kirchner and Beckmann.

In 1984 the estate of Mervyn Horton came to the Gallery, dedicated to the purchase of non-Australian contemporary art. Approval was also given for the Bicentennial wing, designed for the exhibition of contemporary art. This became the basis for a strong contemporary collection, with major international artists such as Yves Klein, Richard Deacon and Francesco Clemente all represented by major examples. These works are displayed on level 2, alongside leading Australian artists of the same generation.

Photography is displayed along with painting and drawing in the collection galleries, where the importance of photography to twentieth-century art is clearly demonstrated. Regular exhibitions of photography and works on paper are also mounted on level 2 and the upper level galleries.

Sano di Pietro
Italy, 1405–1481
Madonna and Child with Saints Jerome, John the Baptist,
Bernardino and Bartholemew 15th century
gold leaf and tempera on panel, 60.5 x 43.2
Gift of John Fairfax and Sons Ltd to commemorate the 140th anniversary
of the founding of the *Sydney Morning Herald* 1971
151.1971

With its gold-ground and tempera technique, this devotional altarpiece is an
example of the international Gothic style that survived in Siena well into the
fifteenth century. Noted for the richness and variety of his palette, Sano di
Pietro was a successful master who ran a busy workshop in that city. He seems
to have been familiar with Venetian religious painting, a certain Byzantine
preciousness being part of his repertoire. A number of Sano's subjects focused
on the life and works of San Bernardino, a controversial local saint the painter
had known personally. It was Bernardino who conceived the device of the Holy
Name in the Sun, an emblem in which twelve solar rays represented twelve
articles of faith promulgated by the Apostles. For this doctrinal innovation he
was charged with heresy. In this panel, Bernardino's participation is restricted to
that of an auxiliary figure. Appropriately, it is the blue-mantled Virgin and her
delightful infant who hold our attention.

Francesco di Simone Ferrucci
Italy, 1437–1493
Madonna and Child c. 1480s
marble, 71.2 x 55.9
Purchased 1971
125.1971

The sentimentality and modesty of this relief reflect changing patterns of devotion in Italy at the time of the first flowering of the Renaissance. The ethereal, queenly Madonnas of medieval art have been superseded by a more human, and altogether more accessible conception of the Virgin. Here is a Madonna to be approached, perhaps kissed, and a Holy Child to be adored. Ferrucci trained in the famous Florentine workshop of Verrocchio, perhaps side by side with the young Leonardo da Vinci. Certainly this marble manifests the essential sweetness that Leonardo elaborated on the basis of Verrocchio's manner. Though an artist of the second rank, Ferrucci surpasses himself in this work. The modulations of drapery, the naturalistic rendering of the figures – especially the rotundity of the infant Christ – and the attention given to Mary's look of dreamy reverie: all these contribute to a work of art that is at once sacred and secular.

Ambrosius Benson
Southern Netherlands, d. 1550
*Portraits of Cornelius Duplicius de Scheppere and his wife,
Elizabeth Donche* c. 1540
diptych: oil on panel, 30.1 x 54 overall
Gift of James Fairfax 1994
301.1994.a–b

Although born in Lombardy, the principal activity of this Netherlandish
painter and portraitist was in Bruges, the northern city which supplied his
audience and his livelihood. A prolific author of devotional panels in the
tradition of Jan van Eyck, Gerard David and even Hugo van der Goes, Benson
had a miniaturist's capability and love of detail. His religious images – by far
the bulk of his output and frequently made for export to France and Italy –
possess a note of introspection which carries over to his secular efforts. In the
case of this flawlessly preserved pair of pendant portraits, the sitters seem as
alert to their own interior imaginings as to any dialogue with each other or the
external world. Small in scale, they were designed primarily for ease of storage,
transport and display. Benson's typically warm palette is well demonstrated,
especially in the clothing.

Domenico Beccafumi
Italy, 1484–1551
Madonna and Child with the infant John the Baptist c. 1542
oil on panel, 92 x 69
Art Gallery of New South Wales Foundation Purchase 1992
231.1992

Reversing the pose of Ferrucci's relief, this marvel of mannerist painting
also shows the new directions of Italian art in the sixteenth century. With its
mysterious luminosity and boldly defined figures, it suggests statuary viewed
by candle-light. Beccafumi has paid homage to Michelangelo in the volumetric
forms of the Madonna and her draperies and the *contrapposto* of her pose.
For the suppleness of flesh and softness of atmosphere, however, Beccafumi has
turned to Leonardo's testing *sfumato* technique. This imbues his altarpiece with
a theatricality that is utterly in accord with the mannerist aesthetic in which
Beccafumi was steeped throughout his long career. As a master trained in Siena,
a city dedicated to the Virgin, Beccafumi produced innumerable versions of this
subject. In this case, the result is a painting of exceptional poetic power.

Agnolo Bronzino
Italy, 1503–1572
Duke Cosimo I de' Medici in armour early 1540s
oil on panel, 86 x 67
Art Gallery of New South Wales Foundation Purchase 1996
78.1996

Though a sense of surface frigidity characterises everything Bronzino produced, emotional heat underwrites his style. As a pupil and adopted son of perhaps the greatest and strangest of mannerist painters, Jacopo Pontormo, Bronzino graduated to artistic maturity with impeccable credentials in that consciously artificial style. That he asserted his own artistic personality, albeit through a steely formality of technique, testifies to the originality of Bronzino's vision. In this magnificent portrait of his principal patron – a work that exists in many replicas and copies – the painter displays a perfectionism it is hard not to think obsessive. Riven with reflections, highlights and shadows, Cosimo's armour alone is an article of transfixing interest: almost reason enough for the painting. It was Bronzino's habit to concentrate on details of costume, jewellery and decoration, to the extent of conceiving the faces of his ducal sitters as polished stones. Apart from this authoritative example, another celebrated version of the work is found in the Uffizi Gallery in Florence.

Nicolò dell' Abate
Italy, c. 1509 – c. 1571
Portrait of a gentleman with a falcon c. 1548–50
oil on canvas, 107.5 x 84.5
Art Gallery of New South Wales Foundation Purchase 1991
167.1991

Nicolò dell' Abate was an Emilian painter active in Modena, Bologna and
ultimately the Fontainebleau of Henry II of France, where he worked with his
compatriot, the equally gifted Primaticcio. He was associated with, rather than
central to, the mannerist movement which was virtually a European court style
in the first half of the sixteenth century. It was in the newly independent genre
of landscape that dell' Abate made his most enduring contribution to the history
of Western art. His classically inspired landscapes are staffed by elegant figures
and typified by pastoral themes pre-empting those of Poussin and Claude. In
portraiture he was a canny observer of the interior life of his subjects, managing
to suggest something of the uniqueness of their psychology. The north Italian
aristocrat portrayed here has an almost indecisive air at odds with his masterful
pose and sporty regalia. Dell' Abate clearly empathised with this equivocal
quality, which he so subtly translates into paint.

Prospero Fontana
Italy, 1512–1597
Deposition 1563
oil on panel, 193 x 116.5
Purchased with funds provided by the Art Gallery Society of New South Wales 1994
219.1994

In this spectacular, if formulaic, altarpiece the decorativeness and artificiality of mannerism can be observed giving ground to the more robust dynamics of the proto-baroque style that emerged in Fontana's native Bologna during this period. The artist occupied an important place in Bolognese cultural affairs, while his daughter and pupil, Lavinia, established a significant reputation as a portraitist. Indeed, her fame eclipsed his for a time. Although the figures in this work derive from the standard Renaissance repertoire, their compression and colouristic variety are Fontana's own. He was especially adept at conveying a mood of heightened emotion within a limited pictorial space. Even the airborne angels bearing the instruments of the Passion are cramped by the ominous cross. Fontana's intention, fully realised, is to force the viewer into direct contemplation of the physical suffering of Christ and its grievous effect on the sacred assembly around him.

Peter Paul Rubens
Flanders, 1577–1640
Constantine investing his son, Crispus, with command of the fleet
1622
oil on panel, 37.5 x 30.2
Gift of James Fairfax 1993
483.1993

Rubens is widely considered the most important artist of the baroque period.
His range, invention and energy as a painter are as apparent in his sketches as
in his finished works. This example of the former illustrates a story from the life
of the Roman Emperor Constantine. Crispus, Constantine's eldest son, is shown
receiving command of the imperial fleet before the campaign against Licinius.
This is accomplished under the aegis of the Goddess of Victory and Neptune,
the Lord of the Sea. Despite such unpromising narrative material, Rubens
avoids bombast, delivering instead a credible tableau in which all participants,
even the allegorical ones, boast the ruddy blush of life. The dynamism of
Rubens's every brush stroke prevails over the provisional nature of this format
to produce a wonderfully complete composition. Nonetheless, it would have
been worked up from a sketch to a full-scale cartoon, only then progressing to
its final form as a woven tapestry for Louis XIII of France.

Jan van Bijlert
Netherlands, 1597/98–1671
Girl with a flute c. 1630
oil on canvas, 108 x 85.8
Purchased 1967
003.1967

A Dutch painter working wholly within
the tradition of Caravaggio, van Bijlert
favoured such low-life settings as taverns,
hostelries and brothels for his human and
still-life subjects. Most of his pictures, in
the fashion of the time, come supplied
with an allegorical or moralistic overlay.
Girl with a flute is a good example,
dressing up seventeenth-century erotica
as a personification of Music. The
woman is either promiscuous or a prostitute: her beckoning
smile and partially exposed breast are contrivances of seduction, both painterly
and sexual. Displayed in a candle-lit interior, this painted coquette would have
quickened as well as embodied the pulse of life. The Pushkin Museum owns
a companion to van Bijlert's picture: a man plucking a lute.

Bernardo Strozzi
Italy, 1581–1644
The release of St Peter c. 1635
oil on canvas, 124.5 x 113
Purchased 1966
001.1966

Bernardo Strozzi's experience as
a Capuchin monk only partly
explains the certainties presented
for contemplation in this masterful canvas. Far more telling
are the formal conventions of
baroque painting that underscore
its every detail, from its diagonal
dynamic to its brazen colouring.
This work can almost be read
as a dictionary of Counter-
Reformation precepts. *The release of St Peter* responds to the Catholic doctrines
that reinvigorated European art at the beginning of the seventeenth century.
These centred on a call to arms to artists for greater realism and a more directly
rendered spirituality. The angel delivering Peter from his bonds is depicted
with the naturalism of an artisan going about a chore, while the saint himself
is shown in glassy-eyed ecstasy – a favourite condition of baroque painting.
Strozzi divides his pigment into areas of flashy impasto and delicate glazing.
Flesh, fabrics, feathers and furry tufts of hair are indicated in brilliant passages
of *alla prima* painting.

Claude Gellée (called Le Lorrain)
France/Italy, 1600–1682
Pastoral landscape c. 1636
oil on copper, 27.9 x 34.7
Gift of James Fairfax 1992
208.1992

Known as the Diamond Claude by virtue of its faceted format, this exquisite
painting on copper is one of a clutch of such works executed by the celebrated
classicist. Claude Gellée was born in Lorrain, but spent most of a productive
life in his beloved Italy, especially Rome and its pastoral environs exemplified
in the Campagna. Initially inspired by northern artists active in that city,
Elsheimer and Bril for example, Claude became fluent in the idealising vocabulary
of Bolognese painters such as Domenichino. Behind his Arcadian landscapes
lay a reliance on forms and relationships found in nature, especially the varied
effects of natural light which are his hallmark. *Pastoral landscape*, with its
lakeside setting, predicts the great seaport subjects of his maturity – works
that profoundly influenced the romantic Turner. Claude's wider influence on
subsequent landscape traditions in Europe is inestimable.

Matthias Stomer
Netherlands, c. 1600–1672?
Mucius Scaevola in the presence of Lars Porsenna
early 1640s
oil on canvas, 152.6 x 205.7
Purchased 1970
004.1970

In the dazzling comet's tail of painters called the *Caravaggisti* – the admirers
of Caravaggio who kept alive his flame for more than a century – Matthias
Stomer stands out for his considered temperament and cool execution. Almost
an academic of the movement, though never an imitative hack, Stomer built a
body of work on the basis of subjects like this. Antiquity in general and Roman
history in particular were his primary source material, reflecting a classicism
which had little to do with Caravaggio's own almost exclusively biblical interests.
Stomer's *Mucius Scaevola in the presence of Lars Porsenna* could be seen to
anticipate the high moral tone, and consequent sober rendition, found in the
works of later neoclassical figures such as David. This painting, after all, posits
a test of faith by fire within a resolutely imperial context – precisely David's
territory. There is a poorly preserved variant in Messina, datable to this Dutch-
born painter's Sicilian period.

Jacob van Ruisdael
Netherlands, c. 1628–1682
*Wooded hillside with a
view of Castle Bentheim*
early 1660s
oil on canvas, 61 x 75
Gift of James Fairfax 1991
256.1991

It is hard to escape the
melancholy which imbues
this painting. Indeed, a
significant part of the appeal
of van Ruisdael to his many
English and Continental
collectors was just this sense of sad foreboding, of abandonment and uneasy
calm. Such works were a source of inspiration, and affirmation, to a later
generation of romantic painters. Constable was particularly taken with van
Ruisdael's work, as were the artists of the Barbizon School. He was not simply
the leading Dutch landscapist of the seventeenth century, but the most forward-
looking, one might say modern, of all northern artists of his day. Van Ruisdael
invested his compositions with something more than a spirit of place: it is
possible to read his paintings as equivalents of mental states. *Wooded hillside
with a view of Castle Bentheim*, a site he was drawn to paint on twelve occasions, is gloomy in the extreme. Yet through the shadowy foreground and steep,
uninviting track, the castle itself, backlit by a burst of splendid clouds, rises like
an apparition of hope.

Frans van Mieris the Elder
Netherlands, 1635–1681
A cavalier early 1660s
oil on panel, 19.3 x 15.3
Gift of James Fairfax 1993
484.1993

Not technically a portrait, this tiny genre piece
pushes the notion of display to an extreme.
The cavalier's material affluence is exhibited
unmistakably; so too is the artist's virtuosity.
The work dazzles, and was meant to. Dutch
painters of this period, which has been called
a golden age, were anxious to impress with their brilliance in oil-painting
technique. Their clients were no less keen to appreciate such tricks of the
painterly trade as meticulous verisimilitude, even *trompe-l'œil*, and elaborate
finish. Interestingly, Renaissance prototypes (mediated through Rembrandt)
form the structural basis of the work. Titian and Raphael both exploited
compositions in which a richly sleeved figure turns into three-quarter view
from a balustrade. These exemplars of Italian portraiture were widely imitated
in northern art. In this instance the artist has probably depicted himself.
A companion piece of his wife exists in Basel. Van Mieris the Elder acquired
his skills of illusionism from his master, Gerrit Dou, Rembrandt's first pupil.

Canaletto
Italy, 1697–1768
Piazza San Marco, Venice 1730s–40s
oil on canvas, 66 x 116.8
Gift of James Fairfax 1996
302.1996

Architectonic in construction and architectural in content, this magnificent *veduta*, or view, sparkles with the very light of Venice. This was subject matter tackled time and again by Canaletto, probably with the aid of a *camera obscura*; yet despite the artist's concern for accuracy, this painting is nowhere dull or perfunctory in its attention to detail. Having worked as a scenographic artist in the Italian perspectival tradition, and as the son of such an artist, Canaletto was ideally placed to become the greatest recorder of the physical glories of the city-state called *La Serenissima*. This is not to say that the human glory of Venice is ignored. Canaletto, here as elsewhere, populated the Piazza with a dizzying and deliciously executed array of merchants, friars, wigged officials, masked revellers, mysterious women, children and dogs. If the majority of such views were intended for consumption by English and other tourists, this has not been to the detriment of their remarkable artistic quality.

François Boucher

France, 1703–70
Portrait of Madame Boucher
c. 1744–45
oil on canvas, 34 x 28 oval
Gift of James Fairfax 1992
118.1992

With his pupil Fragonard, François Boucher is rightly held to epitomise the rococo sensibility in French eighteenth-century painting. Refined in intelligence as much as in taste, Boucher's art is a celebration of surface, not superficiality. His love of silks, satins, velvets, furs and brocades is exceeded only by his devotion to the pearly properties of youthful skin, especially female skin. Whether painting the mythical subjects that characterise his larger commissions, or, as here, an intimate portrait of his wife, Marie-Jeanne Buseau, Boucher brought to the task an attention to detail and a sense of delight that are definitively rococo. This painting wittily, and not at either's expense, juxtaposes the very different beauties of a charming woman and her lapdog. The latter is a canine inclusion not without sexual connotation in the iconography of the period – though Boucher can hardly be thought to portray his spouse in the role of teasing mistress. The slightly generic cast of her face, echoing those of the nymphs and shepherdesses prolifically rendered by this artist, is attributable to the fact that Marie-Jeanne was Boucher's model for almost two decades.

Jean-Marc Nattier

France, 1685–1766
Madame de la Porte 1754
oil on canvas, 82 x 65.5
Gift of William Bowmore 1992
119.1992

Recently established as the portrait of a fellow painter's wife, this image is the last word in high fashion. The sitter's ensemble, overstated for any but an occasion of high formality, capitalises on a rumpled sash winding its attention-seeking way around Madame de la Porte's petite torso. Her overly bright eyes and eggshell skin contribute to an effect of artificiality. Although Nattier was not capable of Boucher's moments of naturalism, this image marks a shift in that direction, and away from the far more formally baroque language of his state portraits. In keeping with the high value placed on harmonious social relations in this age of Enlightenment, the present sitter regards the spectator with a look of courtesy mingled with candour. She is confident, yet not condescending. Her trust in Nattier is clear and clearly reciprocated.

Hubert Robert
France, 1733–1808
An extensive landscape near Paris 1781
oil on panel, 61.5 x 72.5
Gift of James Fairfax 1995
177.1995

Hubert Robert is one of the quiet voices of French painting. In his youth he
worked and studied with Fragonard, a louder talent by comparison, as both
artists mastered the subtleties of a shared rococo style. In 1761 they travelled
together to southern Italy, the wellspring of Robert's essentially classicising
project. Italian view-painters such as Panini and Piranesi authorised his attraction to ancient sites and antiquarian subjects, alerting him to the enduring
possibilities of the fragmentary tradition. Even in his native France, Robert's
landscapes are unmistakably classical in tenor. The Roman Campagna insinuates
itself into this otherwise descriptive scene of the countryside near Paris. Though
it lacks anything so imposing as architectural ruins or sculptural wreckage, one
senses a powerful note of nostalgia in the work. Even so, few views by Robert
are as uncomplicated or as fresh as this, the airiness of the scene prefiguring
nineteenth-century innovations in French landscape painting. The artist shown
at work on the left is conceivably Robert himself.

John Constable
England, 1776–1837
Landscape with goatherd and goats 1823
oil on canvas, 53.3 x 44.5
Gift of the National Art Collections Fund 1961
OB1.1961

The faithful copying of works of art, usually famous ones, by earlier masters
was accepted practice for apprentice painters from the Renaissance to the
nineteenth century. Considered a vital part of visual education, it often implied
homage as well. This is the case with John Constable's loving replication of
Claude's *Landscape with goatherd and goats*. The English painter took pains
to evoke the spirit of his French original, not simply to imitate its surface
appearance. Thus the Constable could not be mistaken for the Claude despite
adhering to it in every important respect of colouring and composition. The
result is an imaginative effort fascinating on its own terms. Constable wrote to
his wife, Maria, at the time, 'I have a little Claude in hand, a Grove scene of
great beauty and I wish to make a nice copy from it to be useful to me as long
as I live... It contains all that I wish to do in landscape'. Seldom in art history
has a prophecy of such modesty proven so extravagantly true: Constable went
on to redefine the landscape conventions of his period.

John Gibson
1790–1866
Narcissus after 1829
marble, 86 height
Purchased 1892
1220

A protégé of John Flaxman, John Gibson gravitated to Rome in 1818, becoming a pupil of the grandest of all neoclassical sculptors, Antonio Canova. Gibson's style was determined by his admiration for, and emulation of, the prototypical masterpieces of Greek and Roman statuary. A resulting academic quality, perfectly in accord with contemporary expectations of taste, became his sculptural signature. Though he experimented on occasion with polychromatic techniques and unusual materials, Gibson's preferred medium was marble, with its traditional associations of purity and chasteness. In this version of the Narcissus legend, inspired by a Roman youth gazing into a fountain, the sculptor transformed an everyday sight into a vision of antiquity. The subject's hairstyle and footwear are dutifully quoted from classical sources.

Ford Madox Brown
England, 1821–93
Chaucer at the court of Edward III 1847–51
oil on canvas, 372 x 296
Purchased 1876
703

Though never officially a member of the Pre-Raphaelite Brotherhood, this colleague of Dante Gabriel Rossetti and William Morris was, by inclination and practice, sympathetic to the realist ambitions of the movement. Born in Calais, Madox Brown studied in Belgium and was influenced by the German Nazarene painters in Rome before his first liaison with Pre-Raphaelitism. Working with pure colours and clear contours on a dazzling white ground, and carefully composing his subjects from well-lit life, Brown achieved a sense of pageantry in this tableau. Its lower portions are especially immediate, an extensive cleaning having revealed the glorious condition of the original paintwork. Though Brown began his original composition in Rome, the final canvas was begun in London in 1847, and completed in 1851. Rosetti modelled for Chaucer, while others of the Pre-Raphaelite circle appear as supernumeraries. It was Brown's desire in this, surely one of the greatest modern British paintings in Australia, to encapsulate an historical moment: the birth of the English language in the person of Chaucer. The Tate Gallery in London possesses a study for the work, exact in detail but much reduced in scale.

Harriet Hosmer
United States
of America,
1830–1908
Beatrice Cenci
1857
marble,
44.1 x 106.3 x 43.8
Purchased 1892
1221

Neoclassicism produced a significant number of women sculptors, many of whom were American by birth. Among them, Harriet Hosmer enjoyed perhaps the greatest celebrity, entertaining dignitaries and connoisseurs in her Roman atelier with the practised aplomb of a *grand maître*. A pupil of John Gibson, her work was widely collected, often on the basis of an interest in her gender as much as her considerable professional merits. Hosmer adapted continental neoclassicism to a personal vision steeped in the classical philosophies of a democratic nation. Capable of producing work on a large scale and to specific order, she was especially proficient in the execution of public monuments. Her smaller works were frequently issued in multiples to accommodate demand. Among her most popular was *Beatrice Cenci*, which exists in several versions.

Eugène Boudin
France, 1825–98
The beach 1864
oil on panel, 30.9 x 47.1
Purchased 1926
1123

Honfleur, Le Havre and the more fashionable Trouville are among the handful of French coastal sites celebrated in the art of Eugène Boudin. A devotee of seascape, it is proper to refer to him as a marine painter. Yet Boudin is really a painter of air. In everything he produced air predominates. It fills his tiny compositions like the wind filling the crinolines of his female figures. Encouraged by Jean Millet, he trained for a time with Isabey, though neither of these established figures could be said to have formed his style. Indeed in some ways, Boudin was more influential than influenced. Monet, for example, revered him. Boudin's impressionist affiliation was so strong that he exhibited at the first of the movement's group shows in 1874.

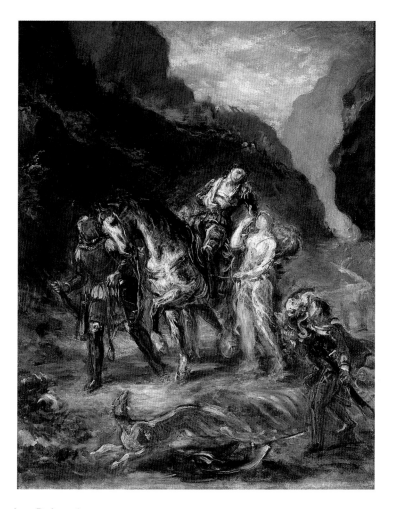

Eugène Delacroix
France, 1798–1863
Angelica and the wounded Medoro c. 1860
oil on canvas, 81 x 65.1
Purchased with funds provided by the Art Gallery Society of New South Wales 1996
443.1996

Representing a romantic prelude to certain aspects of impressionist technique,
this composition from the inestimable Delacroix has a special place in the
collection. It links the formidable tradition of history painting to the subtler
project of modernity. Here is an object less for instruction than delectation.
Almost athletic in handling, the paint is applied in speedy flourishes typical
of Delacroix's late manner. Though the works of his youth and maturity were
frequently large in scale, he produced smaller easel paintings and sketches
throughout his career. *Angelica and the wounded Medoro* is a literary subject
he tackled more than once, though rarely with the freedom and spontaneity
of this version. Like Picasso, Delacroix was a ceaseless re-inventor of his own
forms, which reflected his inner state at any given time.

Edward Burne-Jones
England, 1833–98
The fight: St George kills the dragon VI 1866
oil on canvas, 105.4 x 130.8
Gift of Arthur Moon KC in memory of his mother, Emma, born in Sydney in 1860,
the daughter of John de Villers Lamb 1950
8536

More commonly an excuse for high drama and dynamic design, the legend of
St George inspired in Edward Burne-Jones a typically lyrical response. This
image presents the viewer with something akin to a dream. The knight is hardy
enough, dispatching his beastly (but undernourished) enemy with assurance;
yet this St George is a creature of the mind. The blurry *sfumato* of the forms –
Burne-Jones had yet to perfect his brittle manner – and the elegance of the poses
encourage reverie, not alarm. Burne-Jones was the least ideological of the
Pre-Raphaelites, yet the most enduring, always keeping faith with a moonlit
world of bloodless damsels and epicene saints. Henry James called the Burne-
Jones type 'pale, sickly and wan'. No progressive, the English artist loathed the
impressionists, preferring their symbolist contemporaries, whom he admired
and greatly influenced.

Henri Fantin-Latour
France, 1836–1904
Flowers and fruit 1866
oil on canvas, 71.8 x 58.4
Purchased 1923
4538

Neither his considerable number of mythological paintings, nor his many portraits, have eclipsed in interest Fantin-Latour's fabulous flower pieces. Occupying a contradictory position as modern productions deeply inflected by tradition, they seem to us the most fastidiously crafted of all paintings to have attracted the approval of the impressionists and their circle. Fantin-Latour was by no means an impressionist himself, and some of his fantasy pictures tend more towards symbolism; yet even at its most academic, his touch has the evanescence, the softness, we associate with someone like Manet. Indeed, Manet was his friend and intellectual collaborator. One of Fantin-Latour's most famous canvases records a gathering of artists in Manet's Batignolles studio. The still life reproduced here is the embodiment of elegance. The flowers, freshly picked and perfectly formed, have been set with easeful order in their vase. The opened fruit and table utensils suggest a breakfast piece. Ordinary enough as individual items, as an ensemble their arrangement alludes to ritual.

James Tissot
France, 1836–1902
The widower 1876
oil on canvas, 116 x 74.3
Gift of Sir Colin and Lady Anderson 1939
6697

Though not without a mawkish quality, this atypical work by the French painter James Tissot bespeaks an essential sincerity. The identity of the father clinging so morosely to his child is not known. They may simply have been models. The setting, however, can be identified as the garden of Tissot's London residence in St John's Wood, a property that later passed to his colleague, the 'Olympian' painter Alma-Tadema. *The widower* has the moralising overtones of a Victorian problem picture, and it may be to the English taste for such images that Tissot was deliberately appealing. His liaison with a divorcee – a woman he frequently painted and clearly adored – placed him beyond the pale of conventional society, and beyond its patronage. It is almost tempting to see Tissot himself as the widower of the title, a man unhappily denied his mate. Technically, the work is an exercise in painterly probity: Tissot's rendering of vegetation, fabric and flesh is impressive.

Evariste Luminais
France, 1822–96
The sons of Clovis II 1880
oil on canvas, 190.7 x 275.8
Purchased 1886
712

This demonstration of parental discipline of the Merovingian period remains shocking more than a century after its completion. It says much for the grotesquery of nineteenth-century Salon painting, of which it is so spectacular an example, that *The sons of Clovis II* is still a collection favourite. Alarmed by her sons' rebellion against their absent father, King Clovis, their mother – the regent Sainte Bathilde – has their tendons cut before sending them, immobilised, downstream on a barge to their fate. Though Luminais foreshadows the salvation of the malefactors in the distant shape of a Benedictine monastery, he is clearly more concerned with their present gruesome predicament. His great success with this painting in the Paris Salon of 1880 was not repeated, its cadaverous sensationalism proving a hard act to follow.

George Watts
England, 1817–1904
Alice 1883
oil on canvas, 67 x 53.4
Gift of the Executors of the Estate of the late G. F. Watts 1907
984

From 1843 to 1847 George Watts lived in Italy, studying firsthand the monumental masterpieces of the Renaissance, most notably Michelangelo, Tintoretto
and the Venetian colourists. He sought to achieve in his work a marriage of
sculptural solidity and painterly warmth. Both a painter and sculptor, he
regarded artistic ambidexterity as a duty. Many of the allegorical paintings
Watts produced are bombastic in scale and abstruse in meaning. Nonetheless,
his Victorian public welcomed these often clumsy conceptions as faultless
expressions of genius, going so far as to accord him the title of the English
Michelangelo. Watts portrayed most of the men and women of culture of his
day, amassing a virtual anthology of English society. The ravishing *Alice* shows
him at his understated best. The sitter has been captured in a state of reverie
undisturbed by interruptions from the outside world, and spared the histrionic
excesses more characteristic of this painter's style.

Alphonse de Neuville
France, 1835–85
The defence of Rorke's Drift 1880
oil on canvas, 180.9 x 301.4
Purchased 1882
735

The so-called Zulu War came at the moment of greatest British imperial presence in South Africa. Though understood differently today, in 1879 – the year of the event depicted in de Neuville's famous canvas – the violent exchange was seen in terms of Britain's rightful defence of its own colonial prestige. Rorke's Drift was a small outpost on the banks of the Buffalo River in Natal Province. A large Zulu force, having slaughtered around 900 troops and native levies at nearby Isandlhwana, set upon the eighty soldiers of the Warwickshire Regiment

stationed at Rorke's Drift. The defenders managed to hold off their attackers, usually characterised as an undisciplined horde, in a bloody hand-to-hand battle of Boys' Own proportions. The subsequent awarding of eleven Victoria Crosses confirmed the heroic dimension of the skirmish, though it hardly explains the interest of a Parisian Salon painter in this quintessentially English subject. De Neuville based his pre-cinematic version of events on military reports and survivors' accounts.

Frederick Leighton
England, 1830–96
Cymon and Iphigenia 1884
oil on canvas, 163 x 328
Purchased 1976
210.1976

Not only president of the Royal Academy but a Peer of the Realm, Frederick
Leighton occupied a uniquely privileged place in the artistic and social establishment of Victorian England. The first of many major paintings he exhibited
at the Academy was purchased by Queen Victoria herself – an unbeatable
beginning to a lifetime of official reward and international recognition. Leighton's
taste, like that of his audience, was for ceremonial arrangements of beautifully
draped figures in classical surroundings. The contemporary realities of industrial
England made no appearance in his work, which is unashamedly nostalgic and
idealising. The languorous splendour of *Cymon and Iphigenia* – the tale of a
raw youth brought to moral excellence by the revelation of feminine beauty –
perfectly expresses the technical finesse and intense eroticism of Leighton's
style. Iphigenia's extraordinary undulations betray a sensuous sensibility quite
as much as the artist's obligatory scrutiny of classical statuary. The direct source
of the narrative is Boccaccio's *Decameron*, in which the well-born and handsome
young Galesus was renamed Cymon – meaning beast – on account of his
brutishness. On a mild afternoon in May, Cymon chanced upon the sleeping
Iphigenia, sensing at once that she was 'the loveliest object that any mortal
being had ever seen'. Falling instantly in love, he became a lifelong devotee of
beauty and philosophy.

Edward Poynter
England, 1836–1919
The visit of the Queen of Sheba to King Solomon 1884–90
oil on canvas, 234.5 x 350.5
Purchased 1892
898

When contemplating this picture it is useful to bear in mind that the second half
of the nineteenth century was a period remarkable for archaeological researches
and discoveries, especially by English expeditions. The British Museum was a
treasure house of antiquities increasingly valued by artists as a reference library.
Egypt and the Middle East replaced Greece and Italy as the focus of curiosity.
The visit of the Queen of Sheba to King Solomon can be contextualised against
a craze for orientalist narratives in literature, music and visual art. The wildly
composite architectural system of Solomon's temple is reprised in the frame,
which bridges the temporal and spatial distance between viewer and subject.
The artist has been so obsessed with the accuracy of his details, however, that
the figures seem somewhat doll-like. Trained in Paris under Gleyre, Poynter was
at heart a Salonist for whom artistry resided in weight of detail rather than
dramatic synthesis.

Vincent van Gogh
Netherlands, 1853–90
Head of a peasant 1884
oil on canvas, 39.4 x 30.2
Art Gallery of New South Wales Foundation Purchase 1990
211.1990

Without the obsessive regime of self-instruction and direct observation from
nature that typified his Nuenen period, it is doubtful we would know Vincent
van Gogh today. A late starter, the almost 30-year-old van Gogh made up for
lost artistic time in a fever of drawing and painting that culminated in his first
masterpiece, *The potato eaters*, finished in 1885. Between December 1884 and
the completion of this rustic nocturne, he produced forty bust-length portraits
of peasant types: a series of Heads of the People as it were. Van Gogh's socialist
sympathies are apparent in every one. Vigorously brushed and soberly coloured,
they take substance from the darkness around them. Fiery highlights on flesh
and fabric suggest lamplight. Indeed, *The potato eaters* is lit by paraffin. The
present brooding study in all likelihood shows Antonius van Rooij, paterfamilias
of the group. Van Gogh yearned to share in the social simplicity and moral
certainty of this man. That he could not do so, though painful to him, left open
the way to art.

Auguste Rodin
France, 1840–1917
The prodigal son 1885–87
bronze, 139.5 height
William Farnsworth Bequest Fund 1979
210.1979

Were it not for its palpable bodily presence, this moving bronze might almost seem a manifestation of pure spirit. Flame-like and quavering, the supplicant seems already to have passed beyond filial remorse to paternal absolution. Rodin's pre-emption of symbolist and expressionist imperatives is patent in the work. Unarguably the greatest sculptor of the early modern period – it is almost impossible to call him a nineteenth-century figure – Rodin was also among the most prolific. His Paris studio was large and active, and the French master himself a worker of formidable muscularity. Rodin's reputation for genius, cultivated in part by the artist himself, is justified by the extraordinary variety of his invention and the ardour he brought to even the smallest project. *The prodigal son* characterises Rodin's quest for the life-force within the human form.

Camille Pissarro
France, 1830–1903
Peasants' houses, Eragny 1887
oil on canvas, 59 x 71.7
Purchased 1935
6326

Between 1884 and 1888 Pissarro experimented with the pointillist method of
the younger Seurat. For an avowed anarchist it was perhaps no great step, but
in art-historical terms Pissarro's stylistic shift, however momentary, coincided
with the end of impressionism's avant-garde ascendancy. *Peasants' houses,
Eragny* was painted during this fascinating interlude. Pissarro has fully absorbed
the tenets and techniques of the distinctive style. Form is constructed by discrete
juxtaposition of individual strokes, or 'dots', of pigment. Atmosphere is suggested
by chromatic scintillation. Surface is treated as a single unity. The mechanical
effect which can deaden pointillist painting is obviated by Pissarro's acute sense
of the internal dynamics of design. The cast shadows intruding from the right
are deliberately naive; this was to be an important innovation for the younger
generation of post-impressionists such as Gauguin and Cézanne.

Claude Monet
France, 1840–1926
Port-Goulphar, Belle Île 1887
oil on canvas, 81 x 65
Purchased 1949
8356

Painted in the same year as Pissarro's pointillist canvas, this impressionist seascape by Claude Monet is conservative in comparison. Nevertheless, in the context of Monet's *œuvre* at the time it represents an adventurous advance. This is no conventional example of marine painting. The horizon, a feature generally used by seascapists to stabilise their compositions, is completely occluded by the rocks and cliff faces of Belle Île. These outcrops range with claustrophobic effect across the upper register of the work, appearing as well in the form of cramped promontories on either side of the foreground. The ragged patch of sea thus formed, filled by the painter with countless flecks of paint to indicate waves, is the real subject of the picture. Japanese woodblock prints, commonly available in Paris at the time, provided impressionist and later painters with radical solutions to the problem of representing three-dimensional forms on a flat surface. Few seized these solutions with the alacrity of Monet, or adapted them with such distinction.

Walter Sickert
England, 1860–1942
*Gatti's Hungerford Palace of
Varieties: second turn of Katie
Lawrence* c. 1887–88
oil on canvas mounted on hardboard,
84.4 x 99.3
Watson Bequest Fund 1946
7772

Born in Munich of Danish parents,
Walter Sickert came to England as a
child in 1868. Taught by Whistler
and inspired by Degas, whom he
knew, he became one of the most influential and prolific British painters of his
period. Experimenting with late impressionist and post-impressionist idioms,
Sickert forged a personal practice devoted almost entirely to depictions of
metropolitan life, some of them squalid. He settled permanently in London in
1905, from which time his studio served as a nerve-centre for the younger
'realist' painters of the Camden Town Group. Sickert's love of urban types,
bohemia and the world of variety theatre is apparent in this atmospheric canvas.
Katie Lawrence was a knockabout songstress who frequently headlined at
Gatti's venue. Despite Sickert's interest in working-class themes his art is far
from populist, appealing as it does to sophisticated taste. Daringly, the painter
portrays Lawrence as little more than a footlit smudge.

Etienne Dinet
France, 1861–1929
The snake charmer 1889
oil on canvas, 176.5 x 180.4
Purchased 1890
799

Another of the proficient tech-
nicians of late nineteenth-century
art, Dinet was a French-born
painter–illustrator with a pen-
chant for attention-seeking titles
and striking technical effects.
Both are exploited in *The snake
charmer*, an orientalist painting
that doubles as a touristic
postcard. Exotic in its geo-
graphical setting and sensational in its subject matter, it further trades on scale
as a strategy to arrest the viewer. The figures are large and brilliantly coloured,
seeming to spill into the gallery space. The charmer himself is consciously that,
with a toothy smile and 'authentic' costume. Also noteworthy is the treatment
of bright sunlight which Dinet translates into broad applications of impasto paint
with practised, not to say formulaic, ease. No real attempt is made to create a
composition. Rather, the cropped casualness of a photograph is suggested.

William Henry Margetson
England, 1861–1940
The sea hath its pearls 1897
oil on canvas, 129.5 diameter
Purchased 1897
705

The circlet of crabs carved in low relief on the frame of this painting is integral to its success as a work of art. Echoing the seaside theme, and offering closure to an otherwise excessively open composition, the frame participates in the painting quite as constructively as the bending figure and wave-lapped beach. The cool monochrome of the location suggests an English coastal resort, though clearly Margetson had the Mediterranean in mind. His lovely fossicker is dressed to evoke the ancient classical past more than late Victorian England. Indeed, Margetson's rather dry application of pale pigment echoes Roman fresco technique. Like most of the lesser genre painters and portraitists of his day, he succumbed to the ever-virulent strain of Victorian classicism, being influenced by better-known contemporaries such as Leighton and Poynter. It goes without saying that the pearl of the title is a punning allusion to the maiden herself.

Émile-Antoine Bourdelle
France, 1861–1929
Grande baigneuse accroupie (Crouching bather) 1906–07
bronze, 101.5 x 79 x 115
Gift of Loti and Victor Smorgon 1996
580.1996

The best and truest of Rodin's pupils and followers, Émile-Antoine Bourdelle
passed the flame of Rodinesque ideals to a younger generation of sculptors,
notably Alberto Giacometti and Germaine Richier. Rodin was right to call
him 'a pioneer of the future'. His gift may have been of a different order than
Rodin's, and a lesser one in terms of historical significance, but he was no less
the visionary public sculptor, accepting monumental commissions, and pursuing
them, with the same zeal as his instructor. Though Bourdelle's interest in the
relationship between architecture and statuary is not paramount in *Grande
baigneuse accroupie*, this most sturdy of bronzes typifies his architectonic
tendency. This is sculpture conceived as mass, measured and balanced. The
rolling motion and erotic mood of the figure coexist with formal considerations
equally interesting to the sculptor. The historical link between Rodin's *The
prodigal son* and Giacometti's *Femme de Venise*, Bourdelle's work also sustains
scrutiny on its own terms.

Georges Braque
France, 1882–1963
Landscape with houses Winter 1908–09
oil on canvas, 65.5 x 54
Purchased 1980

This landscape by the co-founder of
cubism was painted in a region of France
frequented by Cézanne: coastal L'Estaque.
Not unnaturally, Braque's faceted brushwork resembles Cézanne's, while at the
same time hinting at the fragmented system
of application he was destined to perfect
with Picasso. Though it had its genesis in
landscape – Braque at La Roche-Guyon, Picasso at La Horta – the cubist
method found its purest expression in still life. This painting has elements of
that genre, from the object-like character of the houses and tree, to their
flattening thrust into the plane of the picture. Braque's shifting of forms in
space, indeed his shifting of space itself, announce the fourth dimension of
cubism. The landscape is understood almost exclusively in spatial terms,
though not without a dramatic connotation specific to the early days of the
movement. *Landscape with houses* has a rawness that would convert to
refinement within the year. The palette of browns, greens and unemphatic
blues is already, at this date, quintessentially cubist.

Georges Braque
France, 1882–1963
Le verre d'absinthe 1911
oil on canvas, 35.3 x 27.2
Purchased 1997

This small but exquisite painting was
produced during that critical two months –
which turned out to be pivotal for modern
art – when Picasso and Braque shared a
studio at Ceret. While the cubist experiment
is as rigorous here as if it were Picasso, the
lyrical touches of colour and the illusionism
of the grapes are very much Braque. The
architectural forms, such as the steps on the
right and the cubic blocks to the left of the absinthe glass, are characteristic
of the equal weight both artists gave to the spaces between objects, and their
concern to integrate objects into the field. As a result, although certain elements
are clearly recognisable – the glass and spoon, the bunch of grapes – others
are obscure. Painted the year before Braque introduced papier collé, *Le verre
d'absinthe* records a key moment of analytic cubism.

Spencer Gore
England, 1878–1914
The Icknield Way 1912
oil on canvas, 63.4 x 76.2
Purchased 1962
OB2.1962

Spencer Gore's *The Icknield Way* is a landscape of preternatural luminosity
and compaction, which bears the stylistic imprint of Cézanne inflected by
the more expressive accents of van Gogh and Gauguin. Lozenge-like
simplifications of natural forms, particularly visible in the trees and clouds,
unify the composition. The ensuing dynamic is both agitated and stable.
Gore contrives to hold fragmentation at bay without loss of pictorial energy.
He animates the work even further by exaggerating colour to a kaleidoscopic
degree. This is topography deeply experienced rather than superficially
observed. It is the artist's masterpiece. Gore was a founder member of the
Camden Town Group, an alliance of younger artists around Walter Sickert.
Popular and promising, Gore's premature death from influenza robbed the
group of a leading light. Paintings of this kind exerted a considerable influence
on the young Sydney painter Grace Cossington Smith, who may have seen
them in London as early as 1912.

Ernst Ludwig Kirchner
Germany, 1880–1938
Three bathers 1913
oil on canvas, 197.5 x 147.5
Art Gallery of New South Wales Foundation Purchase 1984
158.1984

As one of the founding artists of *Die Brücke* group in 1905, Kirchner is
essential to the history of German expressionism, a movement he virtually
personifies. Trained in Munich and Dresden, he was attracted to neo-
impressionism, van Gogh and tribal artefacts, combining influences from all
three in his searingly emotional paintings, drawings and prints. His woodcuts
and woodcarvings combine traditional German folk forms with more primitive
instincts. His oil paintings, ranging from ambitiously large to intimate in scale,
equally show the effects of ethnographic research. The nudes in *Three bathers*
resemble the artist's painted carvings, echoing in turn the sculpted Eves of
medieval art as well as African and Pacific statuary. Wearing lipstick and a look
of enervation, these Berlin day-trippers huddle defensively in the Baltic waves.
Uncannily presaging the coming blitzkrieg, the figures also predict the artist's
own deteriorating health. Conscripted in 1915, Kirchner was discharged six
months later with tuberculosis.

Samuel Peploe

Scotland, 1871–1935
Still life: apples and jar
c. 1912–16
oil on canvas, 51 x 55.8
Purchased 1947
8049

Samuel Peploe is typical of the
many British artists who succumbed to the magnetism of
Cézanne in the early part of the
twentieth century. One of the
so-called Scottish colourists,
a loosely allied quartet of post-
impressionist painters, he made a decisive visit to France before the war, during
which time this well-constructed still life was completed. Generous in its disper-
sal of pigment, it is nonetheless an example of modernist *belle maniere* – refined
and beautiful painting. The surface appearance of this work derives from a
system of square-brushing that links Peploe, via Cézanne, back to artists of the
nineteenth-century Glasgow School like John Lavery. Naturally, Peploe saw
himself as a modern, but he was also a patriot for whom national sentiments
had their place in art. In the 1920s he and his closest colleague, Francis Cadell,
painted views of the Scottish regions which they dubbed 'Ionascapes'.

William Roberts

England, 1895–1980
The interval before round ten
1919–20
oil on canvas, 92.1 x 122.5
Gift of the Contemporary Art
Society, London 1965
OB1.1967

According to the conventional
lineage of modernist art history,
vorticism was the English
progeny of cubism and futurism.
Among its youngest adherents

was the author of this robotic report of a boxing match. By the time he painted
it, however, William Roberts had already passed through and abandoned the
extremes of vorticist practice in favour of a less radical academic cubism. Even
so, *The interval before round ten* is a painting imbued with the edgy virility so
loved by the vorticists, as indeed by futurists such as Marinetti. Aggression in
human behaviour is given visual form in the agitated activity and angular
arrangements of Roberts's design. And design is the right word for this deliberately anti-naturalist composition. The ferocity Roberts brought to bear on his
subjects is akin to caricature. Little fellow-feeling softens his vision of the all-
male madness of pugilism, though the painter delighted in it all the same.
Fernand Léger's interests in proletarian themes, and something of his tubular
style, infiltrate Roberts's work.

Alexander Rodchenko
Russia, 1891–1956
Composition 1918
oil on wooden panel, 93 x 50
Purchased 1997

Painted in the year following the October Revolution by a leading figure in
the Russian avant-garde, this composition exemplifies the ideals of Russian
constructivism. Using transparent oils over a wooden panel – probably taken
from a piece of furniture – Rodchenko has incorporated the curvature and grain
of the wood into his design. This emphasis on the innate qualities of material is
characteristic of constructivism, as is the artist's commitment to abstraction, or
'non-objective' art. Seeking to purge art of its bourgeois values, including the
idea of private ownership, Rodchenko and many of his contemporaries
embraced abstraction as a means of literally emptying art of objects. At the
same time, the unmistakably cubist overtones of the dynamic diagonals and
shallow arcs attest to the rich European heritage of the Russian avant-garde.

André Derain

France, 1880–1954
Still life 1921–22
oil on canvas, 87.2 x 124.5
Purchased 1987

André Derain took as much pleasure in being retrograde as avant-garde. Once the fiery leader of the fauves, an early champion of primitive art and a contender for modernist pre-eminence, Derain made the first of his many stylistic backflips around 1910. When Picasso and Braque were at their most experimental, he chose to investigate early Renaissance art as exemplified in the classical values of order, harmony and detachment. From the 1920s his work was regarded as conservative by his contemporaries, though it coincided with the 'return to order' that characterised post-war European culture. Derain is now regarded as a postmodernist before the fact. Some of his figural and still life subjects influenced painters in the 1980s. This example of the latter genre is particularly grand and impressive, a major work of its period. Recalling an altar set with ritual items, Derain presents his simple objects with a sacramental sense of their placement and interrelation.

Matthew Smith

England, 1879–1959
La chemise jaune c. 1925
oil on canvas, 91.8 x 59.7
Purchased 1952
8737

While many British painters in the early decades of the twentieth century were drawn to the subtlety of Cézanne's technique, Matthew Smith embraced the more dramatic devices of Gauguin and Matisse. Smith spent time in the latter's Paris studio in 1910, albeit without sighting the master, and developed a personal manner based on fauvist principles of pure colour, bold simplification of form and a marked sensuousness of application. *La chemise jaune*, named for the molten yellow slip modelled by the opulent Vera Cunningham, shows Smith's gift for the disposition of fiery hues across a broadly painted composition. Fauve painting is not the exclusive predecessor of the work. Smith was well aware of Delacroix's chromatic experiments almost a century earlier. Indeed, Vera is presented for inspection in the time-honoured guise of an odalisque, in this case in vulnerable repose. The artist produced many images of her, frequently nude. Her Rubenesque roundness recalls the many representations of fruit in the artist's *œuvre*.

Albert Marquet
France, 1875–1947
The Pont Neuf in the snow late 1920s
oil on canvas, 78.2 x 64.7
Purchased 1939
6927

Circumspection and sobriety distinguish Albert Marquet from his fauvist
colleagues and his friend Matisse. Unlike the latter, Marquet never felt the lure
of exotic locations and subjects, let alone scorching colours. Instead he contented
himself with a long series of unexceptional urban views, especially from the
windows of his quayside studio in Paris. Of all the multifarious moods of this
metropolis, he most savoured the quiet and grey. *The Pont Neuf in the snow* is
a perfect expression of Marquet's gift for painterly understatement. As for his
inveterate interest in orderliness, that too is evidenced. Something of the silence,
and everything of the chill composure, of a city in wintertime is apparent in
this image. Seemingly executed with hardly a second thought or indecisive move,
the image is realised in a single unity of tone that is reminiscent of Whistler.
In contrast to many of his contemporaries, artists such as Marquet pursued a
calmer, more reflective, vision of modernity.

Marino Marini
Italy, 1901–80
Rider 1936
bronze, 203 x 94 x 165
Purchased 1979

Evoking a sculptural tradition that flourished in Roman and Renaissance
Italy, this twentieth-century variation of the equestrian theme is less heroic than
the originals which inspired it. Marino Marini produced many such groups of
riders and their mounts with unfailing sensitivity to the pathos of the human
condition. His figures, man and beast alike, seem like cautious participants in a
ceremony more sad than stately. Far from the glorious aftermath of battle, their
mood is one of hesitancy and introspection rather than vigorous movement.
Although Marini's work is similar in subject matter to Italian fascist statuary
of this period, it is entirely different in its spirit of humanism and its gentility
of pose and purpose. Schematic yet immensely supple, his anatomies privilege
individuality over uniformity. Bronze was Marini's favourite material. He
delighted in the textural contrast and formal variety possible in the medium,
producing objects not just of great beauty but of lasting material integrity.

Pierre Bonnard
France, 1867–1947
Self-portrait c. 1940
oil on canvas, 76.2 x 61
Purchased 1972
6.1972

Pierre Bonnard is both the artist and the subject of this picture. Yet as a
self-portrait it is strangely uninformative. The figure appears in shadow,
uncomfortably wedged between the frame of a mirror and the cruciform of
a stretcher. If this is Bonnard, he withholds all clues to his character save a
defining impression of shyness. That it was painted when the artist was seventy-
three, in all likelihood in Nazi-occupied Paris, contributes to an atmosphere
of anxious melancholy appropriate to its historical context. And what of the
curious action of the hands? Is Bonnard wiping his brushes? Preparing to
shave? Shaping up to fight? One thing, at least, is clear: this is the product of
a supreme colourist. Bonnard's reputation was built on a lifelong production
of gloriously chromatic works. Few painters at mid-century could have
orchestrated ultramarine, orange-gold, umber, opaque white and black into
such an intelligible ensemble. Light, refracted through glass vessels, eye-glasses
and mirror glass, promotes these already flagrant tones to the incendiary level
so loved by Bonnard.

Max Beckmann
Germany, 1884–1950
Mother and daughter 1946
oil on canvas, 150.5 x 80.5
Art Gallery of New South Wales Foundation Purchase 1987

Although associated with German expressionism and the New Objectivity
movement, Max Beckmann occupies his own category as a moral fabulist.
His proclivity was for symbolic narratives, often large in scale and complex in
iconography, that highlight the tragicomic fate of humanity. The triptych, with its
sacred associations, was the format he favoured for important projects, producing
a significant number of them at the time of his forced flight from Nazism in 1937.
Beckmann's portraits, still-life subjects, nudes and smaller genre pieces are equally
invested with a sense of the sacramental. Ever the sceptical recorder of the follies
of the world, even his most affectionate works have a cynical edge. *Mother and
daughter* is no exception: it might as easily be read as a prostitute presented
for our inspection by the madam of the brothel. Or perhaps the older woman
signifies exhausted Europe, counterpoised with the vital New World of America.
Beckmann relocated to the United States in 1947 after a decade spent in Holland.

Ben Nicholson
England, 1894–1982
Still life (Alice through the looking glass) 1946
oil and pencil on canvas, 68.6 x 76.2
Purchased 1949

The first thing the viewer notices about this painting is its graphic quality. With its dependence on pencil marks and pallid colours, it hardly seems painted at all. The artist organised his surface into clearly defined, overlapping shapes with little regard to depth or dimensional interplay. The illusionism which was once the mainstay of the oil-on-canvas technique has given way to its opposite, a kind of insubstantiality. Discoveries made by Picasso and Braque before 1914 inform this belated British example of cubism. Ben Nicholson painted his first abstract in 1924 and carved his first purist relief a decade later, though representational motifs occur throughout his career. His father was the Edwardian artist and illustrator, Sir William Nicholson, some of whose pictorial discretion he inherited. Painted near the famed enclave of artists at St Ives, Cornwall, this composition is as devoid of painterly excess and vulgar display as it is full of nuance.

Stanley Spencer
England, 1891–1959
Christ in Cookham
1951–52
oil on canvas
127 x 205.7
Watson Bequest Fund
1952

If Beckmann's religiosity had a decidedly profane dimension, Stanley Spencer's was marked by an almost mystical fervour. His understanding of Christianity had a pantheistic overlay that allowed for the incorporation of his own wilful and eccentric imaginings. Eroticism was an area of human experience to which Spencer's art gave uninhibited expression, though this incident-filled composition is comparatively chaste. A Christ of Romanesque solidity presides over workers, village worthies, children and most of the local football team. The setting is a cottage garden in Cookham, Spencer's rural birthplace which he habitually portrayed as an earthly paradise. Part of a series of canvases executed for the Church Home, *Christ In Cookham* recalls the fastidious images of the Pre-Raphaelites. In this collection it can be usefully compared with Ford Madox Brown's *Chaucer at the court of Edward III*, painted a century earlier. Both artists saw in the structures of English society the worldly articulation of a godly plan.

Henry Moore
England, 1898–1986
Helmet head no. 2 1955
bronze, 34 x 24.7 x 24
Purchased 1955
9195

Echoing the surrealism that was an early influence on the sculptor, this
compact bronze merges mechanistic form with animistic feeling. Its owl-like
outline and interrogative attitude make a direct demand on the viewer. Yet
the secrecy of its internal voids and the implacability of its outward structures
resist all dialogue. The enigmatic objects of Giacometti come to mind, redefined
as they are by Moore's own brand of sculptural rationalism. Regardless of
subject matter, and even at his most primitivistic, the English sculptor invested
his work with a sense of composure and balance. *Helmet head no. 2* rises
with great solidity from a flange-like neck and throat. The shape suggests
a Nazi helmet, unsurprising given Moore's deeply humanistic response to the
sufferings occasioned by the Second World War. By contrast, his far more
easeful bronze, *Reclining figure: angles I* (1980) rests monumentally on its
base outside the Gallery.

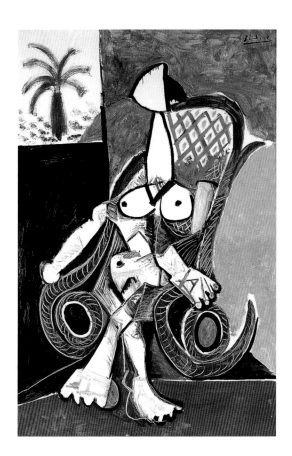

Pablo Picasso
Spain, 1881–1973
Nude in a rocking chair 1956
oil on canvas, 196 x 130.8
Purchased 1981

© Pablo Picasso 1956, Succession Pablo Picasso. Reproduced by permission of VI$COPY Ltd, Sydney 1998
66.1981

By the time he painted this faceless female figure, Picasso was a towering legend
of modern art. Yet to say she is faceless is not entirely accurate: across her torso,
breasts, belly and pudenda the painter has inscribed the disconcerting semblance
of his own features. Her nipples are the tell-tale black pupils of his eyes, her
serrated vagina is his equally aggressive mouth. Having thus invaded her body,
his own erupts in the manner of a physiological mutation. It is not an easy
image, but it is wholly truthful to Picasso's deepest intuitions and experience.
Anger belies the innocuousness of the subject matter. Fear underscores the anger.
It is only very marginally a work of art about appearances. Instead, Picasso enacts
a form of black magic, an exorcising ritual of bodily destruction and psychic
derangement that plays fast and loose with reality – all within the conventions
of the seated portrait. That he did this through the agency of his last great love,
Jacqueline Rogue, setting her violated form in the serenity of his new villa at
Cannes, is admirable and repulsive in equal measure. The gesticulating palm
tree may well allude to Matisse, whose recent death reminded Picasso of the
inescapability of mortality.

Alberto Giacometti
Italy, 1901–66
Femme de Venise VII 1956
bronze, 117 x 16 x 36
Art Gallery of New South Wales
Foundation Purchase 1994
612.1994

Giacometti's significance to modern art grew stronger as the twentieth century drew to a close. The tentativeness of his paintings and sculptures, their state of apparent incompletion and angst, are aesthetic qualities in accord with the temper of our times. Part of an extensive series of single figures and related groups produced in the middle of the decade, *Femme de Venise VII* – from a series displayed at the Venice Biennale of 1956 – explores the enigma of human personality and the impossibility of its ultimate description. Giacometti knew he could never capture the soul of his subjects; even their flesh proved evasive, crumbling away as he worked. Yet he remained dedicated to the quest. His father was an important Swiss post-impressionist in the circle of Cuno Amiet. Adept in that style at an early age, Alberto quickly outgrew its psychological limitations. He moved to Paris in the 1920s, studying with Rodin's successor, Bourdelle, before joining the surrealists in 1930. Finding surrealism, in its turn, insufficient to his ambitions, Giacometti began to sculpt, and eventually paint, in a new and profoundly personal way. His style has no name, and he inspired no movement, yet this indispensable artist left his mark on history as surely as he did on eroded masterpieces such as this. His influence on individual artists such as Francis Bacon and Barnett Newman was profound.

Giorgio Morandi
Italy, 1890–1964
Still life 1957
oil on canvas, 36.6 x 41.9
Purchased with assistance from the Margaret Hannah Olley Art Trust 1997
431.1997

A reticent and quiet man who eschewed the successive fashions of European
modernism, Morandi devoted his artistic career to the unhurried contemplation
of the objects and landscapes of his native Bologna. The objects he painted and
drew were invariably prosaic. Morandi gathered them together into intimate
clusters. An unerring judge of proportion, he imbued these compositions with
an extraordinary sense of unity, realising the lyric possibilities of his objects
through subtle intervals of colour, tone and space. The familiar forms of jars
and pots are simplified, yet their essential qualities seem to be heightened.
In this way Morandi suggests an abstract monumentality: a characteristic
associated with metaphysical painting. The classic composure of Morandi's
work depends on a technique that leaves nothing to chance or improvisation.

Yves Klein
France, 1928–61
Portrait relief PR 3 (portrait of Claude Pascal) 1962
dry pigment in synthetic resin on bronze mounted on primed and gold-leafed board
176 x 94 x 35
Purchased with assistance from the Mervyn Horton Bequest Fund 1990

It was Yves Klein's chosen role to play the contradictory roles of high priest and jester in post-war European art. With more training in jazz and judo than art, the French provocateur began as a creator of mystical monochromes in the 1940s. By the middle of the next decade he had settled on ultramarine as the colour most expressive of spiritual potential, both private and cosmic. He patented a hue called International Klein Blue, using it in a series of works entitled the Anthropometries which were 'painted' with the bodies of living models. Klein had previously used a blowtorch as a brush. His most controversial act, a seminal example of performance art, was to leap 'into the void' from a second-storey window in Paris in 1961. A year later he began the project to record himself and his circle of intimates in a quartet of body casts. *Portrait relief PR 3* belongs to this group, left incomplete at his death. This portrait of Claude Pascal is cast from the poet's body and coloured in International Klein Blue pigment. Seeming to levitate in front of its golden screen, the figure re-enacts Klein's leap into the void. Klein himself was to have been represented, conversely, in gold against blue.

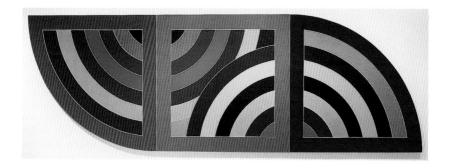

Frank Stella
United States of America, b. 1936
Khurasan gate variation II 1970
synthetic polymer paint on canvas, 304.8 x 914.4
Gift of the Art Gallery Society of New South Wales 1977

Immense in scale and rigorous in geometric ordering, *Khurasan gate variation II* is a major achievement of American minimalist painting. Part of Stella's Protracta series, in which he pushed the genre of the easel picture to architectural dimensions, the work exists both as surface and as solid object. Indeed, the shaped canvases he devised in the 1960s, and continued thereafter to explore, can be seen as attempts to annex sculptural space for two-dimensional practice. Having begun his career in abstract expressionism, the then internationally dominant style, Stella went on to make his reputation with a series of all-black paintings that took their form from the edge of the canvas. The system of repeated striping used in these works has the effect of excluding figural and compositional references, a strategy that was to influence the course of twentieth century art through Donald Judd and other minimalists. For Stella and Judd, the new American painting represented a complete break with the European past. Of all the abstract painters who rose to prominence during this period – among them Morris Louis, also represented in the collection by a major work – Stella has proven the most inventive and enduring. The astonishing visual impact of *Khurasan gate* goes a long way towards explaining this.

Francis Bacon
England, 1909–92
Study for self-portrait 1976
oil and pastel on canvas, 198 x 147.5
Purchased 1978

In this self-portrait, despite the angular and artfully constructed interior – in effect a prison – the subject's flesh dissolves as we watch. It drains downwards, seemingly in a gross enactment of the collapsed hydraulics of the heart. Bacon was no flatterer, either of himself or his other sitters. Among the latter were lovers, intimates and friends, none of whom were spared the devastating scrutiny of his gaze. The whole of his species, for that is surely the term by which Bacon identified himself and his fellows, was prone to corruption and decay. The painter's relation to this spectacle is that of a surgeon, a being whose incisive interventions at the site of decay do not guarantee recovery. Given its grotesquerie, the miracle of Bacon's art is that it is so beautiful. Few painters in the second half of the twentieth century paid such attention to the subtleties of applied pigment and the mechanics of pictorial construction. Bacon was, as this work demonstrates, a master artist.

Philip Guston
United States of America, 1913–80
East Tenth 1977
oil on canvas, 203.2 x 255.3
Art Gallery of New South Wales Foundation Purchase 1988
39.1988

Like Bacon, Philip Guston was a painter of great technical accomplishment.
Behind the apparent artlessness of this work lies a lifetime of painterly experience.
Guston gained success with abstract expressionist canvases in the 1950s and
1960s before his renunciation of abstraction in the early 1970s. At that time the
increasingly dour tenor of his work took form in figurative paintings of extreme
abjectness. These revisited the realist themes of the artist's Work Program
Administration murals of the 1940s, works in which his passion for social justice
and racial equity found its first expression. At the same time, they pre-empted
the return to figuration in American painting of a decade later. *East Tenth* evokes
the bohemian back alleys of New York where Guston had worked with Jackson
Pollock. It is an image of such flagrant seediness that one at first wonders what
the painter intended. A mere reiteration of fact? Ironic comment? Repulsion?
Celebration? Guston felt all these things, finding in problematic paintings like
East Tenth the perfect vehicle for the bathos and sublimity which, in equal
measure, marked his final years as an artist.

Francesco Clemente
Italy, b. 1952
Water and wine 1981
gouache on paper, 243 x 248
Mervyn Horton Bequest Fund 1993
12.1993

Embracing the myths of many cultures simultaneously is a stock-in-trade of
postmodernism; a strategy that Francesco Clemente was ideally placed to exploit.
The artist rose to prominence as one of the principal painters of the Italian
'trans-avant-garde' in the early 1980s. As a resident of three countries – Italy,
the United States and India – he has since the late 1970s consistently drawn
together the threads of these differing societies into a single, and singular,
artistic practice. Though the forms of this painting are essentially those of the
traditional Tamil sign-painters of Madras, Clemente's own private musings and
meanings are unmistakably in evidence. It would not, for example, be acceptable
in any Hindu culture to butcher a cow. Similarly, the water and wine of the
title are more suggestive of Christian than Hindu tradition. Then there is the
symbolic subtext of the image – decapitation as castration, suckling as fellatio,
restraint as bondage – which, it may be argued, belong to the psycho-sexual
milieu of New York. Clemente succeeds in resolving all these elements within a
mytho-poetic whole.

Miriam Schapiro
Canada, b. 1923
Black bolero 1980
fabric, glitter, synthetic polymer paint on canvas, 182.9 x 365.8
Purchased 1982
295.1982

Fundamentally different in approach to the works that precede it here, Miriam
Schapiro's collaged hemisphere is a telling demonstration of the new directions
explored by women artists during this period. Inspired by the often anonymous
domestic and decorative items made by women over the centuries, especially
those making use of salvaged and recycled fabric, *Black bolero* testifies to the
inventiveness possible within traditional craft practices. Patchwork, embroidery,
sewing and découpage are all referenced, with Schapiro consciously shepherding
decoration into the realm of high art. Like a majestic fan, the design unfolds in
patterned ribs of colour across a dark background. The word 'bolero', signifying
both a sensuous dance and an article of female apparel, accurately describes the
object before us. Neither purely fanciful, nor completely practical, it is a brilliant
reconciliation of contrasting conventions.

Giulio Paolini
Italy, b. 1940
L'altra figura 1984
two plaster casts, plaster fragments and two
wooden plinths, 183 x 250 x 190
Mervyn Horton Bequest Fund 1987
349.1987

Two identical plaster busts, neoclassical
in derivation and in pristine condition,
preside over the fallen fragments of a
third. These are the deceptively simple
components from which Italian artist
Giulio Paolini constructs his deeply
affecting drama of the soul. To a reader of
the classics, the scene carries echoes of the
Narcissus myth, in which a beautiful youth falls fatally in love with his own
unattainable reflection. The fate of Icarus is also hinted at. Having fallen to
earth after flying too close to the sun, Icarus represents the impossibility of
attaining absolute knowledge; or, in the case of postmodern art, of representing
ultimate truth. What is perfectly clear is Paolini's formal purity, a defining
feature of his work since the 1960s. At the time of the arte povera movement
his use of materials already indicated an atypical meditativeness and restraint.
Paolini found in the whiteness of plaster an adaptable variant of the tabula rasa.

Frank Auerbach
England, b. 1931
Primrose Hill, autumn 1984
oil on canvas, 121.9 x 121.9
Mervyn Horton Bequest Fund 1985
86.1985

The slow unfolding of form that
occurs when one views a work by
this English master parallels the
process of its making. Frank
Auerbach is a precise and considered worker, a fact that belies his
spontaneous execution. Each stroke
is an intentional contribution to a
final whole, however layered and
textured that may be. Auerbach's subjects, even his landscapes, boast their own
biology, seeming to have been propagated rather than painted. Each one carries
within it the history of its evolution from idea to ultimate object. And these
paintings insist on their physicality. *Primrose Hill, autumn* offers the viewer
much more than a simple record of place. One of the artist's habitual motifs,
the setting is a part of London the painter has internalised through constant
observation. Born in Berlin, Auerbach was in England by 1939. The influential
David Bomberg was his teacher. Art historians usually place Auerbach in the
so-called London School with Lucian Freud and Leon Kossoff, the latter of
whom, is also represented in the collection.

Anselm Kiefer
Germany, b. 1945
Glaube, Hoffnung, Liebe (Faith, hope, love) 1984–86
emulsion, synthetic polymer paint, shellac on photodocument paper on canvas
(linen) with lead, 280 x 380 x 75
Mervyn Horton Bequest Fund 1987
358.1987

In the manner of a nineteenth-century Salon painting, this work exploits scale
to theatrical effect. The sheer enormity of the landscape, into which we are
compelled by irresistible spatial and perspectival manipulations, is not,
however, the most impressive quality of *Glaube, Hoffnung, Liebe*. Its author
is Anselm Kiefer, perhaps the most tenacious German artist in the generation
after Joseph Beuys. While at one level the charred surface of this painting can
be read as a reminder of the European holocaust, this is one of the first works
in which Kiefer follows Beuys's preoccupation with the healing power of art.
Beuys identified with ancient shamanistic traditions in which the healer must
travel to the afterlife and back in order to fulfil his role. Kiefer's propeller
embodies the principle of flight beyond the horizon, or from earth to heaven.
Yet he has made the propeller from heavy lead, suggesting the impossibility of
this passage – a sentiment that also pervades Paolini's work, represented above.
There is melancholy in this idea, and yet for Kiefer embarking on a journey is
more important than knowing the destination.

Richard Deacon

England, b. 1949
Listening to reason 1986
laminated wood
226 x 609 x 579
Mervyn Horton Bequest Fund
1988
156.1988

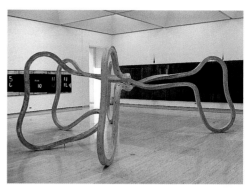

It is no trivialisation of this
delightful sculpture to observe
that it represents a gathering
of ears. Richard Deacon has
bent and laminated strips of wood into the outline of Buddha-like lobes,
presenting the viewer with an immediate sculptural experience. Though
impressive in spatial dimension, the work is surprisingly airy and unstructured.
Deacon shapes his distinctly vernacular material into elastic, linear loops that,
even so, carve out considerable passages of volumetric space. It is impossible
to determine where these constructions end or begin, so seamlessly are they
fashioned by the sculptor. At once a statement of surface and an articulation
of interior tension, *Listening to reason* has all the appeal of public statuary
without its ponderous weight. It makes only one demand on the viewer's
attention: to be understood in the round. It is therefore obligatory to walk
around and in the work. In doing so, one participates in its auditory meaning.

Jannis Kounellis

Greece, b. 1936
Untitled 1984/87 1987 (detail)
steel, wood, plaster, cloth,
gas burner, paint, soot marks
201 x 1093 x 19.5
Mervyn Horton Bequest Fund
1988
393.1988.a–rr

Conceptually vast as well as
physically imposing, this work
by Jannis Kounellis is a masterpiece of modern sculpture and
one of the most memorable objects in the collection. Resembling the side
of a steel ship, or perhaps a sarcophagus of heroic proportions, it stretches
across the entire length of a gallery wall. Known for his poetic yet often
massive installations and independent sculptures, Kounellis deals with the
deepest intimacies of human experience on a universal scale. Here, he invokes
the funerary traditions of his native Greek culture, in which oil lamps are
burned to designate the passage of the human soul from life, through death
into infinity. The bed frame elevated at the upper left of the work signifies the
immemorial site of birth, copulation and death – marked by a burning flame
as matter transforms into elemental energy. Scorch marks at various points
chart previous fiery ignitions. As ever with Kounellis, the implacable abstract
organisation of his work only heightens its fearful emotional content.

Anish Kapoor
India, b. 1954
Void field 1989
four blocks of Northumbrian sandstone and pigment
106 x 330 x 330 installed (variable depending on room size)
Mervyn Horton Bequest Fund 1990
215.1990.a–d

Like Anselm Kiefer's painting, this sculpture by the Anglo-Indian Anish Kapoor
makes its initial impact as a landscape on the grand scale. An assembly of prehistoric monoliths comes naturally to the viewer's mind. Yet there is something
deceptive about these structures: on closer approach they prove to be as thin-
walled and hollow as ceramic pots. Kapoor has purged them of interior bulk,
replacing material solidity with immaterial emptiness, presence with absence.
Drawn to the aureole-like apertures that mark their upper surface, one peers
into the very void. So finite without, the Northumbrian sandstone blocks are
infinite within. The moment of this discovery, repeated each time one looks, is
bound bodily into the work, which thus has a temporal aspect. The forms
function as time capsules: receptacles for meaning and intimation that offer up
their contents only to those prepared to participate in an act – suggestively
ritual – of bending observation. Conventional Western sculpture demands a
self-possessed and possessing gaze. Kapoor's *Void field* invites humility.

WESTERN
WORKS ON PAPER

Andrea Mantegna
Italy, 1431–1506
Bacchanal with a wine press c. 1470–75
engraving, 29.2 x 42.9
Purchased 1938
8486

The resuscitation of the artistic ideals of antiquity that defined the Italian Renaissance is nowhere more compellingly illustrated than in the work of Andrea Mantegna. Born in Padua, and later the court painter to Lodovico II Gonzaga, Duke of Mantua, Mantegna steeped himself in classical researches of a profoundly intellectual kind. As a result, his art is informed by an astonishing richness of historical detail. *Bacchanal with a wine press* belongs to a series of four related mythological images widely circulated in their day, and famous since. Albrecht Dürer is known to have copied them, prizing Mantegna's steely authority of line and extraordinary gift for visual organisation. Like many of his painted and printed designs, the subject is defiantly pagan. Conceived in the manner of a sculptural relief of the kind found on ancient sarcophagi, it could be mistaken for a Roman original. Mantegna's realisation of anatomical form – male, nude and heroic – anticipates whole schools of later classicising artists.

Rembrandt van Rijn
Netherlands, 1606–69
Christ presented to the people 1655
drypoint, 35.5 x 45.2
Purchased 1948
8130

Though it is Christ on whom Rembrandt's multitude fix their interest in this magnificent print, ours is engaged by the multitude itself. Rembrandt was such a purposeful portrayer of human psychology, especially the psychology of the crowd, that the sacred protagonist is overwhelmed by the supernumeraries around him. He is a picture of resignation in a sea of curiosity. A whole society has been summoned into life by the deft and devastating registrations of Rembrandt's drypoint. He subsequently reworked this plate, pushing his depiction of the biblical event towards something far more archaic, even anarchic. Looking at such a work of graphic art, one might wonder what the medium of oil paint could possibly add by way of improvement. Rembrandt took printmaking, especially etching, to expressive levels undreamed of before and rarely equalled since.

Jean-Antoine Watteau
France, 1684–1721
Study of three male figures c. 1712–14
red chalk, 20.6 x 16.4
Gift of James Fairfax 1993
487.1993

Despite the dissolving prettiness which is
their signature quality, the paintings of Jean-
Antoine Watteau are built on solid reality.
Life-drawing and nature study were the
necessary and pleasurable preludes to his
painterly activity. His graphic style reflected
the naturalism of the Italian Bolognese school,
mediated through the tidier protocols of
French academic drafting technique. Watteau
kept his innumerable drawings in large folios as an aid to composition. Two
of the figures in this sheet relate to his canvas, *Love at the Théâtre Français*.
The reclining man serves for the pose of Bacchus in the painting, while the
bagpiper reappears unchanged. Coveted by connoisseurs even during the
artist's lifetime, Watteau's chalk drawings have never fallen from favour. They
epitomise the grace and intelligence central to the best of eighteenth century
art, at the same time seeming to possess analytical and formal attributes we
now think of as modern.

Francisco de Goya y Lucientes
Spain, 1746–1828
The sleep of reason produces monsters
1797–98
etching and aquatint, 21.5 x 15
Purchased 1978
211.1978

Somnolent or despairing, the crumpled
human form which falls prey to vicious
imaginings in this etching could also refer to
the artist's introspection in the wake of a
serious illness that left him deaf. It is certainly
emblematic of the end of a rationalist century,
and a harbinger of romanticism. Above all,
however, *The sleep of reason produces
monsters* is an enigma, in keeping with the
deliberate impenetrability of 'The Capriccios',
the series to which it belongs. Given the
reactionary character of Goya's targets – including the Court and the Church –
he did well to clothe his graphic attacks in strategic levels of strangeness.
Even so, the threat of the Inquisition caused him to withdraw the series from
circulation. Indisputably the supreme Spanish artist of his period, Goya was
a tapestry designer, muralist, portraitist, history painter, printmaker and
draughtsman. Prolific in all these media, he left a vast artistic legacy. Reason
may have slept; Goya did not.

Jean-August-Dominique Ingres
France, 1780–1867
The Hon. Frederick North 1815
pencil, 21.6 x 16
Gift of James Fairfax 1992
120.1992

Using none of his reputed nine languages,
including Latin and Greek, this aristocratic
sitter communicates silently across two
centuries. The artist who drew him, and with
such a grasp of his proprietorial ease, has made
a truly speaking likeness. Ingres trained with
his father, a minor artist from Montauban, and
at the Royal Academy in Toulouse. In 1796 he
entered David's studio, winning the prestigious Prix de Rome. Between 1804
and 1822 Ingres lived and studied in Rome, his spiritual home. After the
collapse of the Napoleonic Empire he earned his living from portraiture, mainly
in pencil and almost exclusively of English tourists to the Eternal City. Some
450 examples are known. *The Hon. Frederick North* boasts the key ingredients
of the Ingres method: an engraved simplicity of outline, subtle modelling of
interior form, and a direct engagement with the subject's face. The result is a
an image of nearly photographic definition.

Honoré Daumier
France, 1808–1879
*Ah! So you want to
meddle with the press!*
1834
lithograph, 30.2 x 43.2
Gift of Mrs H. V. Evatt 1967
DO 33.1967

The unmistakable message
conveyed by this lithograph
has an autobiographical
basis. Prior to its publication Daumier spent six
months in prison for his Rabelaisian caricature of King Louis-Philippe, a
bumbling reactionary whose threats to republicanism and free speech the artist
detested. Daumier's incorruptible worker, in many respects his Statue of Liberty
and something of a self-portrait, stands squarely on the bedrock of freedom.
With clenched fists and defensive stance, he is ready for the good fight, which
Daumier indicates he will win. The enemy, after all, is shown as a pitiful frieze
of Establishment figures up to their shoddy tricks. These shenanigans Daumier
mercilessly pilloried for much of his career in satirical journals such as
Caricature and *Le Charivari*, often at risk to his safety. The authority of this
print, told in every stroke of the lithographer's instrument, is technical as much
as intellectual. Daumier was an admired painter and sculptor as well as a master
printmaker. He spent his final years, blind and impecunious, in a cottage
granted to him by Corot.

Charles Meryon
France, 1821–68
The morgue, Paris 1854
etching, 23 x 20
Purchased 1938
6756

The discovery of his mild colour-
blindness led Charles Meryon to abandon
painting for graphic art, particularly
etching. So amenable did his gift for this
difficult medium prove that Meryon can
be credited with sponsoring its mid-
nineteenth century revival, both in his
native France and in England. The
architectural heritage of Paris became his
definitive subject, but in no routinely illustrative way. Though accuracy of
detail was important to him, far more significant was the subjective terrain
of the emotions. Indeed, Meryon's prints are as attentive to the psychology of
place as to its physical characteristics. He admired the more funereal caprices
of the Italian printmaker Piranesi, investing his own urban views with a similar
strangeness and melancholy. *The morgue* is rightly celebrated as an emblem
of anxiety. Its spiky figures, foretelling the artist's descent into madness, adopt
intemperate gestures rarely seen in European art since Goya. In the twentieth
century Meryon's hysteria was re-articulated by the expressionists.

Paul Gauguin
France, 1848–1903
Breton women at a fence 1889
lithograph, 17.1 x 21.5
Purchased 1976
298.1976

Gauguin's quest for the primitive preceded his ill-fated trips to Martinique
and Tahiti. As a follower of Pissarro
and Cézanne in his Paris years, as a
colleague of van Gogh in Arles soon
after, and then as co-instigator with Emile Bernard of the Pont-Aven School,
he perfected a primitivising technique that could be applied equally to a Breton
pastoral or a Polynesian nude. This print – one of a group of ten zincographs
on distinctive yellow paper known collectively as the 'Volpini suite' – depicts
two women in the regional dress of Brittany. Their characteristic wimples animate
innumerable compositions of the period by this and other artists. Though a
novice to the lithographic medium, Gauguin proved instantly a master. In this
plate the unpredictable undulations of line and Japoniste abbreviations of form
are disruptive, preventing an easy assimilation by the eye. No single element is
represented whole. Instead, the image is constructed from peek-a-boo fragments
that cohere through opposition rather than accord. The farmyard subject is
effectively lost in the process.

Pierre Bonnard
France, 1867–1947
La revue blanche 1894
coloured lithograph, 75.5 x 58.6
Purchased 1978
206.1978

The flair and sophistication of the *fin de siècle* are indelibly stamped on this image. It could serve as an advertisement for a cultural period as opposed to a mere periodical. As a pre-eminent journal of innovation and taste in the 1890s, *La revue blanche* played a vital part in promoting the work of the generation of artists that included Edouard Vuillard and Pierre Bonnard. In association with other young artists, these painter–printmakers formed the Nabis, a collective dedicated to decorative principles and daring design strategies. Bonnard was the most gifted and productive graphic artist in the group. Influenced by the example of Gauguin and Japanese prints, he adapted them to a personal style that was edgy and off-hand, at the same time as being masterfully controlled. In this lithographic poster an imperturbably modish woman is jostled by a child of almost feral physiognomy. Niceties of lettering and layout are abandoned in pursuit of the asymmetrical silhouettes and acidic tints that Bonnard relished at the time.

Edvard Munch
Norway, 1863–1944
The sick girl 1896
etching with drypoint, 13.7 x 17.7
Purchased 1987
473.1987

The greatest Norwegian painter and printmaker, and an individual whose influence on the course of twentieth-century art is inestimable, Edvard Munch was prone to morbid imaginings and depressive episodes throughout his life. These stemmed from the sad and all-too-real experiences of his early years. He lost both his mother and sister to illness, watching them deteriorate, waste and die. *The sick girl* is a print that recalls one of the most significant paintings of his early maturity, a study specific to the deathly events in the artist's family yet universal in its application. Pictured in profile against the tomb-like slab of a pillow, the frail figure represents not so much a sick child as all sick children. It is thus a definitive example of symbolism, the literary style which the artist embraced in his youth. Yet so feverish is Munch's line, and so severe his contrast of dark and light, we have no trouble sensing the searing expressionism to which he progressed in the coming years.

Edgar Degas
France, 1834–1917
After the bath c. 1900
black chalk, 73.7 x 59.8
Margaret Hannah Olley Art Trust 1994
222.1994

The most gifted artists seem able to imbue drawing with the volumetric quality
of sculpture. Degas was such an artist and this is just such a drawing. Seeming
to explain everything essential and nothing inessential in the scene, the work
is no more than a sketch, but nothing less than a masterpiece. With his
colleague Manet, Degas shared the distinction of being the most academically
accomplished of the artists associated with impressionism. In his drawings
particularly, he sought to establish values of permanence and solidity as opposed
to the more transient effects found in his painting. Here, the massive bathtub
is handled with the same candour and concern for corporeal truth as the nude.
In another sensibility, the conjunction of these elements would represent an
erotic site. For Degas, it is merely a point of structural necessity; necessity, and
therefore beauty: the bath is a plinth that prevents the model toppling. Degas's
sensitivity to the forms and actions of the female body arguably mitigates
against a voyeuristic or misogynist reading of his work.

Pablo Picasso
Spain, 1881–1973
The frugal repast 1904
etching, 46.3 x 37.7
Winifred Vere Hole Bequest Fund 1994

The sentimentality in certain of Picasso's images from his Rose and Blue periods at the beginning of the twentieth century is unmistakable. It is also strategic. The Spanish painter had a native interest in emotive themes, especially those arising from the bohemia in which he was steeped in both Barcelona and Paris. *The frugal repast* makes a powerful psychological appeal to the viewer. A thin-lipped woman of brittle demeanour and physique rests her head on a rigid hand as if it were a shelf. Her blind companion palpates her with fleshless fingers. The setting before them is as sparse as a desert landscape. For all this desolation, however, Picasso's self-consciously mannerist style makes it plain that this is not a slice of life but a work of art – a contrived one at that. Old Masters such as El Greco and Rosso Fiorentino were his models as much as the living ones Picasso doubtless observed.

Henri Matisse

France, 1869–1954
Three-quarter length nude with arms raised
1906
woodcut, 34.4 x 26.7
Gift of the Art Gallery Society of New South Wales
1976

© Henri Matisse 1906, Succession H. Matisse. Reproduced by permission of
VI$COPY Ltd, Sydney 1998
222.1976

At one time Matisse was regarded as being as
radical as Picasso. During the period in which he
made this and other memorable prints, he was
the acknowledged, if reluctant, leader of the
fauvist movement. Rather than an organised school, fauvism represented a
propensity in art that took late impressionist and post-impressionist pictoriality
towards something rawer and more expressive. Historically, fauvism is a bridge
to expressionism. Brutal reductions of form as much as brilliance of colour
characterised the style. This black-on-white woodcut is thus a wholly fauvist
work. Despite the simplicity of the composition, Matisse convinces the viewer
of two things: first, that this is a record of a real and fully-rounded human
presence studied from life; and, conversely, that it is no more than a terse and
primitivistic arrangement of lines deployed across a surface. The tension
between these extremes, and the fact of their simultaneous functioning,
contributes to the almost fetishistic status of the work.

Pablo Picasso

Spain, 1881–1973
Still life, fruit, dish 1909
drypoint, 13 x 11
Purchased 1986

© Pablo Picasso 1909, Succession Pablo Picasso. Reproduced by permission of
VI$COPY Ltd, Sydney 1998
60.1986

Drypoint, involving as it does the direct marking of
the metal plate with an engraving tool, requires
of the artist the utmost concentration and control;
it is not a technique for the indecisive. Picasso was
especially adept at this difficult medium. Some of his earliest prints are
drypoints, or etchings with drypoint inclusions. This example of the former is
from the high point of his early cubist phase, during which he and Braque had
established the spatial fundamentals of the style. Like certain paintings of the
same year, this still life takes its time-honoured genre into an entirely new
category. The term 'analytical cubism' has been applied to the style, indicating
the quasi-scientific arena of reality that Picasso and Braque were so keen to
explore. Like an aftershock, a wave of energy rolls across the composition,
dislodging every object from its axis. At the same time an extraordinary sense
of order, which we may call cubist harmonics, stabilises the scene. In the
draperies, bowls, and most of all the talismanic pears, Picasso pays obvious
homage to his predecessor, Cézanne.

Wassily Kandinsky
Russia, 1866–1944
Study for 'Painting with white border' 1913
watercolour, gouache, ink, 39 x 35
Purchased 1982
147.1982

Wassily Kandinsky's artistic personality had been formed in part by the examples of peasant painting he collected as a prosperous solicitor. When he later made his leap to full-time creative practice, he sustained his interest in the decorative principles of Russian and other folk art traditions. This watercolour study for one of Kandinsky's breakthrough abstractions of the pre-war period contains residual representations of a horse and rider: the primitive St George familiar from his earlier work. The background is a landscape complete with rustic village. Yet to read the image literally robs it of its power of association. Kandinsky's intention is to loosen reality from recognisability, to set it adrift. The new vista he unveils is in the realm of the spiritual and the resulting work of art is authentically abstract. With his fascination for theosophical and mediumistic beliefs, and his idealistic faith in the improving potential of painting, Kandinsky was as much a priest of art as a painter.

Percy Wyndham Lewis

England, 1882–1957

Figure composition (Man and woman with two bulldogs) 1912
pen and ink, watercolour, gouache, 30.5 x 21.6
Purchased 1983

The eclectic sensibility of Percy Wyndham Lewis equipped him perfectly for his role as the gadfly of the English avant-garde. It was the avowed mission of this painter, writer, publisher and propagandist to radicalise society through art, to 'blow away dead ideas and worn out notions'. Lewis's explosive rhetoric was often only that, but he managed to found the most important British response to European modernism in a movement he named vorticism. Launched with his 1914 periodical *Blast*, vorticism synthesised the cubist and futurist techniques Lewis had been experimenting with previously. This image from 1912 is already precociously vorticist. The essential steeliness of the style is clear. Jagged lines, sharp angles and metallic colours – an overall effect of shattering – comprise its outward features. The transformation of the figures occasioned by this treatment is brutalising and mechanistic. Lewis was none too gentle in his appraisal of human worth. Here, the bulldogs demonstrate more character than their owners.

George Grosz

Germany, 1893–1953

Murder in Ackerstrasse 1916–17
lithograph, 24.5 x 24.9
Purchased 1984

The history of Western art is not so empty of violent images as to render this one either surprising or tasteless. Martyrdoms, complete with disembowellings and decapitations, were a mainstay of Christian iconography. Nonetheless, the unflinching George Grosz does shock with this matter-of-fact portrayal of a modern crime of passion. In its very ordinariness of observed detail it is disturbing; as though an alarm clock and a lucky horseshoe had the same weight as a bloodied hatchet and a headless corpse. And where is the victim's head? This, the most crucial detail of all, is missing. Conjecture as to its whereabouts is one of the most unsettling aspects of this gruesome print. The timid murderer and presumptive rapist, aghast only at his own momentary strength, washes his hands in a basin inadequate for such an act of hygiene. Associated with both the Dada and the expressionist movements, Grosz was a vigilant anti-militarist and humanitarian who applied his art like a scalpel to the ills of society. His particular target was the moral corruption of his native country, Germany, in the period between the two world wars.

Egon Schiele
Austria, 1890–1918
*Poster for the Vienna Secession
49th Exhibition* 1918
colour lithograph, 63.4 x 48.2
Purchased 1979
167.1979

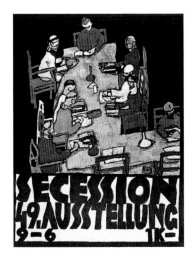

Schiele studied at the Vienna Academy,
coming under the influence of the heightened
art nouveau of Gustav Klimt. He rapidly
evolved his own style, redirecting the
symbolist intensity of his mentor towards
a more psychological, and indeed more
modern, focus. In this Schiele echoed the
new psychoanalytical theories of Sigmund
Freud as well as his own subjective and
often neurotic intimations. His view of human nature, graphically evidenced
in the prolific drawings, paintings and prints that constitute his short career,
was filtered through a prodigious eroticism. This poster for the last Secessionist
exhibition in which he participated is based on a slightly earlier painting,
photographically transferred to the lithographic plate before being reworked
by the artist. Suggesting a Christ-like centrality not out of keeping with his
personality, Schiele represents himself at the head of a table of friends, a number
of whom have the tonsures of monks. Beyond its collegiate message, the print
impresses as a formal arrangement of stark reductivity.

Kurt Schwitters Germany, 1887–1948
Theo Doesburg Netherlands, 1883–1931
Kleine DADA Soirée (DADAsofie) 1923
lithograph, folded horizontally and vertically,
29.8 x 29.8
Purchased 1984
268.1984

Collective projects and collaborations characterised the second wave of modernism in
Europe. Dada, surrealism, constructivism and
other international styles emphasised and
exploited the creative affinity and social conscience of artists. In this humorous
poster Kurt Schwitters, the famed pioneer of collage, teamed with the Dutch-
born Theo Doesburg to advertise a Dada performance, and turn typography
on its head. The resulting image is at once striking, confusing, intriguing and
attractive. Despite its strategies of inversion and miscalculation, the obligation
of conveying useful information to the viewer has been fulfilled. In struggling
to decipher the text one is brought closer to the poster, both physically and
in terms of its content. This perceptual strategy is a hallmark of Dada, a movement with close links to cabaret, theatre and performance. *Kleine DADA Soirée*
would not look out of place in a contemporary cultural context; indeed the
Dadaist heritage of artists such as Schwitters resurfaces in graphic conventions
from pop art to punk rock.

Robert Rauschenberg

United States of America, b. 1925
Cardbird VI 1971
photographic screenprint, collage,
corrugated card, 66 x 69 (irregular)
Anonymous gift 1973

© Robert Rauschenberg 1971, VAGA. Reproduced by permission
of VISCOPY Ltd, Sydney 1998
19.1973

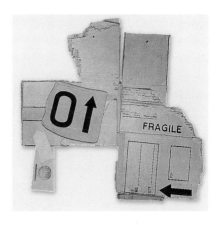

Reality meets artifice in this beguiling
example of *trompe-l'œil*. One might
even call it duplicitous, since it aims to
mislead the viewer as to its outer
nature and inner import. As cleverly as
any artist before him and with no less
attention to his craft, Rauschenberg presents a perceptual conundrum rich in
potential decipherment but finally inscrutable. In 1971 this pioneer of American
pop art exhibited a group of collages called 'Cardboards', named after the banal
material he was then exploring as a medium. At the same time, he produced a
number of printed simulations of these pieces, dubbing them 'Cardbirds'. This
work is the sixth in that series. To all intents and purposes it is indistinguishable
from the originals. Rauschenberg has even added real packaging tape alongside
the photograph-ically screened tape on the simulation. What at first has the
appearance of a rather uninspired found object becomes, on closer scrutiny, an
elaborate and sustaining artwork. Since the 1950s, when the young artist
worked with his friend and colleague Jasper Johns, Rauschenberg has been
fascinated with the nexus of high art and low culture.

Miriam Cahn

Switzerland, b. 1949
Lesen im Staub, das wilde Lieben
(*Reading in dust, the wild love*)
1984 (detail)
charcoal on paper, 59.5 x 84
Mervyn Horton Bequest Fund 1985
195.1985.1-4

A detail of a larger work, this primitivistic
fragment is a compelling fusion of the
ancient and the contemporary. Reminiscent of prehistoric cave painting, it
also evokes the tactile art of modern primitives and children. The process Cahn
used to produce the image contributes to its spiritual quality: having crushed
the charcoal across the surface of the paper, she drew directly with her fingers
without benefit of light. Working 'blind' in this fashion ensured that none of
the conventional tricks of illustration came between the artist and her interior
vision. By blowing away the dust at the end of the session, the drawing was
revealed. The precise nature of the resulting shadowy figures and shapes cannot
be determined, though a condition of ecstatic suspension operates throughout,
warranting the 'wild love' of the title. Cahn is not alone among contemporary
women artists in drawing upon the archives of archetype and myth. The
American Nancy Spero is arguably a recent precursor.

WESTERN
PHOTOGRAPHY

El Lissitzky

Union of Soviet Socialist Republics, 1890–1941
Untitled (Pressa catalogue) 1928
photocollage, ink and paint on photographic paper, 14.9 x 10.9
Purchased 1997
61.1997

El Lissitzky was one of the most important and influential artists of the early
twentieth century – he worked as an architect, designer, painter and photographer.
A contemporary of Chagall's in the early 1910s, he later founded the construc-
tivist movement with Naum Gabo, Tatlin and Rodchenko. *Untitled (Pressa
catalogue)* is an original photocollage with ink and paint additions. The *Pressa*
catalogue was designed by the artist in his role as the main designer and the
Soviet Union's official commissioner for the international *Pressa* exhibition in
Cologne in 1928 which was devoted to the press, publishing and printing
industries. Lissitzky's designs for the *Pressa* exhibition marked a turning point
in his career, when he finally succumbed to figurative and documentary imagery,
making use of a combination of photography, typography, painting and design.
Lissitzky's contributions to abstract art in the 1920s are well established, however
his important experiments in photography, photomontage, graphic and exhibition
designs in the late 1920s and throughout the 1930s remain controversial.

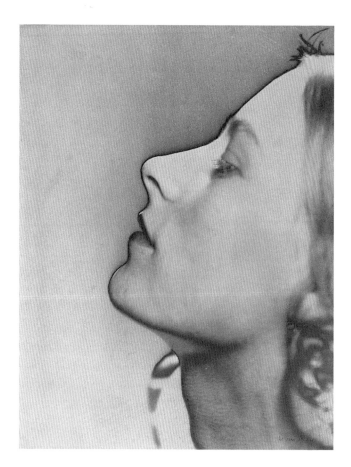

Man Ray

United States of America, 1890–1976
Untitled (solarised portrait, profile) 1930
gelatin silver photograph, 28.5 x 22.1
Purchased 1987

The history of photography in the twentieth century is unthinkable without
the diverse contributions and technical innovations of Man Ray. Though he
began as a painter, his work spanned an extraordinary range of artistic media.
Painter, collagist, film-maker, writer, photographer and cultural eminence,
he brought to these roles a common enthusiasm and invention. Born in
Philadelphia, Man Ray was attracted to avant-garde circles in New York and
ultimately in Europe. Alfred Stieglitz and Marcel Duchamp were significant in
his development, though to neither did he owe artistic allegiance. It was in Man
Ray's character to be independent. While he is historically identified with the
Dadaists he joined in Paris in 1921, and subsequently with surrealism, he was
never constrained by the requirements of any particular movement or style. The
artist's photographic work, of which his experimental 'rayographs' and solarised
images are perhaps the most famous, also encompassed fashion, documentation,
portraiture and still life. This beautiful example of the solarisation technique has
the gravity of an Egyptian relief, and the elegance of a perfume ad.

Brassaï

Transylvania/France, 1899–1984
Filles de Montmartre 1932
gelatin silver photograph, 39.3 x 29.1
Purchased 1986
237.1986

By changing his country and his name, an
obscure Transylvanian artist who trained in
Budapest and Berlin became Brassaï: one of
the great photographers of the twentieth
century. His mission, for it had that evan-
gelical aspect, was to record Paris by night.
For Brassaï, the nocturnal milieu of that city,
its cafés, bars and brothels, had unfailing
appeal. It was not the architecture so much as
the inhabitants of this world that intrigued him. He shared bohemia with them,
a fact that invests his work with both intimacy and partisanship. Though
Brassaï seems always sympathetic to his subjects, many of his images are also
profoundly analytical. This is one. *Filles de Montmartre* portrays two women
for whom the title 'ladies of the night' is not pejorative. Their trade is as
obvious and as time-honoured as their make-up. The image is a complex
exchange of gazes: the photographer's at the women; theirs at him; the reflected
barman's at the unfolding scene. Complicity is the keynote. That Brassaï
ultimately requires ours does not prevent enjoyment of his art.

Werner Mantz

Germany/The Netherlands
1901–1983
*Untitled (Schunck
Department Store)* 1934
gelatin silver photograph,
16.6 x 21.8
Purchased 1983
266.1983

Werner Mantz's photography
is synonymous with the
exemplary documentation of
German and Dutch modernist
architecture of the 1920s and 1930s. Mantz trained as a photographer in
Munich though his home and later studios were in Cologne where he began to
work with architects such as Walter Ripbahn, Bruno Paul and Erich Mendelsohn.
His sensitivity for the play of light over pure form has made him one of the most
important architectural photographers of the twentieth century, to the extent that
his photographs – such as *Untitled (Schunck Department Store)* – transcend simple
documentation and become objects of aesthetic pleasure in themselves. This is as
much due to Mantz's ability as a printer as his ability as a photographer. Mantz
settled in The Netherlands after 1933 and increasingly worked as a portrait
photographer. His work was largely forgotten until the 1970s when his abilities,
in many ways the equivalent of those of Atget or Blossfeldt, were recognised.

Edward Weston

United States of America, 1886–1958
Dunes, Oceano 1936
gelatin silver photograph, 19.2 x 24
Purchased 1989
140.1989

Dunes, Oceano is an excellent example of Edward Weston's mature work. This photographer is one of the major figures in American photography and his images have become icons in the history of the medium. The young Weston worked in California mainly as a portrait photographer and in the soft-focus pictorialist mode. In the early 1920s his work began to change as he came under the influence of Alfred Stieglitz and his circle, and appreciated the formal and modernist possibilities of working with the camera. By the late 1920s Weston was photographing vegetables and other natural objects in monumental close-up. Weston was influenced now by music and sculptural form, and when he photographed landscapes such as the dunes at Oceano in the 1930s his ability to encompass such vastnesses had been informed by his earlier concentration on small and humble objects. The folds and ridges of the dunes in this photograph are richly poetic and reveal Weston's avowal 'to know things in their very essence'.

André Kertész

Hungary, 1894–1985
Nude 1939
gelatin silver photograph, 16.7 x 18.2
Purchased 1989
141.1989

In 1925 the Hungarian photographer André Kertész moved from Budapest to Paris, where he quickly established his reputation in a series of solo exhibitions. Among his professional achievements, Kertész had the distinction of advising Brassaï to take up his *métier*. A formalist for whom structure, pictorial balance and abstract values were presiding interests, Kertész was by the same token a diarist with a canny eye for anecdotal details and psychological states. Eroticism of a witty, if occasionally cold, variety is evidenced in his many arrangements of female nudes. Often solitary, these nudes have something in common with autoerotic figures in the paintings of Balthus. This image is remarkable in combining candour with inscrutability – what, after all, is the naked subject thinking? Her body is offered complacently to view, her psyche not at all. Voyeuristic scenarios are commonplace in the work of Kertész, to the extent that he appears to view the world through a keyhole rather than a camera lens. In 1936 the photographer moved to New York, working for publications including *Harper's Bazaar* and *Vogue*.

Christo Bulgaria, b. 1935
Jeanne-Claude France, b. 1935
Wrapped coast, Little Bay, Australia 1969
gelatin silver photograph, photographer Harry Shunk
62.3 x 77.5
Gift of Chandler Coventry 1972
© Christo 1969
14.1972

The use of concealment to bring a subject more clearly into view is a strategy
explored both imaginatively and extensively by Christo and Jeanne-Claude.
Indeed, this paradox lies at the heart of their practice. Since the 1960s they
have specialised in a process of wrapping that has placed them at the forefront
of environmental art. Christo and Jeanne-Claude made an indelible contribution
to the development of conceptual art in Australia in 1969 when, at the invitation
of Sydney collector and patron John Kaldor, they conceived and carried out the
wrapping of Little Bay. This prominent foreshore site south-east of Sydney is
precipitous and rocky, presenting formidable technical and logistical problems
for the volunteer collective of artists and students who assisted with the project.
Integral to the sculpture was the collaborative participation of these individuals,
some of whom went on to public notice. For ten weeks a 2.4-kilometre strip
of natural landscape lay hidden beneath a synthetic – but breathing – material.
Preparatory drawings and documentary photographs extended, and became
part of, the work. Indeed, proceeds from the sale of similar items helped to
finance it.

Cindy Sherman
United States of America, b. 1954
Untitled 1982 1982
Type C photograph, MP#113, 114.3 x 75
Mervyn Horton Bequest Fund 1986
© Metro Pictures
372.1986

American photo-artist Cindy Sherman simultaneously recreates and deconstructs
the archetypes of modernity. Since the early 1980s she has proven to be a
fearless performer of private rites in the public domain, and an exacting
technician. Taking her cue from the image bank of mass culture, in which
scenes of B movie sultriness like this abound, Sherman transforms herself in a
series of extraordinarily detailed photographic tableaux, recently taken to the
point of grotesquery. She has managed, through these masquerades, to pinpoint
social anxieties and second guess cultural modulations with an almost prophetic
capacity. In this image of bruised but defiant femininity – a stereotype of such
arrant trashiness as to raise the question of self-exploitation – Sherman plays
with the expectations of her audience. She knows that her viewers, if not literate
in art as such, will almost certainly be literate in entertainment. Sherman's
photographs depend on this understanding, for without it they are simply
examples of the genre she so painstakingly seeks to subvert.

Gerhard Richter
Germany, b. 1932
Ema 1992
cibachrome photograph, edition 11/12, 227.5 x 153.5
Mervyn Horton Bequest Fund 1993
14.1993

This extraordinary work, commissioned for the Ninth Biennale of Sydney, is less a two-dimensional image than a part of the environment. The woman of the title, naked and blurred though she is, strides into view and seems about to step, like Pygmalion's Galatea, into the real space of the museum. This is not disturbing so much as intriguing, a response compounded by the difficulty of identifying the technique Richter has used in the work. Is it a photograph or a painting? In fact, it is a photograph of a painting, derived in turn from an original photograph of Richter's wife, Ema, descending a staircase in the manner of Duchamp's famous nude. Such circular complexities are part and parcel of Richter's practice, for which the description 'conceptual' is the least limiting we have. Active since the 1960s, the German artist has consistently played with the crossover point of artistic conventions, in the end establishing a richly allusive convention of his own.

Australian Collection

Australian Collection

Visitors to the Australian rooms of the old wing of the Gallery may experience immediately the golden age of Australian painting and an essential history of the institution. Here may be found the auspicious beginnings of the collections of the Art Gallery of New South Wales symbolising a powerful sentiment within the Gallery, from its establishment, to represent local artists. This early commitment to local art blossomed in the 1880s and 1890s with the acquisition of some of the greatest of all Australian paintings.

The Gallery pursued this policy to a varying degree into the twentieth century, however it was not until the 1950s and early 1960s, activated by the appointments of professional staff, that the Gallery began to seriously flesh out the Australian collection retrospectively, with works by earlier colonial artists and, surprisingly, the earliest modernist school in Australia. Iconic works of this formative period of modernism did not enter the collection until much later, from about 1960. These may be found by the visitor by moving from the old wing to the twentieth-century Australian rooms in the newer part of the building.

It was also in the 1960s that the Gallery began to substantially establish the Aboriginal collection now presented in the beautiful Yiribana Gallery for Aboriginal and Torres Strait Islander art in the lower eastern part of the building. The Australian collection allows viewers to look backward and forward – from inherited traditions of the early nineteenth century through to an identifiable Australian way of seeing and interpreting the landscape and its people as well as international influence, to the modern and postmodern age and beyond – to glimpse the challenges of the approaching millennium.

John Glover
England, 1767–1849
Natives on the Ouse River, Van Diemen's Land 1838
oil on canvas, 78.5 x 115.6
Purchased with assistance from Mr and Mrs J. K. Bain 1985
48.1985

John Glover enjoyed two careers, first as a prodigious painter in the eighteenth-century picturesque manner in his native England (he called himself the English Claude) then as a nineteenth century colonial landscapist in his adopted Tasmania. The simplicity, one might say naivety, of his Australian manner is exemplified in this pellucid re-imagining of Aboriginal life. Bright tonalities and verdant colouring contribute to the Edenic scene, belying the atrocities to which the native inhabitants of the island were being subjected. Like W. B. Gould, Glover concentrated his artistic activity in and around what was then Van Diemen's Land. His mainland reputation was not secured until well into the twentieth century, though then with undiminishing certainty.

Maurice Felton
Australia, c. 1805–1842
Portrait of Mrs Alexander Spark 1840
oil on canvas, 142.5 x 114
Purchased 1974
117.1974

Between his arrival in Sydney in 1839 and his death three years later, Maurice Felton, naval surgeon and sometime painter, exhibited landscapes, animal studies and society portraits to considerable acclaim. This portrait's sitter was the wife of an art collector and patron elaborately resident in semi-rural Tempe. Her desire to be portrayed as a woman of substance is as apparent as Felton's eagerness to accommodate it. Mrs Spark boasts a queenly cargo of fur, fabric and jewellery, brought off with as much care as her creamy skin and curvaceous lip. The inclusion of botanical and geographical details – Sydney Harbour and the datura blossom for example – would have allowed any reasonably informed observer in England to identify the setting. As elsewhere in colonial portraiture, the leather-bound book hints at a cultivation that was, if not an accomplishment of the sitter, then assuredly an aspiration.

W. B. Gould
Australia, 1803–1853
Flowers and fruit 1849
oil on canvas, 65.8 x 76.8
Purchased 1956
9196

In a period when still-life painting of any kind, let alone the showy variety instanced here, was rare in Australia, Gould produced a significant body of flower pieces and related nature studies. Transported to Tasmania for theft in 1827, he worked variously as draughtsman, coach painter, scenographer and botanical illustrator. Gould's conventionalised but highly proficient style confirms a background in china painting and the lesser applied arts, though he claimed loftier derivation from no less than the Royal Academy. His principal activity was in Launceston and Hobart, where he died an emancipated citizen in 1853. Now darkened, this picture was once more brightly coloured, but even in its current state it conveys a sense of opulence and fertility.

Eugene von Guérard
Australia/Germany, 1811–1901
A figtree on American Creek near Wollongong, NSW 1861
oil on canvas, 83.7 x 66.1
Purchased 1996
398.1996

The son of a court painter in Vienna, von Guérard arrived in Melbourne in
1852. Early gold-field studies were followed by an astonishing series of pastoral
panoramas documenting the estates of wealthy colonial settlers, especially in
western Victoria. Von Guérard's New South Wales subjects are rarer, but equal
in their quality of invention. This meticulous essay in the minor sublime is
typical of the artist's sophisticated response to the Australian landscape. The
mighty tree rises from ferny undergrowth against a luminous sky: a totem of
nature unconstrained. Photographic conventions are arguably referenced in this
work, von Guérard being no stranger to the new medium.

Eugene von Guérard
Australia/Germany, 1811–1901
Sydney Heads 1865
oil on canvas, 56 x 94
Bequest of Major H. W. Hall 1974
122.1974

By the time he completed this breathtaking vista, the industrious von Guérard
had won a considerable, if not consistently remunerative, colonial following.
He became Master of Painting at the National Gallery School in Melbourne,
as well as a curator of that collecting institution. In these roles, and through
his many important commissions, von Guérard set an impressive professional
example to colleagues, students and buyers. It testifies to the faithfulness of
his vision that this bird's-eye view remains, almost a century and a-half later,
unmistakably and gloriously Sydney. The picture itself was worked up from at
least one preliminary drawing and painted in Victoria.

Louis Buvelot
Australia/Switzerland/Brazil, 1814–1888
At Lilydale 1870
oil on canvas, 76.1 x 101.6
Purchased with funds provided by the Art Gallery Society of New South Wales 1990
244.1990

The Swiss-born Buvelot arrived in Melbourne in 1865. By consensus one of the progenitors of Australian landscape painting, he brought to the subject a familiarity with the techniques of the Barbizon School and a flexibility of handling that suited colonial conditions. This exceptional example of his mature style records farmland near Lilydale, Victoria. Buvelot constructs the picture according to clear – and time-honoured – divisions of foreground, middle-ground and distance, united by an ameliorated Antipodean atmosphere. *At Lilydale* provides a brilliant foretaste of the Heidelberg School, Australia's response to the *plein air* tradition, while standing on its own multiple merits as one of the finest Australian landscapes of its category.

Lucien Henry
Australia/France, 1850–1896
Waratah 1887
oil on wood, 51 x 35
Gift of Marcel Aurousseau 1983
238.1983

This Beaux-Arts graduate and Paris Communard was exiled from France to New Caledonia, settling in Sydney after his reprieve in 1879. As both teacher and practising designer, Henry made a vital contribution to the Sydney art scene during two of its most active and experimental decades. Fascinated by the pictorial possibilities of native flora and fauna – especially the waratah, the floral emblem of New South Wales – Henry produced superlative designs for stained glass, interior decor, architecture and items of applied art. Although his painstaking technique adds to the flower's three-dimensionality, the graphic organisation and intense colouring of this resplendent image cannot account for the almost surrealistic impact of the protuberant bloom at its centre.

John Peter Russell
Australia, 1858–1930
Madame Sisley on the banks of the Loing at Moret 1887
oil on canvas
45.7 x 60.9
Margaret Hannah Olley Art Trust 1996
768.1996

While his compatriots Arthur Streeton and Tom Roberts were still coming to terms with *plein air* painting, the Australian painter John Peter Russell had already superseded it, imbibing impressionism at its source and from its masters. A friend of Monet, Toulouse-Lautrec, van Gogh and Alfred Sisley, Russell was likeable and industrious. Financially independent, he regularly rescued needy colleagues, pursuing his own career without commercial constraint. Russell's portrait of Vincent hangs in the van Gogh Museum in Amsterdam. *Madame Sisley* is a faultless display of his impressionist credentials. Deft and casual, the work is as much a performative event as a depictive record, an autumnal trace of the moment Madame Sisley ambled with a book by the long-shadowed banks of the Loing.

Tom Roberts
Australia, 1856–1931
*Holiday sketch at
Coogee* 1888
oil on canvas, 40.3 x 55.9
Purchased 1954
9078

Echoing an equally
celebrated painting of
the same subject by
his younger colleague,
Charles Conder, this
bright and breezy
depiction of the Sydney
ocean beach is spirited, almost summary, in execution. Roberts was visiting
from Melbourne at the time, which perhaps lent his work a note of impatience.
The site in question is verifiably Coogee, in this case populated by overdressed
day-trippers from town. *Holiday sketch at Coogee* is an early testament to
the outdoor culture that still conditions the Australian character – and a
textbook display of *plein air* technique. The pigment is applied in flicks and
flurries that replicate the glancing sunlight of an April day.

David Davies
Australia,
1864–1939
*From a distant
land* 1889
oil on canvas
80.9 x 115.6
Purchased 1968
OA15.1968

A letter from
abroad occasioned
mixed emotions
in the colonial
recipient. What
news would be
conveyed from 'home', what questions answered and travails revealed? Who
had married, died, prospered, failed? Who would be arriving on the next boat,
or compelled to embark on it? There are clues enough in this narrative tableau,
but it is the quality of light rather than any anecdotal properties that makes
it interesting to modern viewers. Ballarat-born and trained in Melbourne by
George Folingsby and Frederick McCubbin, Davies subsequently spent time in
Paris and St Ives, Cornwall, where he encountered French and English *plein air*
painting first hand. His exquisite *A summer evening* (1895) is also a collection
favourite.

Charles Conder
Australia, 1868–1909
Departure of the Orient, Circular Quay 1888
oil on canvas, 45.1 x 50.1
Purchased 1888
829

It is probable this bravura composition inspired Arthur Streeton to paint *The railway station, Redfern* some years later. For a brief but dazzling interlude, Charles Conder was the most precocious of the young painters then disrupting the traditional outlines of Australian art. He was also the one most given to compositional daring. Painted a mere five years after he arrived from England as a 15-year-old, this Whistlerian experiment in tone is Conder's graduation piece as an artist. The modernity of its setting, its Japoniste inflections and studied informality make it a definitive example of aestheticism. Little wonder Conder gravitated to Paris and London in the 1890s, making his mark in the circles of Toulouse-Lautrec and Oscar Wilde.

Julian Ashton
Australia, 1851–1942
The prospector 1889
oil on canvas on hardboard, 213.4 x 116.9
Purchased 1889
4554

Ashton's gift for paraphrase is highlighted in this heroic representation of an
Australian type. It is less a portrait than a character study reminiscent of the
illustrations the artist had come to the colony to prepare for Melbourne's
Illustrated Australian News in 1878 and, later, for the *Picturesque Atlas of
Australasia* and the *Bulletin*. Ashton's prospector is a beguiling fellow, stained
by his labours and tanned by the sun. That this is a city-dweller's version of the
frontier experience, and therefore somewhat theatrical, does not rob it of
human vitality. Ashton went on to instruct several generations of important
painters through his Sydney Art School. He became a trustee of the Gallery in
1888, championing the purchase of Australian art.

Arthur Streeton
Australia, 1867–1943
Still glides the stream and shall forever glide 1890
oil on canvas, 82 x 153
Purchased 1890
859

The first of Arthur Streeton's landscapes to be purchased by a public institution –
in this case virtually still wet – *Still glides the stream and shall forever glide*
remains among his most poetic. A depiction of the Yarra River in Victoria
winding down from the Dandenong Ranges, it consciously romanticises the
uneventful scrubland and placid pastures of the Heidelberg flats where painters
such as Streeton and Roberts first began working in a quasi-impressionist style.
The atmosphere is as literary as the title. Streeton's aim was to evoke a mental
state as much as record an actual place, though he added identifiable plant
forms to the foreground at the behest of a pedantic Gallery trustee.

Arthur Streeton
Australia, 1867–1943
Fire's on 1891
oil on canvas, 183.8 x 122.5
Purchased 1893
832

The single year that separates this unforgettable dossier from Streeton's previous notation, *Still glides the stream and shall forever glide*, might as well be twenty. *Fire's on* is an achievement of startling maturity for an artist not yet twenty-five, an indication of the rapid development of his talent as he worked within the periphery of the admired Tom Roberts in the ever-changing environs of Sydney and Melbourne. In deliberate synchrony, the vertical format and faceted brushwork of this painting convey the mineral structure of the blasted cliff face so searingly depicted. Streeton conveys the reality of this place in an almost journalistic degree of detail. The viewer observes the rush of open sky, the profiled stands of eucalypt, the nation-building enterprise of a rail-line pushed through rock – noting, finally, a worker's corpse borne from the tunnel and a woman's headlong descent to him. The painting is thus both dramatic and obstinately without incident, like the Australian continent itself. Streeton allows the mass of rock – disturbed by geological shifts and industrial intervention alike – and the square-brushed cobalt above, to speak in their own immemorial tones.

Tom Roberts
Australia, 1856–1931
Eileen 1892
oil on canvas, 49 x 36
Purchased 1892
998

Some of the most vivacious portrayals of human personality in all Australian
art were produced by Roberts in the final decade of the nineteenth century;
indeed much of his income was derived from portrait commissions. He made
memorably energetic studies of men of influence in Sydney – Sir Henry Parkes
and Cardinal Moran for example – while his portraits of women often suggest
an affinity between artist and sitter. The subject of this stunning portrait is
Mrs Eileen Tooker, an Irish beauty whose husband owned a property in
Rockhampton, Queensland. Eileen's profile, conceived according to the aesthetic
taste of the time, is draped in a sheer veil, its mystery inciting allure. Roberts's
similarly side-on *Smike Streeton age 24* (1891) is also in the collection.

Arthur Streeton
Australia, 1867–1943
The railway station, Redfern 1893
oil on canvas, 40.8 x 61
Gift of Lady Denison 1942
7209

Although landscape was Streeton's métier, he was sufficiently its master to adapt its principles with ease to city and maritime views. This remarkable rendition of one of Sydney's busiest transport interchanges, on the current site of Central Station, lacks none of the atmospherics of his purely natural subjects. It has the added virtue, especially for a contemporary audience, of suggesting transience, even speed. The wet, windy expanse occupying most of the image, punctuated by the activity of steam-engines, carriages and commuters, is realised with a confidence that pulls up short of glibness. The painting resulted from a single three-hour session in front of the scene.

Sydney Long
Australia, 1871–1955
By tranquil waters 1894
oil on canvas, 111.1 x 183.7
Purchased 1894
689

Long's *By tranquil waters* was acquired by the Gallery while the artist was still a student. Little wonder: it is wholly delightful. Bearing evidence of the techniques of his instructors, A. J. Daplyn and Julian Ashton, and echoing boyish bathing scenes by Roberts and Streeton, the work is nonetheless stamped with the quality of bucolic fantasy that was Long's special proclivity. He became a productive painter, etcher and teacher, influential in artistic circles in Sydney and eventually active in England. The refined colour and rich application which characterise this work would soon give way to flatter, more graphic tendencies – as in *Pan* (1898), also reproduced. Landscape became his preferred genre.

Tom Roberts
Australia, 1856–1931
The golden fleece 1894
oil on canvas, 104 x 158.7
Purchased 1894
648

Painted by Tom Roberts in the 1890s, a period of change in the pastoral
industry, *The golden fleece* records a way of life as it passed into myth. This
heat-filled hymn to the nobility of human labour and the necessity for commercial
enterprise is an Australian classic. Roberts, with Arthur Streeton and Frederick
McCubbin, founded the Heidelberg School, setting Australian art on a course
of experiment. Here, the rough-hewn shearing shed at Newstead North station
in New South Wales suggests a temple, its central aisle marked by the ritual
movement of manual shears. *The golden fleece* – aptly named for the epic
contribution of wool to late-colonial prosperity – was the second painting by
Roberts of a sheep-shearing subject, and his first to enter a public collection.
Acquired by the Gallery in the year of its execution, the painting has enjoyed
national popularity ever since. The reasons for this are to be found in its
celebration of the social rites of masculine labour, its reassuring dourness and
its superb evocation of the conditions of Australian heat and light. On the
occasion of its purchase in 1894, a writer for the *Bulletin* observed that it was
'undoubtedly the picture of the year... a work bearing evidence throughout
of the most careful study. This is emphatically a picture typifying a phase of
Australian life that is rapidly passing away, and the trustees have done wisely
in securing it for the National [Art] Gallery [of New South Wales]...'

Tom Roberts
Australia, 1856–1931
Bailed up 1895/1927
oil on canvas, 134.5 x 182.8
Purchased 1933
833

Bailed up is as fixed in the cosmology of Australia as the Southern Cross, as laconic as the Australian character itself. Roberts executed the picture largely *en plein air* between February and April 1895, building a perch in a stringy-bark tree for better vantage. The Cobb and Co. coach, horses and most of the mannequin-like figures were added indoors. The early reception of this picture was mixed, the artist reworking it thirty-two years later. It tells us a little about the strategies of bushrangers, its nominal subject, and a great deal about the regional landscape of the Inverell area: about high summer conditions of light and heat, and about the bodily attitudes of men and animals caught at a moment of anticlimactic lassitude. Roberts's vision of the bush, as opposed to bushranging, lends this masterpiece its sustaining interest and power. Nobody before had ever quite captured the hovering torpor of an Australian midday, and arguably nobody since.

E. Phillips Fox
Australia, 1865–1915
Art students 1895
oil on canvas, 182.9 x 114.3
Purchased 1943
7319

This array of feminine forms, as rhythmically statuesque as figures on a classical relief, is one of the treasures of the collection. Eclipsed in renown by his own *The ferry*, Fox's *Art students* remains a vivid demonstration of his compositional and colouristic skill. Polka-dotted prettiness is mediated by the sobriety his young subjects bring to their task, and by certain grubbily realist touches like the oil-spattered floorboards and squished paint-tube. The discarded crust is a remnant, not of lunch, but of bread used as an eraser. Melbourne-born Fox trained at the National Gallery School, took academic instruction and impressionist tips in Paris and discovered *plein air* painting firsthand in St Ives – all factors which inform his work. He was married to, and survived by, the equally gifted painter Ethel Carrick.

W. C. Piguenit
Australia, 1836–1914
The flood in the Darling 1890 1895
oil on canvas, 122.5 x 199.3
Purchased 1895
6105

Few canvases in the Art Gallery of New South Wales, indeed few anywhere in Australia, match the cinematic aplomb of Piguenit's *The flood in the Darling 1890*. The sparkling sweep of this composition, its sense of a scene observed firsthand and faithfully reported, the dazzling manner of its application leading to near-miraculous evocations of water and sky: these qualities lend it iconic status. Tasmanian by birth and essentially self-taught, Piguenit travelled widely and worked prolifically, understanding nature as a spectacle both beautiful and cruel. His twenty-three years with the Colonial Survey Department served him in good stead when he began his second career as a painter. Topographical accuracy charged with a notion of sublimity formed the basis of his approach to landscape. He was vocally averse to the broader techniques of the *plein air* manner. Piguenit did indeed witness the event depicted here, having moved to New South Wales in 1875. He settled in Sydney's Lane Cove in 1880, producing many local river views as well as subjects from the Blue Mountains, the Murray River and, as here, the Darling River. In 1902 he was asked by the Gallery to paint a landscape featuring Mount Kosciuszko, a commission in honour of Australian Federation. Yet despite the majesty of the resulting landscape, *The flood in the Darling 1890* remains the work by which Piguenit is best known.

Frederick McCubbin
Australia, 1855–1917
On the wallaby track 1896
oil on canvas, 122 x 223.5
Purchased 1897
572

With an evident empathy for rural labouring life, and a nationalist message in
keeping with its 1890s date, this much-admired painting by a principal member
of the Heidelberg group entered the collection in 1897. McCubbin studied
under the masterful von Guérard at the National Gallery School. With fellow
pupil Tom Roberts he explored the Studley Park area around Melbourne in
the 1870s; then, on Roberts's return from England, the Box Hill region in the
1880s. With the participation of Arthur Streeton and others, this led to the
birth of the Heidelberg School. McCubbin exhibited in the famous Exhibition
of 9 x 5 'Impressions', small *plein air* paintings of Australian landscapes and
related subjects, but his gift found truest expression in larger statements such as
On the wallaby track. This tableau includes the boiling of a 'billy' of water for
tea, an act of almost mythic significance in Australian culture.

Gordon Coutts
Australia, c. 1869–1937
Waiting c. 1896
oil on canvas, 90.2 x 59.7
Purchased 1896
5893

A mélange of sentiment and social observation, this popular painting is the artist's most esteemed Australian work. Trained in his home town of Glasgow, Coutts continued his studies in Melbourne in 1888. The femininity of the sitter in this painting and the fashionability of her attire were trademarks of Tom Roberts's portrait and genre styles at the time, suggesting the influence of the older artist. The light-filled though unbroken execution of this painting is closer to Manet than Monet, and it is Manet's sedentary mademoiselles waiting in empty cafés who are recalled.

Sydney Long
Australia, 1871–1955
Pan 1898
oil on canvas, 107.5 x 178.8
Gift of J. R. McGregor 1943
9017

One might with justification nominate this painting as an example of Australian art nouveau. Viewed through subaqueous gloom, the human and natural forms swoon like river reeds. Music is both depicted and evoked. A pagan principle that would prove highly attractive to a whole generation of Sydney artists, especially Norman Lindsay, is announced to Australian art. For all its extraordinary beauty, perhaps because of it, the painting contradicts the robustly nationalist imagery of Long's more famous contemporaries. This has not detracted from its enduring popularity in the collection, nor its frank advertisement of the beauties of regional landscape.

Tom Roberts
Australia, 1856–1931
The camp, Sirius Cove c. 1899
oil on canvas on paperboard,
25.4 x 34.6
Purchased 1940
6928

This tiny work belatedly records the artists' encampment at Little Sirius Cove, Sydney Harbour, which Roberts and Streeton shared with bohemians and hangers-on in the early 1880s. By this stage married and comparatively prosperous, Roberts presents the site as an idyll, perhaps a memory, but nonetheless in photographically sharp focus. Flawlessly constructed and crisply executed, it has the precision of a jewel. This, and other water views by Roberts, such as *An autumn morning, Milson's Point, Sydney* (1888), also in the Gallery, helped establish the harbour as a symbol of the city itself. The trademark device by which Roberts dragged the loaded brush across the surface had a profound effect on Arthur Boyd, whose 'Shoalhaven' series is a veritable homage to Roberts and Streeton.

George W. Lambert
Australia, 1873–1930
Across the black soil plains 1899
oil on canvas, 91.6 x 305.5
Purchased 1899
550

Hailed as the picture of its year in Sydney, *Across the black soil plains* was immediately acknowledged as a contribution to the archive of nationalist imagery being assembled by painters such as McCubbin, Roberts and Streeton. Its somewhat self-conscious muscularity reflected the artist's own, promoted in the face of more effete qualities. Lambert had some early training at the Art Society of New South Wales and with Julian Ashton, but precocity was his real tutor. He was a bower-bird of styles, with a preference for van Dyck. This particular work took out the Wynne Prize for landscape, and was, as it remains, widely reproduced.

George W. Lambert
Australia, 1873–1930
Miss Thea Proctor 1903
oil on canvas, 91.5 x 71
Purchased under the terms of the Florence Turner Blake Bequest 1961
OA12.1961

A pupil and protégée of Lambert, Thea Proctor was an indispensable fixture in the cultural life of Sydney during the 1920s. Not only did she embody style, she dictated it. Her pronouncements on taste, published with her designs in trend-setting journals such as *The Home*, were regarded as definitive. Her decorative watercolours and prints remain esteemed. Portrayed here as an ingénue by Lambert during their London years, Proctor was rumoured to be his lover. Returning to Sydney from England and Europe, she formed, with him, the modernist-friendly Contemporary Group of artists in 1926. In this portrait Lambert captures her elegance and self-possession, if little of her deeper personality – which she took pains to conceal.

Hans Heysen
Australia, 1877–1968
The coming home 1904
oil on canvas, 106.4 x 184.6
Purchased 1904
5733

Hamburg-born but irrevocably associated with his adopted South Australia, Heysen's mere name has the power to summon landscape in the minds of most Australians. There was a time when this supremely talented watercolourist and oil painter seemed to hold copyright on the very look of the continent; certainly the look of its trees. *The coming home* reflects Heysen's youthful interest in the Romantic scenes of Victorian and Edwardian pastoral painting. This is, after all, a version of farmyard life without sweat or slog. A languor, perhaps indebted more to Alfred Lord Tennyson than to actual twilight, pervades the air. Heysen's sure touch and sweet sensibility contribute to the accessibility of the work.

Bertram Mackennal
Australia, 1863–1931
The dancer 1904
bronze, 168 x 71 x 69
Purchased 1910
700

For much of his working life Mackennal, sculptor and sculptor's son, was the most famous expatriate Australian artist of them all. The first from this country to be elected a member of the Royal Academy, he achieved the professional advancement in England that so eluded Tom Roberts. Based upon his ability to work speedily, and completely within the dictates of convention, Mackennal's career was in essence that of an official iconographer. State and establishment commissions came his way, especially memorials. *The dancer* attests to his less public side, the part of his artistic identity that admired and imitated Rodin, with whom he had contact. The surface animations of symbolism and art nouveau, the twin influences of his youth, speak through the simpler planes of this Rodinesque nude.

Hugh Ramsay
Australia, 1877–1906
The sisters 1904
oil on canvas on hardboard, 125.7 x 144.8
Purchased 1921
849

Beyond its veracity as a double portrait – in fact a composite of the artist's
three sisters – and its specification of fashion and femininity at a precise
historical date, this canvas is imbued with an unsettling subtext. Ramsay
identifies in his sisters' eyes the watchful cognisance of his own ill-health.
His death soon after surprised no-one, certainly not these satiny seraphs, one
of whom even has wings. The poses derive from the canon of melancholy and
mourning. A bravura production from a painter not yet thirty, *The sisters* is
a stylistic marriage of John Singer Sargent and Diego Velázquez, yet an image
of extraordinary originality. Ramsay's confident massing of form within
cropped confines, his nuancing of tonal gradation and textural effect combine
to produce an unforgettable work of art.

Rupert Bunny
Australia, 1864–1947
A summer morning c. 1908
oil on canvas, 222 x 181.5
Purchased 1911
666

Salon painting as a precept and as a practice had no more loyal adherent than
Rupert Bunny. Born and educated in Melbourne, Bunny began a lifetime of
European travel and residence in 1884. The success of his academic and
essentially escapist project in Paris and London was real, complicit though it
proved to be with the self-delusion of an age on the edge of war. Bunny's
dedication to the good life resulted in some of the most sumptuous paintings in
Australian art history, and the most admired. This is one of them. The artist's
wife, kittenish herself, plays with a lapful of cats. Her companion accepts a
basin of milk from a meaningfully shadowed maid. As upholstered in privilege
as they are in their lacy day-gowns, Bunny's women are the late-picked fruit of a
century whose heyday had passed. Despite his stylistic conservatism, the painter
kept a finger on the pulse of taste. He responded to post-impressionism and
fauvism, albeit belatedly, in a series of brilliantly coloured compositions on
classical themes in the 1920s. During that decade, Bunny returned twice to
Australia, settling permanently in 1933. Music, in which he had always had a
parallel interest, became increasingly important to him: even so palpable a
painting as *A summer morning*, with its plump depictions of fabric and flesh,
has a musical ethereality.

George W. Lambert
Australia, 1873–1930
Holiday in Essex 1910
oil on canvas, 183.8 x 230.6
Purchased with assistance from the Art Gallery Society of New South Wales
and the Marshall Bequest Fund 1981
157.1981

The royal sitters of Velázquez are silent participants in this impressive pageant
of the Australian artist's family. Casual in pose yet courtly in demeanour,
Lambert's wife, Amy, and two of their sons peruse the world with proprietorial
condescension. Every inch an image intended for public display, *Holiday in
Essex* confirms Lambert as one of the flashiest stylists of his generation.
Sydney having proved too dowdy, he left for London and his destiny in 1900,
becoming a fixture of Edwardian artistic circles and a champion of academic
values in art. Despite his conservatism, Lambert was an incomparable teacher
of drawing, influencing many of the Sydney modernists on his return to
Australia in the 1920s.

E. Phillips Fox
Australia, 1865–1915
The ferry c. 1910–11
oil on canvas, 114.6 x 152.4
Purchased 1949
8171

Though distanced by at least three decades from the high-water mark of
French impressionism, *The ferry* retains the distinction of being the most
flamboyantly impressionist image ever produced by an Australian painter,
both in subject matter and handling. Completed in Paris in 1911, but recalling
earlier visits to beachside resorts like Deauville – indeed, seeming to evoke
an entire, and entirely vanished, *belle époque* – this masterpiece of the artist's
maturity was belatedly purchased for the collection in 1949. Since then it has
achieved a notice unmatched by even the most blue-and-gold of Streeton's or
Roberts's *œuvre*. This is surely due in part to Fox's magisterial response to
perspective problems: linear, spatial and atmospheric. The design is Japoniste
in its complexity, an influence probably absorbed via post-impressionism.

Grace Cossington Smith
Australia, 1892–1984
The sock knitter 1915
oil on canvas, 61.6 x 50.7
Purchased 1960
OA18.1960

With this reductive but richly nuanced work, the young Grace Cossington
Smith challenged the predominance of academic painting in Australia.
The artist's first exhibited painting, *The sock knitter* is also the first post-
impressionist image executed in Australia, and arguably our first frankly
modern work of art with its echoes of figures such as Cézanne and Matisse.
It is, furthermore, the first Australian picture to credibly displace masculine
labour, replacing it with an iconography of feminine fortitude. Cossington
Smith studied in Sydney with Anthony Dattilo-Rubbo, a Neapolitan Salonist
instrumental in the roster of moderns that included Roland Wakelin and
Roy de Maistre. She travelled little, worked conscientiously and lived quietly,
her fifty-year career distinguished at every stage by the vitalist doctrine of
colour inaugurated in this image. The subject of the painting is the artist's
sister Madge, depicted here knitting socks for soldiers as a contribution to
the war effort. She is seated in the garden studio built for Cossington Smith
by her supportive father, a renowned Establishment solicitor. This anecdote
aside, the figure is uncompromisingly conceived as a formal shape against
a formalised background.

Roland Wakelin
Australia, 1887–1971
Down the hills to Berry's Bay 1916
oil on canvas on hardboard, 68 x 122
Purchased 1961
OA18.1961

Although compositionally conservative, this landscape is correctly regarded as Wakelin's post-impressionist manifesto. A pupil of Dattilo-Rubbo, a colleague of Cossington Smith and Roy de Maistre, the New Zealand-born Wakelin participated in the mild-mannered modernism that became Sydney's 'house style' between the wars. Recalling Streeton's paintings of the harbour city from the 1890s, *Down the hills to Berry's Bay* also harks back to colonial views by Joseph Lycett and Conrad Martens, and anticipates the work of Lloyd Rees and Brett Whiteley. It exemplifies post-impressionism in the clarity of its hues and in the broken system of their application. At other times Wakelin's tendencies were variously tonalist, impressionist, fauvist and notionally abstract.

Roland Wakelin
Australia, 1887–1971
Synchromy in orange major 1919
oil on cardboard, 30 x 40
Mervyn Horton Bequest Fund 1983
50.1985

What convinced the cautious Wakelin to embark on an interlude of avant-gardism around 1919 can only be surmised. In that year, with Roy de Maistre, he showed 'colour harmonies' – tiny chromatic experiments without precedent in Australian painting. Older by a few years than his co-exhibitor, Wakelin was feasibly fired by a spirit of competition and camaraderie. *Synchromy in orange major* is a landscape, but one in which the structural underpinnings of place have been extracted, stripped, and presented for pure aesthetic consideration, not for descriptive purposes. A rare handful of related studies survive, Wakelin having revoked the enterprise in 1920.

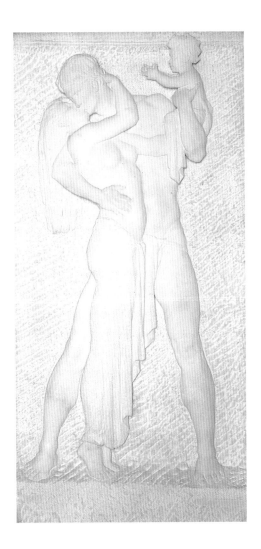

Rayner Hoff
Australia, 1894–1937
Idyll: love and life 1926
marble, 106.7 x 52 x 13
Gift of Howard Hinton 1926
1323

A relatively short Australian tenure – from 1923 to his death following a
surfing accident in 1937 – did not prevent Rayner Hoff transforming the face
of Australian sculpture. No active practitioner of the period is more associated
with art deco, for example, or with the redirection of monumental statuary in
Sydney towards an expressively inflected classicism. Hoff's sculpture is robustly
erotic, but never prurient, embodying a paganism which is different in quality
and kind from the coarser work of Norman Lindsay. *Idyll: love and life* might
be described as chaste, despite the languor of its poses. Hoff taught drawing and
sculpture at East Sydney Technical College, whose students revered and imitated
him. Although met at the time with public outrage, Sydney's official Anzac
Memorial in Hyde Park remains his enduring testament.

Elioth Gruner
Australia, 1882–1939
Spring frost 1919
oil on canvas, 131 x 178.7
Gift of F. G. White 1939
6925

Painted in the same year as Wakelin's and de Maistre's experiments in colour harmony, Elioth Gruner's *Spring frost* seems retrograde in comparison, a throwback to the pastoral tradition of colonial art. In fact, that tradition endured healthily into the twentieth century, reinvigorated by painters such as Gruner, an urbane artist with an openness to ideas and an unfailing fluency in the oil-on-canvas medium. Taught by Julian Ashton, it is believed he gave instruction in turn to de Maistre. The broken brushwork in the foreground of the painting also reflects the influence of Phillips Fox on Gruner as well as his younger contemporaries, especially Wakelin and Cossington Smith. Painted according to nineteenth century *plein air* conventions, *Spring frost* is also distinguished by a contemporary succinctness of form. This is one of the collection's most requested images for postcards, posters and reproductions.

Roy de Maistre
Australia, 1894–1968
Rhythmic composition in yellow green minor 1919
oil on paperboard, 85.3 x 115.3
Purchased 1960
OA17.1960

By its title alone this startling composition declares an interest in music. Roy de Maistre had been a student at the Sydney Conservatorium, bringing to painting a musician's awareness of rhythm, repetition and repose. Certainly this work is 'scored' according to synaesthetic principles. The context for de Maistre's cross-disciplinary approach is found in nineteenth-century chromatic theory, theosophy and the quasi-scientific researches of post-impressionism itself. During the First World War he promoted the benefits of colour-therapy for shell-shocked soldiers, painting rooms at a Sydney infirmary. *Rhythmic composition in yellow green minor* can be read as the translation of visual sensation into pure colour.

Roy de Maistre
Australia, 1894–1968
Woman with parasol at Palm Beach 1927
oil on hardboard, 32 x 43
Bequest of Mervyn Horton 1983
49.1985

Like Wakelin, de Maistre recanted the incipient abstraction of his colour
harmonies in favour of a blander, more saleable, variation of modernism.
Habitually broke, neither of them could afford the luxury of avant-gardism
for long. This image is a slice of middle-class life destined for return to it.
De Maistre understood this, but it did not blight his authorship of some of
the lushest landscape and genre paintings of the 1920s. Never uninteresting,
he is no less than compelling in this solar homage to Sydney's Palm Beach.
Having expatriated himself to England in 1930, de Maistre honed an adapt-
ably academic cubism that influenced his admirer, the young Francis Bacon.

Margaret Preston
Australia, 1875–1963
Implement blue 1927
oil on canvas on paperboard, 42.5 x 43
Gift of the artist 1960
OA7.1960

Preston's single-minded pursuit of the grail of modernism led to paintings and prints that are simply incomparable. Hers was no sudden eureka of discovery: she studied originally with Frederick McCubbin and the pedantic Bernard Hall. Years of academic training, overseas tuition and sheer industry preceded Margaret Rose McPherson's transfiguration into an artist of tenacious and polemic repute. She was a learned educator who put artistic theory into pictorial practice. *Implement blue* has the exterior fixity, and internal energy, of the modern machines she often eulogised. The very word 'implement' suggests a mechanistic category for which still life would be an all too inappropriate designation.

Margaret Preston
Australia, 1875–1963
Western Australian gum blossom 1928
oil on canvas, 54.6 x 44.5
Purchased 1978
93.1978

Preston believed that the simple and familiar were fit subjects for painting.
In this indisputable masterpiece she puts a native posy in a plain pot against
a paper placard. Only in orderliness is the arrangement decorative. *Western
Australian gum blossom* operates on a dogged disregard for prettiness. Every
element – the proto-abstract fields of black and white, the huddled leafage,
hardy gum nuts and multiple flower-heads – appears consensual and concrete.
The work acknowledges cubism, while reflecting the artist's own finesse with
relief-print techniques: the pigment seems 'placed' rather than simply painted.
That it might also invoke the cruciforms and squares of constructivism is not
out of the question. Yet the reason this painting is so esteemed lies above all
in its unapologetic Australian character.

Grace Crowley
Australia, 1890–1979
Portrait of Lucie Beynis 1929
oil on canvas on hardboard, 79 x 64.5
Purchased 1965
OA14.1965

Another graduate of Julian Ashton's
Sydney Art School, succeeding Gruner
as a teacher there in 1918, Crowley
studied in France with the late-cubist
painters André Lhote and Albert Gleizes
throughout the 1920s. Her continental
researches with colleague Anne Dangar
led to the formulation of a highly
rational approach to painting, a sort of
classicising cubism, which she put into
practice on her return to Sydney in the
1930s. With Ralph Balson, and long after the pioneering attempts of Wakelin
and de Maistre, Crowley eventually came to paint an important series of pure
abstract paintings in the 1940s. *Portrait of Lucie Beynis* was completed at
the close of her Paris period; indeed, it may be read as an exercise in Parisian
chic. The subject, a fellow artist, is conceived as an emphatic diagonal, the
compositional element Crowley believed the most dynamic of all. Offsetting
this, planes and lozenges of warm colour lock the figure architectonically.

Arthur Murch
Australia, 1902–1989
Beach idyll 1930
tempera on canvas
on plywood
35.5 x 59.1
Purchased with
assistance from the
Visual Arts Board,
Australia Council
Contemporary Art
Purchase Grant 1975
57.1975

The strain of Arcadianism in Australian art of the twentieth century has its
roots in *fin de siècle* productions such as Sydney Long's *By tranquil waters*
and *Pan*, as well as in work by the Lindsay clan, Rupert Bunny and George
Lambert. Arthur Murch assisted Lambert on public projects in Sydney in the
late 1920s, absorbing his colleague's figural style though not his artificiality.
A brilliant designer and colourist with a fine poetic sensibility, Murch was
given to portrayals of femininity and motherhood. *Beach idyll* bears this out
in a rendition of family life Edenic in splendour. If a hint of the pub painter
intervenes, with the image just a dune away from the beach-themed beer
advertisements of the day, this only serves to confirm the irrepressible
Australianness that underpinned Murch's classical overlays.

Grace Cossington Smith
Australia, 1892–1984
The curve of the bridge 1928–29
oil on cardboard, 110.5 x 82.5
Purchased with funds provided by the Art Gallery Society of New South Wales
and James Fairfax 1991
1.1991

Inseparable from Australian modernity, the 'great bridge at Sydney' was the
largest engineering enterprise undertaken here between the wars. As the
cantilevers rose to meet mid-air, a nation imagined itself completed. Of the
many artists and photographers moved to record the soaring superstructure,
Cossington Smith was surely the most inspired. In the industrial grossness of
girders she saw, and painted, ethereality. Even here, in the more earth-bound of
two defining versions of the subject, the steel colossus hovers into frame like a
sci-fi mothership. Viewed from the North Shore, the unfinished bridge brackets
a city it has since come to symbolise – not least through the vision of this artist.
Her agitated attack, sustained across the entire composition, reverberates
through air, iron and earth alike.

William Dobell

Australia, 1899–1970
The boy at the basin 1932
oil on wood, 41 x 33.2
Purchased 1939
6788

William Dobell's destiny in portraiture
is not infallibly forecast in this genre
piece, but intimations of his insight
abound. The room and its obsessively
observed contents, not least the som-
nambulant semi-nude, are charged
with a singular intensity. The art-
historical model is Vermeer, though
Rembrandt would soon prevail as
Dobell's pre-eminent Dutch master.
Lavish, yet decorous too, the paint
assumes a pink-grey skin of almost
living promise. After early training at
Julian Ashton's, Dobell graduated in 1931 from the Slade School in London,
a city whose streetlife he wittily, sometimes spitefully, documented over the
ensuing decade. The satirical character of Dobell's Australian work finds gentler
expression here in the affectionate mockery of a lazy English sleeper awakened.
Originally, the figure was intended for inclusion in an outdoor beach scene.

Nora Heysen

Australia, b. 1911
Self-portrait 1932
oil on canvas, 76.2 x 61.2
Gift of Howard Hinton 1932
943

The determination required to build
an artistic career – and build it
independently of a famous father –
is the psychological subtext of this
self-portrait. Heysen summons help
from art history: Vermeer's *The artist
in the studio cradling her head like a
friend*. With a number of equally dour
self-portraits from her apprentice
years, this painting has the meticulous
finish and confrontational tone found
in the German New Objectivity
movement. The artist studied in London under Bernard Meninsky, her painting
style reflecting his, and that of other English masters such as Augustus John and
Henry Tonks. On her return to Australia she was the first woman to win the
Archibald Prize for portraiture, in 1938.

Jean Broome-Norton
Australia, b. 1911
Abundance 1934, cast 1987
bronze, 128.5 x 67.5 x 22
Purchased 1985
427.1985

Of the many gifted students who came under the sway of Rayner Hoff at East
Sydney Technical College, Jean Broome-Norton, Lyndon Dadswell and Barbara
Tribe were the most diligent, each advancing to self-sufficient careers. So adept
was Broome-Norton in the Hoff manner that she assisted in completing his King
George V monument in Canberra after his death. Her independent statuary,
of which the art deco *Abundance* is a notable example, is suppleness itself. Her
plaster reliefs for corporate buildings in Sydney during the 1930s and 1940s,
and her subsequent activity as a jewellery designer for Hardy Brothers, point to
the determined decorativeness of her style, though not to any exclusion of
vitality or eroticism. She was Hoff's match in both.

Grace Cossington Smith
Australia, 1892–1984
The Lacquer Room 1935
oil on paperboard on plywood, 74 x 90.8
Purchased 1967
OA10.1967

For many, this jubilant interior is Sydney in the 1930s. Painted during
Cossington Smith's suburban sequestration in Turramurra, it serenades the
simple thrill of a trip into town. The misnamed Lacquer Room of the title
was an American-style soda fountain in retailer David Jones's Elizabeth Street
store, although there are some who remember the Lacquer Room in Farmer's
department store and feel the composition may reflect both. An excuse for the
interplay of complementary colours and conflicting tangents, the composition
answers the café paintings of van Gogh with gusto. Enshrined in the mass
cultural image bank of Australia, it has decorated book covers, postcards,
calendars and telephone directories, and inspired the wishful efforts of
countless imitators.

Herbert Badham
Australia, 1899–1961
Breakfast piece 1936
oil on hardboard, 59 x 71
Purchased 1936
6381

Teacher, author and administrator,
Badham found little enough time
to paint even without being
slowed by the demands of an
academic technique. His realist
values were an amalgam of those
of his teacher, Julian Ashton,
and – as with Nora Heysen – a certain contemporary shift towards classical
strategies. *Breakfast piece* is a collusion between portraiture and still life.
The woman enacts her morning ritual of newspapers, toast and tea with an
abstractness close to boredom. Distanced by some thought other than the
breakfast articles around her, she does in fact become an article herself, an
elaborately limbed furnishing that catches Badham's eye as unemotively as the
egg-cup and cutlery. The chequered tablecloth lends a note of festivity.

John D. Moore
Australia, 1888–1958
Sydney Harbour
1936
oil on canvas
91.5 x 122.5
Purchased 1936
6382

The paintings, more
usually watercolours,
of John D. Moore
have a patrician tenor
that puts them with
Badham's at the
classicising end of the
modernist scale. Never one to distort or improvise, Moore's precision is of a
kind the surrealists exploited, finding strangeness in exactitude. Despite the
graphic rendering, which speaks of his architectural training, Moore's art is
imbued with a dreamy dullness of atmosphere, a relentless suspension of things
in heavy space. Topographically faultless, this harbour view is scenographic, one
might say theatrical. Scudding clouds, calm waters and carefully constructed
objects contribute to an autumnal hymn to Sydney Harbour.

Ralph Balson

Australia, 1890–1964
Portrait of Grace Crowley 1939
oil on canvas on cardboard,
108.8 x 64.3
Bequest of Grace Crowley 1980
123.1980

The teachings of Grace Crowley and Rah
Fizelle, promoted through the school of
modern painting they set up in Sydney in
1932, require no more vindication than the
work of Ralph Balson, their pupil and friend.
By trade a housepainter, English-born Balson
painted the rooms of the Crowley–Fizelle
academy, using them in lieu of the studio he
did not possess. This portrait of his mentor
and intimate is executed in a quasi-abstract
style, a prelude to the complete non-figuration
he unveiled to the Australian public in an
historic solo exhibition in 1941. Crowley's features retain a vestige of three-
dimensionality where all else fractures into planes. Her character, too, holds out
against the flattening assertions of Balson's brush. The painter was, by turns, an
ardent devotee of geometric abstraction, abstract expressionism and tachism.

Margel Hinder

Australia, 1906–1995
Mother and child 1939
ironbark, 125.5 x 38 x 38
Purchased 1994
554.1994

Arriving from the United States in 1934
with her Australian partner, Frank Hinder,
this prolific sculptor was well-versed in
contemporary international developments
in art. In Sydney she studied with Eleanore
Lange, a German-born artist–teacher, and
began experimenting with local timbers and
stone. *Mother and child* shows how quickly
she accommodated Australian materials,
and a certain Australian robustness as well.
Though strongly influenced by English
sculpture of the interwar period, especially
that of Henry Moore and Jacob Epstein,
Hinder's truer inspiration came from her
interest in vitalist philosophies and theories.
The self-contained poise of this image soon
gave way to a restlessness more resonant of
modern times.

Charles Meere
Australia, 1890–1961
Australian beach pattern 1940
oil on canvas, 91.5 x 122
Purchased 1965
OA20.1965

Many exponents of the belated art deco that flourished in Sydney in the 1930s and 1940s experimented with beachscape, a sub-genre of marine painting much suited to the art of an island nation. None did so with the monumental impulse of Charles Meere. His strategy was to populate an average ocean beach, the Coogee of Roberts and Conder, say, with gods of the surf and caryatids of the sand. Grand in scale, aggrandising in intent, *Australian beach pattern* carries echoes of the Renaissance and antiquity, with a dash of naturism thrown in. American murals of the 1930s are also suggested. No day at the beach was ever so balletic as this, but Meere conveys the worship of sun, sand and sea that has often been seen to epitomise Australian culture. The sobriety of Meere's colouring adds to the already sacramental effect of the figures.

Eric Thake
Australia, 1904–1982
Archaeopteryx 1941
oil on canvas, 41.9 x 52
Purchased 1964
OA6.1964

Famed for his ingenious linocuts,
Thake's rarer watercolours and oils
constitute a more haunting body of
work. Associated with the unregulated
manifestation of surrealism in Australia,
he produced a few images that are indispensable to it. *Archaeopteryx* is among
these. With a directness derived from his experience as a graphic artist and
medical illustrator – and hinting at the wittiness of his later war work – Thake
creates a composition of immediate legibility. The naturalistic eggshell has given
issue to a surrealistic flying machine reminiscent of Marcel Duchamp and Max
Ernst, its lizard-like head and feathered body evoking the prehistoric creature of
the title. Thake's inspiration for this image was a book by Willi Ley in which
Australia is described as a world's-end warehouse of nature's experiments.

Eric Wilson
Australia, 1911–1946
Abstract – the kitchen stove 1943
oil, paper on plywood, 145.5 x 79.7
Gift of the New South Wales Travelling
Art Scholarship Committee 1946
7663

The synthetic cubism of Picasso and
Braque, concluded at least twenty years
before this Sydney variant, permitted
decorative invention of an elaborate
order. Eric Wilson investigated the style
in a series of large-scale, complex
compositions that signify, with those of
his compatriot John Wardell Power, an
impressive Australian response to the
movement. J. S. Watkins and Julian
Ashton were among Wilson's early
teachers, hence the realism he pursued
in parallel with a more modernist
practice. In London he studied with
Mark Gertler, Bernard Meninsky and
Amédée Ozenfant, the last painter's
purist aesthetic especially influencing his
manner. His own teacherly influence on Australian art in the 1940s, though
considerable, was curtailed by an early death. *Abstract – the kitchen stove*
testifies to the works he might have achieved as much as to those he did.

Sidney Nolan
Australia, 1917–1992
Self-portrait 1943
synthetic polymer paint on hessian sacking on hardboard, 61 x 52
Purchased with funds provided by the Art Gallery Society of New South Wales 1997
412.1997

In his early work Sidney Nolan stood out as one of the most dazzlingly original artists of his generation in Australia. Painted when Nolan was just twenty-six, this self-portrait displays all the irony, intelligence and economy of his more mature work. In its graphic and psychological precision, the image prefigures Nolan's abiding fascination with the topography and psyche of his country. Painted at Dimboola in the Wimmera district of Victoria during the artist's military service, *Self-portrait* also foreshadows the naive style of the Ned Kelly series of 1946–47. In the early 1940s, however, his influence was not Henri Rousseau, but child art: Nolan had seen mask-like faces with striped foreheads painted by the so-called 'haptic' children in Viktor Löwenfeld's book *The Nature of Creative Activity*. What is so remarkable about this image is its unsettling combination of a childlike rawness and immediacy – heightened by the pure visual impact of the bold primary colours – with the figure's shrewd and tenacious gaze.

James Gleeson
Australia, b. 1915
The sower 1944
oil on canvas, 76.2 x 50.8
Purchased 1966
OA13.1966

A literary imagination and a masterful
technique have typified the art of James
Gleeson since the days of his indenture at
East Sydney Technical College in the mid-
1930s. Among the first Australian artists,
loosely grouped as they were, to embrace
surrealism, Gleeson remains its last legiti-
mate defender, although his colleague and
occasional collaborator Robert Klippel can
be accorded that distinction in sculpture.
Gleeson's abiding loyalty to surrealist
doctrine has been matched by a continual
output of surrealist paintings. *The sower* is a hideous vision of a world at war,
a dystopia in which the presence of Salvador Dali is both patent and perfectly
integrated. Giving form to fear and flesh to nightmare, Gleeson's shocking
emblem provides an antidote to both.

Russell Drysdale
Australia, 1912–1981
Walls of China 1945
oil on hardboard
76.2 x 101.6
Purchased 1945
7631

Having made precocious
modernist paintings on
mainly urban themes
under the direction of
Melbourne's George Bell,
Russell Drysdale graduated
to a more conservative
though considerably more personal manner. As a result of a 1944 *Sydney
Morning Herald* commission to record the drought in western New South
Wales, he confirmed his own deep connection to the Australian landscape,
especially at its most extreme. He was entranced by the hardy types who
inhabited the outback towns and far-flung properties: drovers, publicans,
pastoral workers, transients and, towards the end of his career, the Aboriginal
people whose own relationship to land suggested something of his own. *Walls
of China* is based on Lake Mungo, a prehistoric lake flanked by massive white
sand dunes, where human remains dating back 40,000 years have been found.
Realised in Drysdale's signature palette of reds and golds, the painting's
expressive, even distorted, forms are redolent of the majesty of ruination.

Sidney Nolan
Australia, 1917–1992
The camp 1946
synthetic polymer paint on hardboard, 89.7 x 121.5
Purchased 1978
207.1978

Haphazard as his artistic training was in the 1930s, the virtually self-taught
Sidney Nolan absorbed the tenets of surrealism, abstraction and expressionism
at a precocious age. His literary curiosity brought him to the work of philoso-
phers such as Kierkegaard and poets such as Rimbaud and the French symbolists.
Although uneven, his Eurocentric culture was broad and open, not unlike the
Australian terrain he would paint so memorably. A driving force in Melbourne's
Angry Penguins movement in the 1940s, Nolan illustrated its journal and
provided its theorists with a living exemplar. The deceptively naive narratives
he painted on the subject of bushranging folk hero Ned Kelly in 1946 and
1947 are part of the visual inventory by which Australians know themselves.

Russell Drysdale
Australia, 1912–1981
Sofala 1947
oil on canvas on hardboard, 71.7 x 93.1
Purchased 1952
8700

Among Drysdale's most acclaimed works are his tributes to the ramshackle towns of country New South Wales. The subject of this fine example is Sofala, a mining settlement encountered by Drysdale and Donald Friend in 1947, and subsequently visited by Margaret Olley, David Strachan, Jean Bellette and other members of the so-called Sydney Charm School. Caught in a moment of melancholic muteness which reflected Drysdale's own emotional state as much as any architectural reality, the township could nevertheless be identified on the basis of this work. Fond of the recessions afforded by verandah posts, roof lines and roadways, Drysdale exaggerated perspective for psychological effect. In that sense *Sofala* is a regional response to the metaphysical art of de Chirico and to the surrealists, in whose work Drysdale took some interest.

Robert Klippel Australia, b. 1920
James Gleeson Australia, b. 1915
Madame Sophie Sesostoris (a pre-raphaelite satire) 1947–48
painted wood, 49.5 x 10 x 10
Gift of James Gleeson and Robert Klippel 1970
SA3.1970

At an early point in the London association of James Gleeson and Robert
Klippel, these like-minded Australians collaborated on this fabulous bibelot,
a unique embodiment of surrealist fancy. With its hint of T. S. Eliot and
fetishistic overtones, *Madame Sophie Sesostoris* mixes high modernism and
primitivist impulses, more or less dissonantly. Though resisting rational
interpretation, it is a remarkably intelligent sculptural statement. Klippel had
some training with Lyndon Dadswell in Sydney, followed by an unsatisfactory
half year at the Slade School. He and Gleeson co-exhibited at a London
gallery specialising in surrealism, visited the movement's founder, André
Breton, in Paris and established a creative dialogue of uncommon duration
and fruitfulness. Gleeson, a professional art critic, wrote an exemplary
monograph on Klippel.

Arthur Boyd
Australia, b. 1920
The expulsion 1947–48
oil on hardboard, 101.6 x 122
Purchased 1986

Born into a prolific, extended family of artists, Arthur Boyd had the good fortune to be raised in a culturally munificent family environment in rural Victoria. Blessed as he was by this advantage, it was a prodigious visual capability that made him a great artist. As a painter, potter, printmaker, patron and patriot, Boyd cut a swathe through the whole of Australian culture. His first success came in a suite of full-blooded biblical subjects in the 1940s, of which this is a striking example. Though he went on to produce other equally expressive works, typically in series, images like *The expulsion* have made an indelible impression on the national consciousness. The Old Masters, studied in reproduction, and the landscape of his own country encountered firsthand are the twin sources of Boyd's vision. Here, an Adam and Eve out of Masaccio are expelled from their bush Eden by a believably blokey angel.

Sidney Nolan
Australia, 1917–1992
Pretty Polly mine 1948
synthetic polymer paint on hardboard, 91 x 122.2
Purchased 1949
8169

While the mythography of Ned Kelly never lost its appeal for him, and continues
as the primary signifier of his art-historical status, Nolan proved himself capable
of immense range as a painter. This seemingly effortless recollection of a mine
near Mount Isa in Queensland betrays the conscious, one might say boastful,
clumsiness of a master working in the manner of a primitive. Certainly the
French naive painter Henri Rousseau – promoted by Picasso and the Parisian
avant-garde at the beginning of the twentieth century – provided Nolan with
the inspiration and the confidence to paint intuitively. *Pretty Polly mine* is one
of the most popular paintings in the collection, principally by virtue of the
'innocence' of its style. In a place where parrots drop dead on the wing from
heat, the 'Polly' of the title is no surrealist confection. The gent in Sunday best
surveying the unreliable source of his wealth is imported from the photographic
conventions of the nineteenth century. He is of the race of explorers, including
the ill-fated Burke and Wills, whose presence in the landscape was a frock-coated
anomaly. This struck Nolan as simultaneously comic and tragic, an opposition
at the heart of his *œuvre* and a key to the character of settler Australia.

Frank Hinder
Australia, 1906–1992
Subway, Wynyard 1948
tempera on hardboard, 22.9 x 19
Purchased 1967
OA17.1967

No local artist played as inventively on the variations of modernist painting and sculpture, or for such a sustained period, as Frank Hinder. Having trained with Dattilo-Rubbo at the Royal Art Society of New South Wales, the young Hinder completed his education in Chicago and New York, legendarily modern cities. Returning to Sydney in 1934 with his American wife, the sculptor Margel Hinder, he began a busy career of practice and pedagogy covering – and reflecting – six decades of art in Australia. The kinetic-luminal sculpture of Hinder's later years is only now being assessed. This painting, characteristic of the ongoing interest in cubism that motivated much of his work, displays a rhythmic sureness of construction. It echoes an earlier Wynyard subject in the collection, Grace Cossington Smith's *Rushing*, of c. 1922.

Sali Herman
Australia,
1898–1993
Near the docks
1949
oil on canvas,
50.7 x 96.8
Purchased 1949
8278

Having studied in Zurich and Paris, Swiss-born Sali Herman arrived in Melbourne in 1937 as a mature post-impressionist artist. This did not prevent his attendance at the George Bell School nor his development of an authentically Australian urban style in Sydney, the city he made his home from 1938. Associated with a circle of artists around Kings Cross, notably William Dobell and intermittently Russell Drysdale, Herman devoted much of his career to representations of inner city architecture and life. His streetscapes of Paddington, Darlinghurst, Woolloomooloo, Surry Hills and similarly venerable residential and light-industrial precincts form a catalogue of characteristic views comparable to those Maurice Utrillo made of Paris. *Near the docks* conveys the desultory, almost abandoned beauty of a down-at-heel neighbourhood – Herman's favourite motif.

William Dobell
Australia, 1899–1970
Margaret Olley 1948
oil on hardboard, 114.3 x 85.7
Purchased 1949
8164

Rubens, Rembrandt and Renoir preside over this magnificent portrait. The sitter, now a senior celebrant of domestic and still-life subjects, was then an apprentice painter much depicted by her fellow artists, including Russell Drysdale, Donald Friend and Dobell. It is Dobell's baroquely florid image of Olley that is today inseparable from our notion of them both: portrayer and portrayed have merged in a veritable fountain of paint. It won the Archibald Prize in 1948, barely salving the hurt over Dobell's more controversial win in 1943 with an alleged caricature of painter Joshua Smith that infamously led to litigation. Dobell envisaged Olley as a welcoming, indeed maternal, presence, flushed with vitality and spectacularly in the pink of health. This is in contrast to his usually more acerbic repertoire of the feminine.

Lloyd Rees

Australia, 1895–1988
The harbour from McMahon's Point
1950
oil on canvas
77.2 x 99.7
Purchased 1950
8478

As a demonstration of technical skill this work would be extraordinary enough, but in it Lloyd Rees reanimates traditionalist landscape.

Despite the artist's modesty, *The Harbour from McMahon's Point* tackles Arthur Streeton at his own game. Though it lacks the seductive blue-and-gold of the earlier *plein air* painter, the brown-and-white of this wind-swept work just as accurately defines the Sydney foreshores. Rees was besotted by the harbour since first arriving from Brisbane in 1917. He captured its every mood over a long and fertile career. From early pencil sketches displaying an attention to detail reminiscent of Dürer to late oil paintings of deliquescent indistinctness, Rees's Sydney was as complex and changing as the city itself.

John Passmore

Australia, 1904–1984
Miller's Point, morning 1952
oil on hardboard, 50.8 x 61
Marshall Bequest Fund 1952
8672

John Passmore's abstracted vision is at odds with the realist one of Rees. The latter had little truck with the spatial distortions of Cézanne, whereas Passmore idolised the great French painter. Son of a Sydney stevedore, Passmore studied inconsistently under George Lambert before establishing a career in commercial art, travelling to Europe in 1933 with colleagues Paul Haefliger and Jean Bellette. On his final return to Australia in 1950 he became one of the most inspirational teachers at the Julian Ashton School and East Sydney Technical College. John Olsen, later to develop a new approach to local landscape, was among his devotees. This delicate but durably constructed work is indicative of Passmore's most Cézannesque moments. Specifics of the built and natural environment are subsumed in a generalising pattern of painterly marks. A growing, perhaps even inevitable, interest in abstract expressionism underlined Passmore's participation in the historic Direction I exhibition in 1956.

Godfrey Miller
Australia, 1893–1964
Still life with lute 1954–56
pen and black ink, oil on canvas on hardboard, 64.5 x 82.5
Purchased 1956
9286

At one with Passmore in his admiration for Cézanne, Godfrey Miller was the more cerebral of the two Sydney artists. Born in New Zealand where he studied as an architect, Miller moved to Warrandyte, Melbourne, in 1919, followed by extensive European wanderings from 1929. He was able to live modestly well by independent means. With a melancholy temperament exacerbated by the horrors of the First World War, he matured into one of the irreconcilable loners of Australian art. Even so, Miller influenced many students through his long teaching tenure at East Sydney Technical College. His universalist philosophies lent an esoteric quality to his ideas, though Miller was never less than plain-spoken in his pictorial expressions. *Still life with lute* is a stately investigation of cubist principles with a musical resonance entirely in keeping with its subject.

Grace Cossington Smith
Australia, 1892–1984
Interior with wardrobe mirror 1955
oil on canvas on paperboard, 91.4 x 73.7
Purchased 1967
OA11.1967

That the intuitive artist need travel no further than her home to find a subject was proved by Cossington Smith as early as 1915. From late in her career comes this glittering and powerful reiteration of that truth. By the simple device of an outswung door, which is yet a miracle of reflected light, the artist entices the external world into this interior space. In patches of purest pigment she renders the furnishings of the room – cupboard, carpet, bookshelves, bed – as well as the verandah and garden beyond. One of a sequence of such interiors painted between 1954 and 1970, and for which she is justly renowned, *Interior with wardrobe mirror* confirms Cossington Smith as a laureate of the domestic sublime.

Ian Fairweather
United Kingdom/Australia, 1891–1974
Roi soleil 1956–57
gouache on paperboard on hardboard, 99 x 72.5
Purchased 1957

The elusive, not to say eccentric, personality of the Scottish-born Ian
Fairweather found a unique place in Australian art. Restless and anti-
materialistic, Fairweather was a gipsy of geography and of style. Though he
spent periods in Melbourne and Darwin, the reclusive painter is renowned
for his residency on Queensland's Bribie Island from the early 1950s. His
intellectual habits, and unfailing attraction to Eastern philosophies and faiths,
found their expression in his painting. His calligraphic approach to picture-
making, increasingly complex and layered, proved an elastic system for the
translation into surface of ever-deepening levels of sensation and thought.
Roi soleil, not the largest Fairweather in the collection, is among his most
popular creations. A casual depiction of a boy on a buffalo, it is also an
articulation of formal, symbolic and spiritual ideals. No painter active in
Australia in this period enjoyed an equivalent prestige with younger artists.

John Olsen
Australia, b. 1928
Spanish encounter 1960
triptych: oil on hardboard, 183 x 366
Purchased 1960
OA29.1960.a–c

This pupil of Passmore, admirer of Fairweather and irrepressible observer of the world around him exhibited as a student in the celebrated Direction I exhibition in 1956, an event he also helped to organise. Between 1957 and 1960 he travelled and studied in England and Europe, a first trip to Spain confirming his taste for the dramatic gesture in art. While he can be understood as an abstract-expressionist painter at this point, such a reading grossly underplays the naturalist imperative that operates in Olsen's style, augmented by a gift for narrative and a love of the humorous. *Spanish encounter* is grandiose without being verbose; a mural-sized confession of faith in linearity and speed. Painted on his return to Sydney in 1960, it charts the course of a European grand tour within the never-suppressed contour of Olsen's Australian character.

Fred Williams
Australia, 1927–1982
Trees on hillside II 1964
oil, tempera on hardboard, 91.4 x 121.9
Purchased 1965
OA6.1965

By his own acknowledgement an inheritor of the tradition embodied in von Guérard, the Heidelberg School and early twentieth-century painters such as Elioth Gruner, Fred Williams is the Australian landscapist par excellence, a painter's painter possessed of prodigious talent. His capacity for placement, for the telling mark, could be impeccable. A landscape by Williams at his greatest is so reliably right in its organisation and tone that formal perfection takes on moral value. An early death cut short his career, but Williams's formidable body of work was by then wholly fixed in the visual culture of his day. A prolonged, patient apprenticeship in Melbourne and London preceded his emergence as a mature painter and artist–etcher. This powerfully composed and exquisitely crafted work of art, like others by Williams in the collection, draws praise from lay and professional audiences alike – a warrant of his democratic appeal.

Oliffe Richmond
Australia/United Kingdom, 1919–1977
Sentinel 1962
bronze, 147.5 x 29 x 24
Purchased 1967
SA2.1967

Much of the active career of this Hobart-born sculptor was spent in London,
where he lived and taught from the late 1940s until his death in 1977. Inspired
by the work of Henry Moore, Richmond was a full-time assistant to him in
1949–50, continuing to count the revered English sculptor a mentor and friend.
The carving techniques of his compatriots Ola Cohn and Lyndon Dadswell were
of early significance to Richmond, their monumental effects giving way in his
work to more attenuated forms. Richmond produced a sequence of standing
figures in bronze, a material that suited his increasing interest in the
scarification and corrosion of sculptural surface as a metaphor for inner states.
Sentinel epitomises these stark, aggrieved, yet rigidly armoured personages.
Though the reductionism of Giacometti is operative, Richmond's own
excavatory strategies and emotional defensiveness dominate.

Tony Tuckson
Australia, 1921–1973
White lines (vertical) on ultramarine 1970–73
diptych: synthetic polymer paint on hardboard
213.5 x 244.6
Gift of Annette Duprée 1976

As an assistant director of the Art Gallery of New South Wales, Tony Tuckson
was ideally placed to study and promote the historical art and living artists of
his adopted country. His endeavours on behalf of Aboriginal culture are especially praiseworthy. Born in Egypt of English parents, Tuckson was attached to
the Royal Australian Air Force as a pilot instructor in 1942. His youthful art
training was reactivated at East Sydney Technical College after the war. Though
administrative duties kept him from full-time creative practice, Tuckson painted
prodigiously in private. His belated first solo exhibition in 1970 was a revelation
to colleagues and the public alike. Having transcended an expressive-figurative
style inspired by Picasso in the 1950s for a maturer, gestural abstraction by the
end of the 1960s, he seemed to paint in a state of divine urgency. In *White lines*
Tuckson borrows from tribal practices of body-marking and the calligraphic
notation of Fairweather to create an ecstatic abstract.

Jeffrey Smart
Australia, b. 1921
Central Station 1974–75
synthetic polymer paint on canvas, 86 x 100
Purchased 1976
241.1976

Having at an early stage explored the peripheries of surrealism, vestiges of
which inform his work even now, Jeffrey Smart resolved upon a pristine
academic technique as his personal trademark. Applied to an inexhaustible
repertoire of urban and industrial motifs, and pursued through the dutiful
regimes of a nineteenth-century Salon painter, Smart's artistry has resulted in
an *œuvre* of nearly classical order and probity. *Central Station* is nominally a
Sydney subject, but in keeping with the internationalism of Smart's world-view
it could be anywhere in the developed West. His is an art of cities and satellite
towns, of airports, fuel-stations and autobahns. If he paints a field, you can be
sure it will house a billboard. The role of human beings in this machine-tooled
universe is as wry, disaffected but not inconsolable embodiments of modern
ennui. Edward Hopper's Depression America, as well as Poussin's Arcadian
Europe, are Smart's psychological referents.

Brett Whiteley
Australia, 1939–1992
The balcony 2 1975
oil on canvas, 203.5 x 364.5
Purchased 1981
116.1981

Controversy dogged the life and career of Brett Whiteley, not all of it resolved in the aftermath of his drug-related death. What is not debatable about this Australian wunderkind is his creation of some of the most splendid evocations ever made of Sydney Harbour, a subject he took up with a vengeance in mid-career and made his own. Early classes at Julian Ashton's and design work at Lintas preceded his rise to notoriety in the 1960s, a decade bracketed by English success and American failure. Whiteley returned to Australia from New York, via Fiji, in 1970. With respectful nods to forebears such as Duccio, Rembrandt, van Gogh, Matisse, Francis Bacon and Lloyd Rees – a virtual mentor – he developed a brazen style typified by whiplash lines, collaged inclusions and impro-visatory accents. *The balcony 2* justifies his inveterate boastfulness about his own gifts. This nocturnal composition is imbued with all the breeziness of the natural setting itself, and Whiteley's own aesthetically heightened response to it.

Rosalie Gascoigne

Australia, b. 1917
Enamel ware 1976
wood, kitchen utensils, 113.3 x 51 x 14.3
Purchased 1976

© Rosalie Gascoigne 1976. Reproduced by permission of VISCOPY Ltd,
Sydney 1998
236.1976

Rosalie Gascoigne is one of an elite group
of Australian sculptors whose activity has
increased and deepened with maturity.
Gascoigne, indeed, was not at liberty to sculpt
full-time until later in life. Arriving from
New Zealand in 1943, marriage and family
responsibilities slowed, yet also enriched, her
eventual artistic blossoming – an event presaged
in horticultural work, Japanese ikebana
studies and an interest in informal assemblage.
Gascoigne's method is characterised by judi-
cious and frequently inspired juxtapositions of
found objects, the serendipity of her materials
always conditioned by conceptual clarity. In her untrivial and
original way she is a landscape artist, displaying a sensitivity to seasonal
rhythms and subtle shifts of mood most notably found in Aboriginal art.

Inge King

Australia, b. 1918
Planet 1976–77
stainless steel, 53.5 x 55.1 x 18
Purchased 1982
218.1982

Among the most fastidious of the
post-war generation of abstractionists,
Inge King has spent a lifetime pursuing
the ideal of formal perfection in
three-dimensional practice. *Planet* is
a sculptural statement of unerring
purity, a seamless confluence of
volume, void and surface. Though not
without a suggestion of anthropomorphism in the centralised metallic head, it
withholds feeling, refuses inquisition and stands as a starkly self-sufficient icon
of the artist's aesthetic resolve. Half ritual object, half cosmic artefact, *Planet* is
imbued most of all with a sense of its own durability. King, who was born in
Germany, studied in Berlin, London and Glasgow before relocating to Australia
in 1951. Initially working as a jeweller, she graduated to welded sculpture in
black steel. Much of her output has been in the realm of large-scale public
statuary. In recent years she has executed a number of quirkily figurative
sculptures, though not at the cost of her always operative abstract values.

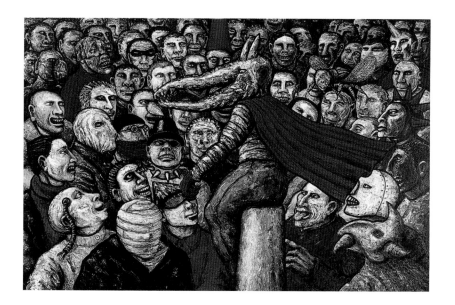

Peter Booth
Australia, b. 1940
Painting 1981
oil on canvas, 197.5 x 304.5
Purchased with assistance from the Visual Arts Board, Australia Council 1981
203.1981

Along with a handful of other repellent images unleashed by him, Peter
Booth's *Painting* stands out as one of the indisputable benchmarks of its era.
Born and educated in Sheffield, the young Booth arrived in Australia in 1958,
continuing his studies in Melbourne, the city which remains his home. His
early creation of hard-edged abstract paintings led to his inclusion in The Field
exhibition in 1968, a turning-point for him as much as for modern Australian
art. By the late 1970s, fearing he had reached an impasse with a body of
completely monochrome works, and pre-empting an international revival of
figuration in painting, Booth plunged into a fevered period of grimly morbid
invention. Humanity was portrayed as a race of victim–idiots tormented by the
bloodied and bloodthirsty monsters of its own imagining. Bosch and Goya are
Booth's antecedents, though not his prototypes, for there is something utterly
of the twentieth century in these ghoulish spectres of modernity.

James Gleeson
Australia, b. 1915
The arrival of implacable gifts 1985
oil on canvas, 198 x 245
Purchased 1985
225.1985

Not even this artist's apocalyptic paintings of the 1940s prepare one for the
operatic excess of his later work. With his painterly activity minimised by
curatorial and critical duties throughout the 1960s and 1970s, Gleeson stored
up a visual treasury that spilled out prodigiously on his retirement from public
life. The period from the early 1980s was no less than his watershed as a
painter. The obsessions of his youth – poetry, dream, the subconscious, culture,
the male nude and the cosmos – reasserted themselves in the form of gigantic
canvases that consolidated one career while inaugurating another. The very
processes of creation and disintegration take shape in this surrealist landscape
of the imagination. He continues to pay homage to the masters of Western art –
the sky in this tempestuous picture is an inverted Turner seascape – while
marking out audacious new levels of technical achievement. At lower left, from
behind a visceral outcrop, Gleeson's pleased but not prideful self-portrait
contemplates a gene pool of his own invention.

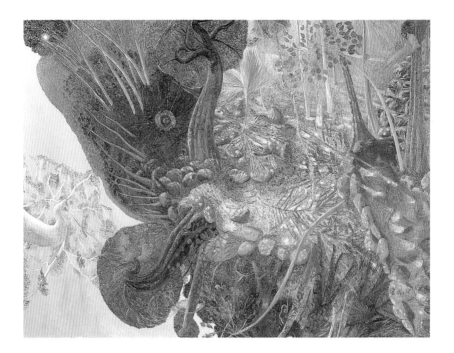

William Robinson
Australia, b. 1936
Creation series – man and the spheres 1991 (detail)
triptych: oil on canvas
182.5 x 243.5 each panel; 182.5 x 730.5 overall
Purchased with funds provided by the Art Gallery Society of New South Wales 1994
593.1994.a–c

Though success came to William Robinson in mid-career, he seemed on course
from the beginning for a kind of greatness. By no means ignorant of the major
progressive movements of his youth and maturity, he chose from an early age
to pursue what he saw as the inexhaustible possibilities of representational art.
From the giddy temptations of Bonnard and the French domestic intimists, he
moved to more robust and greatly more externalised passions – his farm and
farmyard animals, his family environment and pastoral vicinity, and eventually
the scrubby hills of his Queensland Arcadia depopulated of all but a pantheistic
presence. *Creation series – man and the spheres* puts the case for Robinson's
status as an artist of the romantic sublime. A more recent body of panoramic
machines has tackled the coastal zone of Australian identity, reflecting the
artist's own move from hinterland to seaboard.

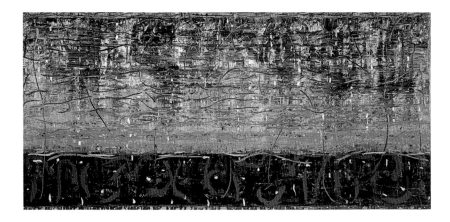

Michael Johnson
Australia, b. 1938
After Sirius 1987–88
oil on Belgian linen, 210 x 450
Purchased with assistance from the Moët and Chandon Art Acquisition Fund 1988
130.1988

As Peter Booth evolved a figurative sensibility out of abstract practice, so Michael Johnson, at roughly the same time, moved from cerebral abstractions towards a more emotive stance in painting. His work remained abstract, but became more palpably the product of a response to landscape and the forces of external nature and internal feeling. *After Sirius* is by any account an exceptional example of lyricism in paint. This canvas records no heady experiment in the materiality of a medium, but the mature exercise of virtuoso technique employed in the service of grand ideas. Despite the artist's evident relish for the sensual properties of pigment, a certain intellectual and formal decorum prevails over oily promiscuity. Johnson's extensive history of exhibition and the critical acclaim he receives here and abroad rank him as one of Australia's premier painters.

Robert Klippel
Australia, b. 1920
Wooden prototype for Adelaide Plaza bronze, Opus 714, Adelaide 1988
1988
assembled wooden parts, 300 x 350 x 135
Purchased 1989
57.1989

The surrealist fondness for serendipity, the happy accident, survived in Klippel's
method long after his devotion to the movement ended. Yet to call this massive
construction accidental is to misunderstand the organising intelligence behind it.
Robert Klippel is one of the inveterate assemblers of art. He surveys the universe
in terms of objects, and those objects in terms of their potential for linkage,
interrelationship and affinity. The wooden industrial casting blocks he has used
as components in his work since the 1980s are ideal articles for such a project.
This monument, with its tinted and textured patina, vividly announces its
volumetric occupation of museum space. Few sculptures in the collection are
as commanding. Rather than intimidating the viewer, however, it is a work
that welcomes approach. The figures Klippel seems to summon in the work
are not in the least malign; on the contrary, they possess the playfulness of
chess pieces or toys.

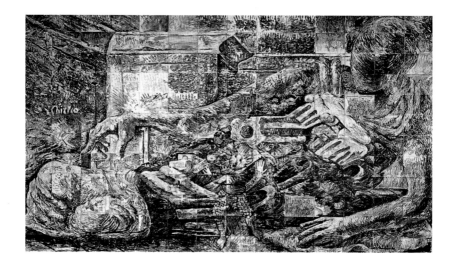

Imants Tillers
Australia, b. 1950
Pataphysical man 1984
168 canvas boards: synthetic polymer paint, charcoal, pencil
25.2 x 38 each panel; 304 x 532 installed
Murray-Will Bequest Fund 1985
1.1985.a–llllll

As the child of Latvian immigrants to this country, Imants Tillers participated
in one of the defining experiences of post-war Australian society. Located
physically in his new country, he was nonetheless dislocated from it in respect
of his parental tongue and family history. Though resolutely Australian in
his education, habits and speech, Tillers was ever able to intuit his difference
from the apparent norms of Australian culture as well. He chose to make this
intuition both the focus of his art and, ironically, the ultimate proof of his
citizenship. Tillers's roots in conceptual art of the 1970s, quite apart from
his architectural background, give to his paintings a sense of rationality and
organisation. Each of his multi-panelled works, invariably numbered by unit,
is released into public life as the promise of a greater whole. Though it is
proper to speak of postmodernism in regard to his interests and strategies,
Tillers's true capability as an artist cannot be restricted to one or other stylistic
category. If anything, his work is as vehemently 'outside' style as that of his
contemporary Susan Norrie.

Ken Unsworth
Australia, b. 1931
Suspended stone circle II conceived 1974–77, constructed 1985
103 river stones, wires, 400 diameter
Purchased 1988
356.1988.a–yyyy

Delight, fear, curiosity, puzzlement: these are among the many responses
visitors to the Gallery feel when faced with the gravity-defying grace of Ken
Unsworth's *Suspended stone circle II*. At the sheer level of craft, or science if
you will, it is compelling. Like a weird but supremely logical enactment of
a law of physics, it has a lesson to teach. The sculpture is as conceptually fluid
as it is precise in its balance. Committed to experimental performance, painting
and sculpture since the 1960s, Unsworth is as concerned with the mystery of
intuitive sensation as with the reality of objective experience. The river stones
in this work have been carefully, indeed lovingly, selected on the basis of unities
of shape, weight and weathering – the modules of minimalism parodied, and
bettered, by nature. A collection crowd-pleaser, the aesthetic stature of this
sculpture is undiminished by its popularity.

Simone Mangos
Australia, b. 1959
Salt lick 1986
salt, nails, 30 x 34 x 34
Purchased 1987
348.1987

Since making this quintessentially conceptual piece, almost an anti-sculpture,
Simone Mangos has progressed to large-scale installations in which natural
substances such as honey and wood are used to increasingly poetic effect. In
essence, Mangos makes time her medium. It is difficult to imagine any of her
works being complete without it. *Salt lick*, for example, will actually cease to
exist when the salt block has corroded the iron nails – a process that becomes,
as we watch, the subject of the work. Mangos is probably making the point
that all art is given to change, and indeed to ultimate collapse. The special
achievement of *Salt lick*, which has intrigued visitors since its first display in
the Gallery, is to make this sobering insight into entropy a matter for reverie.

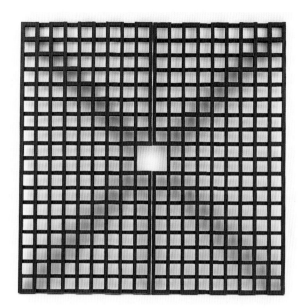

Hilarie Mais
England/Australia, b. 1952
Grid doors II 1987
two timber grids, oil paint, 200 x 234 x 36.5 installed
Purchased with funds provided by the Rudy Komon Memorial Fund 1988
506.1988.a–b

Combining order and informality, containment and release, the sculpture of
Hilarie Mais takes as its fundamental principle the reconciliation of opposites.
Fully cognisant of the conventions of minimalist art-making, and equally able
to exploit them, Mais's work resists stylistic categorisation. Her use of grids,
ellipses, circles and squares – that deathless geometry of abstract form – is
neither copyist nor perfunctory. Mais's selective powers allow her to adopt
certain systems, certain inflections, to do with the construction of abstract
objects and apply them to an original vision. The resulting artworks are usually
perceived as sculptures, but they might also be viewed as paintings. Indeed,
some of them are painted to the point of impasto. For Mais, colour itself can
function as a sculptural element, as it does in this vividly chromatic work,
which is meditative rather than emotive in effect.

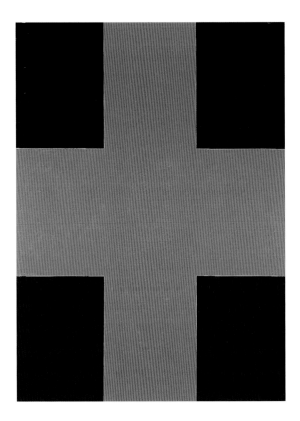

John Nixon
Australia, b. 1949
Black and orange cross 1992
synthetic polymer paint on hardboard, 243 x 152.6
Purchased with funds provided by the Rudy Komon Memorial Fund 1998
51.1998

If minimalism is the movement against which Mais must be comprehended, for John Nixon constructivism is the key. The flawless and seemingly inevitable abstractions of twentieth-century masters such as Mondrian and Malevich provide Nixon with his point of departure. Beyond formal values, Malevich's social idealism and belief in the transformative role of art have influenced Nixon's approach to contemporary art production. The notion of the discrete and self-sufficient artwork, though not rescinded by him, has been subjected to systematic interrogation and re-conceptualisation since Nixon began his career in 1973. The ongoing sequence of non-objective self-portraits which has occupied him since the early 1980s, and for which he is internationally known, posits a view of artistic identity at odds with the expressive-romantic clichés more usual in Australian portraiture. Nixon has been an articulate defender of this position, arguing his case in room-scaled installations and thematic exhibitions of admirable authority over many years.

Susan Norrie
Australia, b. 1953
Model seven (from the series 'Room for error') 1993 (detail)
seven panels: oil on canvas
152 x 61 x 3 each panel
Moët and Chandon Art Acquisition Fund 1995
103.1995.a–g

Both in the elaborately figural paintings she unveiled in the 1980s, and in the more sculptural, indeed more experimental, practice she pursued in the 1990s, Susan Norrie's creative trademark is a call to contemplation. While one may speak of her style, Norrie's art has consistently resisted stylistic categorisation. More speculative and cerebral than much of her earlier work, *Model seven* also registers at the deepest level of human reflection. As deliciously executed as anything the artist has ever done, the painted surfaces have the lush and softly radiant finish found in Chardin. They suggest the texture and elasticity of skin. And with good reason: the text replicates an arcane recipe for embalming fluid, an interesting if unsettling metaphor for the preservative character of oil painting itself.

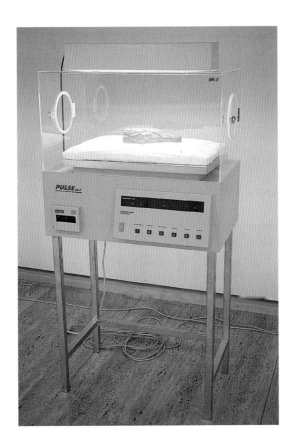

Maria Kozic
Australia, b. 1957
Pulse Mk2 1994 (detail)
4 incubators and mixed media, 148 x 74 x 49 each
Purchased with funds provided by the Rudy Komon Memorial Fund 1995
504.1995.a–d

In the generation of Australian artists now entering their first maturity, the Melbourne-based Maria Kozic is exceptional for the diversity of her practice as well as the consistency of her vision. Though she frequently borrows from the repertoire of post-war international artistic movements, especially pop art, her strategy involves no cold-blooded appropriation. Rather, it is true to call Kozic a passionate artist, both in terms of her opinions and ideas, and in her pursuit of fitting forms for them in her art. While uncompromisingly polemical, her work is also experiential. From public billboards potent with feminist content to smaller private images tinged with surrealist fancy, she maintains a profoundly personal identification with the objects of her manufacture. Self-portraiture of one kind or another is her preferred mode. In a painting called *Pulse Maria*, she once depicted herself covered in a life-giving – yet somehow draining – arterial filigree. Similar veins emboss the objects in the incubators in this work: a hammer and an arm, for example. The preciousness of existence and the terror of its sudden termination are here, as ever, her themes.

Mike Parr
Australia, b. 1945
Bronze liars (Minus 1 to 16) 1996 (detail)
16 bronze and beeswax sculptures, dimensions variable according to room size
Purchased 1996
564.1996.1–16

No contemporary artist in Australia has more courageously plumbed the
maelstrom of the psyche than Mike Parr. He came to prominence in the 1970s
with a series of provocative body-based performances and actions, some of
which he re-interpreted for audiences in the 1990s. Physical endurance, pain
and actual mutilation were the tools he used to construct a performative
œuvre of unrivalled emotionality. A shamanistic intent informs his output in
conventional media as well. This phenomenal set of sculptures in the deliberately
academic material of bronze is a case in point. In simple terms, the sixteen busts
represent the artist's features in various states of transmogrification and decay:
the autobiography of a mind. Past, present and future emphatically collide,
and equally emphatically coalesce. Parr returns himself to the condition of clay
moulded by the will of a Creator, who is also himself. By passing among the
beeswax plinths that support the busts, viewers transcend the private world of
Mike Parr to participate in a cosmic moment of unmaking and remaking.

AUSTRALIAN
WORKS ON PAPER

J. W. Lewin
Australia, 1770–1819
The Gigantic Lyllie of New South Wales 1810
pencil, watercolour, 53.9 x 43.2
Purchased 1968
WA9.1968

Perhaps Lucien Henry's *Waratah* (1887) matches this floral subject in graphic distinction, but Lewin's *Gigantic Lyllie* is a vastly more spectacular, and hence more appropriate emblem for the colony which nourished it. If such a statement can be made of an essentially descriptive effort by a colonial illustrator, Lewin unleashes the drama of the plant, its sensual extravagance. With justification the Sydney merchant Alexander Riley referred to Lewin's botanical watercolours as 'worthy of the Palace of a Prince'. Having established the constitutive forms of the flower-head, he deploys them as a single grand decoration against the blank support. Lewin was inspired to paint this variety of lily on at least three occasions, the earliest in 1805.

Joseph Lycett
Australia, 1774–c. 1825
*View of the Heads,
at the entrance
into Port Jackson*
c. 1822
watercolour, 21.4 x 28.9
Purchased 1978
97.1978

Entering Sydney
through the sandstone
embrace of the Heads
was, for most visitors,
a moment of emotional relief. In an era dominated by ocean travel, and in a
continent completely surrounded by sea, the notion of safe harbourage had a
vital connotation. The Heads signified a voyage's end, or promised its beginning.
Lycett understood this. Recidivist forger the Staffordshire lad may have been,
but there is little falseness in his art. Painted in the year he left the colony for
an unhappy end in the environs of Bath, this watercolour reveals him at his
understated best. His depictions of Aboriginal tribal life, not evidenced here,
are noteworthy for their sensitivity.

John Skinner Prout
England, 1805–1876
*The Tank Stream,
Sydney* c. 1842
pencil, watercolour,
opaque white
highlights, 25.5 x 37.5
Purchased 1913
1034

Active in Sydney
and Hobart, this
Plymouth-born
painter, lithographer
and teacher built a
reputation on modest skills and much industry. Often compared to Conrad
Martens, though not always favourably, Prout excelled as a portrayer of the
natural rather than the built environment. His fern-filled Illawarra subjects are
especially likeable. Though not among these, *The Tank Stream* is one of the
most widely studied of his works. It is hard for today's residents to imagine
Sydney as it was in the opening decades of the nineteenth century. What
remains of the stream in question, which supplied water for drinking and gin-
making, is now lost under the high-risen city.

Conrad Martens
Australia, 1801–1878
View of the Heads, Port Jackson 1853
watercolour, opaque white, gum, 54.2 x 76.4
Purchased with assistance from Overseas Containers Australia Ltd 1986
44.1986

Enlivened by Turneresque inflections, this moody glimpse of the Tasman Sea
through the Heads is a technical triumph. Indeed, so much was it admired that
in the following year a second version was produced for another client. Martens
painted the harbour on many occasions and from numerous vantages. Neither
he nor his clients ever wearied of its watery effects: Venice its lagoon, Sydney
its harbour! If his ideas sometimes erred on the side of glibness, in this instance
he has produced an artwork of consummate invention. Martens's year-long
stint as a topographer with Charles Darwin on HMS *Beagle* caused him to
modify the romanticism in which he was trained and adopt a more dispassionate
approach to nature. Even so, the picturesque and the sublime continued to
characterise his colonial style: this is indeed Coleridge's 'painted ship upon a
painted ocean'.

S. T. Gill
Australia, 1818–1880
Overlanders c. 1865
pencil, watercolour, scraping out, 33.5 x 58.5
Purchased 1946
7721

S. T. Gill arrived in Adelaide in 1839. At that point an amateur painter and fashioner of silhouettes, he made himself a graphic artist of distinction. His principal activity was in South Australia and Victoria, especially the gold-fields, though a productive period in New South Wales between 1856 and 1864 resulted in an important body of work. Gill's rumbustious scenes of rural and frontier life are inseparable from our mental image of Australia's settler beginnings. This watercolour typifies his style and interests. Gill had an anecdotal understanding of human personality and an illustrator's grasp of the natural world. The overlanders depicted here were hardy souls who 'upped stumps' in pursuit of greener pastures.

Tom Roberts
Australia, 1856–1931
Louis Buvelot 1886
pen and black ink, 28.1 x 22.2
Gift of Miss Helen Lempriere 1960
DA1.1960

It is appropriate that Roberts should be represented in the drawing collection by this vigorous portrait of an artist as an old man. Buvelot was his favourite among the preceding generation of colonial landscapists, one whose artistic imperative he and his friends Frederick McCubbin and Arthur Streeton saw themselves extending. Affection and respect inform the work, as well as Roberts's considerable energy as a draughtsman. The drawing was used as the basis for an etching, the largest of the painter's handful of known prints. The image contributes to the inventory of men and women of distinction to which Roberts devoted much of his Australian career.

Oswald Brierly
Australia, 1817–1894
Whalers off Twofold Bay, New South Wales 1867
watercolour, opaque white, 86.3 x 147.7
Purchased 1901
6294

Whaling and other maritime pursuits provided Brierly with subject matter for a lifelong career. Trained in England as an artist and naval architect, and passionate about the sea, he was uniquely equipped for the role. He arrived in Sydney with the explorer Benjamin Boyd in 1842, proceeding to manage Boyd's interests at Twofold Bay near Eden, New South Wales – the setting for the tumultuous event in this work. Details of rigging, ship construction and manoeuvring are carefully observed, though the whales appear somewhat mechanical. In late life Brierly, who made a world voyage with the Duke of Edinburgh in 1868, was appointed marine painter to Queen Victoria.

Julian Ashton
Australia, 1851–1942
A solitary ramble 1888
watercolour, chinese
white highlights
35.5 x 25.7
Purchased 1888
18

Few among Ashton's prolific
number of watercolours approach
this composition in either luminosity or vivacity. His facility in
the medium surpassed his sometimes heavy touch as a painter in
oils. *A solitary ramble* has won
generations of admirers, seizing as
it does the eternal brilliance of the
Australian sun. Not so much an
impressionist work as a naturalist
one, it nonetheless functions within
the favoured repertoire of the
French movement. Monet's parasol-protected demoiselles are not distant at all
from this southern charmer, in either temperament or time.

B. E. Minns
Australia, 1864–1937
Aboriginal woman, Sydney,
New South Wales 1895
pencil, watercolour, 40.3 x 28
Acquisition date not known
4379

As we see from Lindt, the
representation of Aboriginality in
settler art is fraught with problems.
Even Tom Roberts's *Aboriginal head*
(Charlie Turner) (1892), also in the
collection, betrays a sentimentality
by no means intrinsic to the sitter.
Minns was a prolific though often
imprecise painter of the natural and
social environment of the colony,
creating many quasi-ethnographic
essays of this kind. He trained under
Lucien Henry and A. J. Daplyn,
forging a loosely impressionist style
more suited to landscape than the
figure. Minns's response to his
subject is, however, clearly
approving.

Arthur Streeton
Australia, 1867–1943
*A surveyor's
camp* 1896
pencil, watercolour
36.3 x 62.8
Purchased 1896
30

This might be a
template of Aus-
tralian *plein air*
painting. It displays
the 'tricks' of the technique in concentrated and quickly communicated form.
The setting near Richmond, New South Wales, locates the work geographically
just as the dazzling execution locates it in an artistic movement and an historical
period. In addition, Streeton's ability to work up an intelligible statement from
a vocabulary of unintelligible marks is demonstrated here as persuasively as in
the formidable *Fire's on*. The subject is similar too: the continuing mission of
colonial man to build and to civilise.

John Peter Russell
Australia, 1858–1930
*Les Aiguilles de Coton, Belle-
Île, France* 1897
watercolour, gouache, opaque white
54.5 x 37.5
Purchased 1974
66.1974

The technical progression from
Russell's earlier oil painting and
this, its progeny in a medium he
came to prefer, testifies to his
real (and largely realised) professional ambitions. He was not a
dilettante. Any of his impressionist mentors might have claimed
this work. Russell had a gift for
placement and an eye for searing
bicolours such as blue-and-
yellow. Belle-Île, the Brittany
retreat of the title, was frequented
by academic and impressionist
artists alike. Russell lived there
with his wife, an erstwhile model of Rodin's, entertaining Australian artists
such as John Longstaff and Bertram Mackennal. His correspondence with
Tom Roberts, with whom he had travelled in Spain, is an invaluable resource.

Norman Lindsay
Australia, 1879–1969
The picnic god 1907
pen and black ink, 38.7 x 30.7
Purchased 1943
7331

Complete nudity, anticlericalism and bourgeois outrage were the unaltering ingredients of the Norman Lindsay manner. An eccentric of Australian art, he was one of several artistic siblings born in Creswick, Victoria. A black-and-white penman of real adroitness, as this drawing confirms, a less persuasive painter and an all-purpose literary gadfly, Lindsay left his inky imprint on Australian culture for seven decades. He sculpted, and built fastidious model ships as well. The spirit of Rubens is responsible for much that is good and all that is execrable in his *œuvre*. *The picnic god* reads like a colloquial take on classical myth. Lindsay's paganism, it goes without saying, was essentially literary.

Hans Heysen
Australia,
1877–1968
Summer 1909
pencil, watercolour
56.5 x 78.4
Purchased 1909
4804

A more dextrous
exercise in the
devilish medium
of watercolour
would be hard to
conceive. Before
and above any of
his other artistic accomplishments, Heysen was a prodigy of technique.
This is not to say a work like *Summer* lacks feeling or intellect, just that
it impresses itself thoroughly as the product of an executive act. As for the
subject, Heysen's much-painted eucalypts, one might almost speak of their
personality. For the painter, as for the indigenous people whose presence was
never introduced into his art, the forms of the gum-tree were charged with
anthropomorphic potential.

J. J. Hilder
Australia, 1881–1916
Timber getters 1910
watercolour, 22.2 x 27.5
Gift of Howard Hinton 1917
89

The vogue for watercolours
and the sustained public
interest in national landscape
collide happily in the work of
J. J. Hilder. Queensland-born,
he was essentially self-taught
in the watercolour medium,
which he commanded with an
authority equalled only by Hans Heysen and Blamire Young. *Timber getters*
takes its cues from the Heidelberg School, Sydney Long and the English
aesthetic movement, with Hilder supplying his signature touch of atmospheric
fluidity. The image coheres for the viewer from pools of pure colour. Hilder's
early death from tuberculosis robbed Australian art of a unique sensibility,
though a substantial body of his work survives.

Margaret Preston
Australia, 1875–1963
Circular Quay c. 1925
hand-coloured woodcut, edition 19/50, 24.7 x 24.4
Purchased 1964
DA28.1964

Margaret Preston was instrumental in popularising woodblock technique in
the busy milieu of interwar Sydney. Not for a moment was she intimidated by
the tendency to coarseness which is at once the medium's weakness and its
strength. Preston's fearlessly experimental attack led to designs of great vigour
and visual distinction. Typically, the cutting tool is allowed to leave its trace
across the whole composition, so that the energy of actual execution, as of
first inspiration, is conveyed in the final image. Preston liked to hand-colour
her prints. *Circular Quay* has been illuminated in this way in bold shades of
red, green and yellow: colours with strong post-impressionist associations.
The design is almost primitive in its simplicity, belying the finesse of Preston's
methods.

Thea Proctor

Australia, 1879–1966
The bay 1927
watercolour on silk, 20.4 x 20.1
Purchased 1927
© Thea Waddell
4382

While it is true that Proctor dabbled in a
graphic vocabulary verging at times on rococo
frivolity, she was arguably as robust a designer
as Preston. In prints, drawings and watercolours
produced over several decades of dedicated
activity, she promoted an escapist elegance with the matter-of-factness of an
ardent modernist, which indeed was how Proctor saw herself. Capable of
academic life-drawing of easeful certainty, and aided by her talent for commercial
illustration, she also made a reputation as an interior decorator and all-round
cultural authority. Proctor's views on fashion and taste were promulgated through
magazines such as *The Home*, Sydney's answer to the great European journals
of style. This watercolour is unusual in her *œuvre* in containing an identifiable
landscape. Otherwise, it is Proctor at her purest. The medium is handled with
admirable poise, blending stylistic discretion with emotional restraint.

Jessie Traill

Australia, 1881–1967
*Sydney Bridge IV: the ants' progress
1929* 1929
etching with foul biting, edition 2/25
39.8 x 25.2
Purchased 1975
201.1975

Melbourne-trained Traill made a unique
contribution to Australian graphic art,
particularly in her preferred field of
etching, which she studied firsthand with
the English master of the medium, Frank
Brangwyn. The compositional strategies
and tonal contrasts of Whistler were
passed, through Brangwyn, to the highly
receptive Traill, who exploited them in a
series of imaginative and much-admired
prints on industrial and rural themes. Her
investigations of the construction of the
Sydney Harbour Bridge comprise, with those of Grace Cossington Smith, a
powerful testament to urban progress, as well as to the vitality of work by women
artists during the 1920s and 1930s in Sydney. In Traill's prints, nineteenth century
aestheticism feeds fluently into twentieth century modernism, mediated through
a knowledge of Japanese woodblocks. The elongated vertical of this example
does, in fact, echo the classic pillar prints of the *ukiyo-e* school, with flatness
and recession held in knife-edge balance.

Lloyd Rees

Australia, 1895–1988
Sydney skyline from McMahon's Point 1932
pencil, watercolour,
27.2 x 33.5
Purchased with assistance
from the artist 1986
304.1986

It is hard to nominate which of Rees's aesthetic achievements in this drawing is most dazzling. Is it his uncanny investment of blankness with the weight of reality; or his confident massing of architectural forms one against the other in structurally sustainable sequence? Is it the delicacy of his application of watery washes of tone to the paper support, neither too much nor too little in degree or intensity? Is it the suggestion he is able to make of a summery palette of colours through virtual monotone? Or perhaps his conjuring of a burgeoning metropolis by means of fragmentary indications? All these attributes contribute to the majesty of *Sydney skyline from McMahon's Point*, a work in which the nobility of ordinariness is definitively evoked.

Lionel Lindsay

Australia, 1874–1961
Goat and rhododendron c. 1933
wood engraving, 16.9 x 15.2
Purchased 1935
6341

Brother of the notorious Norman, Lionel Lindsay first came to prominence as an illustrator for mass-appeal publications like *The Bulletin*, Australia's premier outlet for the work of graphic artists, designers and cartoonists. In the last category Lindsay was a beloved master. He was also largely responsible for the revival of etching, and especially wood engraving, that enlivened the conservative end of art practice in his day. Lindsay's work stands as a counterpoint of some substance to the modernism he so publicly repudiated. As this astonishing print proves, he was a bravura technician. Margaret Preston, at her most daring, hardly disposed black so decisively against a blank support. *Goat and rhododendron* achieves botanical and naturalist accuracy, but not at the cost of an essentially abstract tendency. In this respect at least, Lindsay was more modern than he thought.

Francis Lymburner
Australia, 1916–1972
Nude (The vulture) c. 1942
pen and black ink, 20.3 x 25.4
Purchased 1989
14.1990

A romantic to the last, adhering to his
figurative ideals in the face of several waves
of abstract and abstract-expressive fashion,
Francis Lymburner is loosely identified with
the so-called Sydney Charm School. Born in Queensland, he moved to Sydney
on the eve of the Second World War, bringing with him a love of Matisse,
Gaudier-Brzeska and Asian art: influences he tried to resolve in his own work.
His drawing style was initially and devastatingly linear, winning Lymburner
the respect of his peers if little financial recompense. The Lymburner line was
curled, confident and fast. By contrast, his oil paintings took a more tonal,
even muddied, path to completion. Often darkly sensuous, and occasionally
erotic, they betray the Parisian prototypes that increasingly informed his manner,
especially during a decade spent abroad in 1952–63. This drawing tackles a
characteristic subject, the female nude, with the adroitness and supple
modulation of form that are Lymburner's trademarks in the medium.

Donald Friend
Australia, 1915–1989
The incinerator
1944
pen, ink, gouache,
watercolour
42 x 62
Purchased 1984
7.1984

A significantly more
celebrated ambassador
of Sydney 'charm'
than Lymburner,
Donald Friend shared
many of the same art-
historical influences. From the outset a formidable draughtsman, Friend's graphic
powers never deserted him over a lifetime of creative activity, continuing to
enliven even the least of his productions. Having studied under Anthony Dattilo-
Rubbo in the 1930s, Friend began the series of expeditions in search of the
exotic that marked his career. Nigeria, the South Pacific, Sri Lanka and Bali,
quite apart from fabled Australian townships like Sofala and Hill End, were
among his destinations. For the period 1966-84 Bali was his home and chief
inspiration. *The incinerator* is from a series of surprisingly sombre drawings –
surprising in view of Friend's more usual vivaciousness – on wartime themes.
He served as a gunner with the Australian army, publishing a famous account of
his experiences. Absent from this work is Friend's brilliantly decorative colour,
but not his remarkable compositional and textural skill.

Jon Molvig

Australia, 1923–1970
Carcase no. 2 1958
reed pen and red ink
37.5 x 50.8
Rudy Komon Memorial Fund
1985
10.1985

One of the few genuinely
vocational expressionists of his
generation, Jon Molvig was a
Sydney-trained painter who
moved north to Brisbane, making it his permanent home from 1954. There,
as a teacher and exhibiting practitioner, he exerted a profound influence on
Queensland's artists and art community over two decades. He gathered around
himself a loose assembly of colleagues called the Half Dozen Group. Molvig's
strengths were an emotional directness and a terrific energy of gesture. Like
Boyd, subjects from Aboriginal and white settler history formed part of his
repertoire. *Carcase no. 2* is an image which instantly recalls those produced by
Sidney Nolan and Russell Drysdale, though neither of those artists brought to
the subject quite the same expressiveness. Molvig experiences the dead beast at
a very personal level: one might almost call this image a psychological self-
portrait. The genre of portraiture, not incidentally, is one this artist explored
with passion and insight.

Kevin Connor

Australia, b. 1932
Study, '8 am Haymarket' 1964
pen, brush and black ink on ivory wove paper
25.9 x 20.6 sheet
Gift of Margaret Connor 1998
152.1998

Kevin Connor has carved himself a lasting
niche in the shifting domain of expressionism.
From the harassed, haunted urban-dwellers
who populate his early Haymarket subjects
to the equally fraught occupants of his later
portraits, he has captured something of the
soul of Sydney. Beginning as a commercial
artist and gradually devoting himself to full-
time professional painting, Connor won a Harkness Fellowship in 1967,
enabling him to study in the United States. His contribution to Australian art is
unusual in being informed by existentialism and other philosophical interests.
Connor's painterly and graphic style is characterised by bold registrations of
form, pentimenti and furious surface activity – all elements of a visual language
with which the artist explores the psychology of place. His most recent paintings
exploit sheer scale, adding a physical dimension to their psychological impact.
The typically smaller works on paper achieve the same end through their intensity
of expression.

Ken Whisson
Australia, b. 1927
Man seated 1967
pen and black ink, 39.4 x 40.7
Purchased 1984
8.1984

Limiting himself to the barest essentials of
form, and relying on a crackling line, Ken
Whisson conjures entire worlds of feeling on a
single page. The unnerving communicativeness
of this ink drawing is typical of the prolific
number of such conceptions produced in his native Australia and adopted Italy.
From the confines of a small yet oddly spacious interior – as though Whisson
leaves room for any possibility – a grim male nude addresses the viewer, more
observer than observed. The artist gives us the impression that the tetchiness of
this figure is the native condition of humanity. Whisson studied at Melbourne's
Swinburne College in the 1940s. Lessons with Danila Vassilieff and contact
with Albert Tucker, Joy Hester and Noel Counihan influenced the psychological
rawness of his style. For all the remarkable asperity of his drawings, Whisson is
perhaps better known as a painter of magnificently tensed and intensely
coloured industrial landscapes.

Arthur Boyd
Australia, b. 1920
The narcissus emblems 1983–84
etching, artist's aquatint,
proof for edition of 25, printed
by Mati Basis, London
60.5 x 42.6
Anonymous gift 1993
Reproduced with permission of Bundanon Trust
384.1993.15

As if acknowledging the European
tradition to which painter–printmakers
such as Rembrandt and Goya belong,
Arthur Boyd has produced a stellar
body of original prints since the late
1950s. These definitively graphic
productions, characterised by an
exaggerated expressivity, return to
the artist's painterly themes as well as
striking out in novel directions of their
own. In this image, the authority of Boyd's biting line is undiminished, as is
his grasp of the formal balance between oppressive blackness and liberating
blankness. Impressive, too, is his continuing ability to work at the level of
myth and archetype: the cosmos invoked in *The narcissus emblems* is racked
and writhing, but always redemptive. The techniques of drypoint, lithography,
etching and aquatint have all been exploited by this artist, who has continued
to experiment even in venerable old age.

AUSTRALIAN
PHOTOGRAPHY

J. W. Lindt
Germany/Australia, 1845–1926
Untitled (Aboriginal man holding club) c. 1873
albumen photograph, 17.3 x 13.1
Purchased 1984
314.1984

Notwithstanding the problematics of stereotype and condescension that bedevil
this period, the German-born Lindt's photographs of Aborigines strain after
an attainment of individual character. Despite a pose indicative of classical
rather than colonial conditions, and a setting contrived in the studio, a sense
of the unique presence of the subject is conveyed. While such albumen prints
cannot be relied upon in the matter of cultural authenticity, they provide a rare
and precious visual record of a few of the people whose immemorial occupation
of the continent was despoiled by European settlement.

Unknown (Kerry & Co.)
Australia, est. 1893–1910
Blue gums c. 1893–1910
albumen photograph, 14.1 x 18.3
Purchased 1989
210.1989

Charles Kerry and the photographers at Kerry & Co. produced a succession of
benchmark photographs around the turn of the nineteenth century that speak,
even now, to the heart of the Australian experience. By 1898 Kerry's Sydney
studio was the largest in the country, producing individual photographs, thematic
albums and especially postcards for national and international distribution.
Blue gums contains all the elements of the Kerry & Co. style: technical skill,
compositional balance and a congratulatory tone.

Charles Bayliss
Australia, 1850–1897
Shearing shed from
the album *Collection
of a country property,
New South Wales*
c. 1890–97
albumen photograph
13 x 20
Purchased 1984
149.1984.2

Like *The golden fleece*
by Tom Roberts, this
photograph conjures both the romance and the reality of the shearing
shed. It is a work of literal brilliance, light streaming through rows of
windows to illuminate shed, shearers and interloping bosses. Posed in part,
and commissioned by the owner of the property, it still has the effect of
a spontaneous moment arrested in time. Among the elite of Australia's
nineteenth-century photographers, Bayliss was a tireless recorder of colonial
life, which he documented within an agenda of undisguised nationalism.
These are the workers, he implies, and this the industry, that made
Australia great.

John Kauffmann
Australia, 1864–1942
Turkey c. 1910
carbon photograph
28.8 diameter
Gift of John Bilney 1978
131.1978

Though he slots con-
veniently into the category
of late nineteenth and
early twentieth century
photographic production
called pictorialism,
Kauffmann possessed a
distinctly individual vision.
Turkey is a hen-house portrait
that contrives to ennoble its subject
at the same time as honouring its

mundanity. It is painterly, not to say impressionistic, in conception and
in presentation, bringing to mind similar tributes to this feathery bird by
Claude Monet and Hans Heysen. The dapper, introspective Kauffmann
studied in England and Europe but reached artistic maturity in Adelaide,
joining the South Australian Photographic Society in 1897. The collection
carries his work in depth.

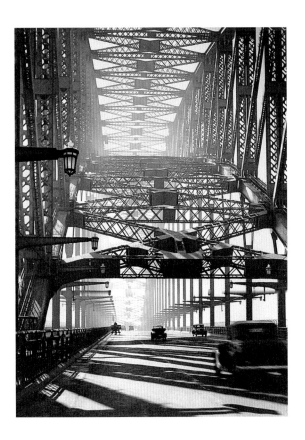

Harold Cazneaux
New Zealand/Australia, 1878–1953
Sydney Bridge c. 1934
gelatin silver photograph, 29.7 x 21.5
Gift of the Cazneaux family 1975
121.1975

It was in Sydney that New Zealand-born, Adelaide-trained Cazneaux ultimately made the photographs on which his high historical reputation is
justifiably based. His personal vision helped to shape a nation's understanding
of itself in the first half of the twentieth century. Emerging from the poetics
of the pictorialist tradition, Cazneaux nonetheless admired, and imitated, the
racier, more hard-edged themes of modernist photography. His interest in
contemporary European photography, especially that of the German Weimar
Republic, confirmed his subject matter as urban, industrial and documentary.
The building of the Sydney Harbour Bridge provided him with a project
perfectly formed for his artistic needs. Here, in but one of many superlative
examples, Cazneaux contrasts the uncompromisingly mechanistic structure
with a subtle tracery of light and shadow.

Olive Cotton
Australia, b. 1911
Tea cup ballet c. 1935
gelatin silver photograph, 37.3 x 29.6
Gift of the artist 1980
218.1980

Olive Cotton was a friend, model, assistant and professional peer of Max Dupain's, running his studio during his wartime absence before she moved from Sydney to country New South Wales. From an early age, Cotton displayed an interest in photography, a medium for which she had a strong, unforced gift. Her stylistic signature combines subtle lighting effects, elaborately orchestrated even in the field, and an uncanny insight into the internal character of things. Her sense of atmosphere is especially vivid: clouds, skies and wind frequently figuring in her work. *Tea cup ballet* is among her most formal compositions, as strictly posed and lit as the theatrical performance it references. Arms akimbo, the 'dancers' form a *corps de ballet* holding back for a solo turn. Inevitably recalling the still-life paintings of Margaret Preston and Grace Cossington Smith, this photograph occupies its own sure place in the repertoire of favoured images of the 1930s.

Max Dupain
Australia, 1911–1992
Sunbaker 1937
gelatin silver photograph, 37.9 x 42.8
Purchased 1976
115.1976

If a single photograph of the twentieth century can be claimed to enshrine
the Australian ethos, it is this. In *Sunbaker* Max Dupain combines landscape,
anatomy and social document in one compelling image that does, indeed, go
some way towards summarising the aspirations and beliefs of a sun-loving
nation. Even today, in the era of a less monocultural, and less acceptingly
solar, Australia, few would dispute the national truths embodied in this image.
Radically foreshortened by Dupain's close-focused lens, the figure dominates
the visual field like a human Uluru. It is slothful, yet tensed for sudden action.
At any moment the bather's right arm, a leonine paw, will flex to raise the
resting torso. Dupain joined the studio of noted pictorialist Cecil Bostock in 1930.
By the end of the decade he had formed the Contemporary Camera Groupe
and produced an essential body of surrealist, modernist and commercial
photographs.

Axel Poignant
England, 1906–1986
The swimmers, Milingimbi, Arnhem Land 1952 (printed 1983)
gelatin silver photograph, 43.2 x 32.8
Purchased 1983
161.1983

The English origins of Axel Poignant were no impediment to his production of a body of photographs regarded as definitively Australian. Poignant came to Western Australia under the Dreadnought Scheme which brought British youths to this country to work on rural properties, not always happily it must be said. In Poignant's case he developed a deep love for, and understanding of, Australia's natural environment which was reflected in the essentially documentary cast of his *œuvre*. More particularly, he found the traditional way of life of Aboriginal communities a fit subject for his craft. *The swimmers, Milingimbi* has become one of the most widely reproduced images of Aboriginality, partly for its expression of untroubled adolescence and partly for its properties as a pictorial arrangement. The foreground figures – set against a sunken stand of trees in the middle distance – breast the waves in a way that suggests the sequential action shots of Eadweard Muybridge.

David Moore
Australia, b. 1927
Migrants arriving in Sydney 1966 (printed later)
gelatin silver photograph
30.2 x 43.5
Gift of the artist 1997
429.1997

David Moore began his professional career in the commercial studio of Russell Roberts in 1947 as a fashion photographer, a role to which he brought considerable talent but little lasting enthusiasm. He progressed to the more creative studio of Max Dupain in 1948 before basing himself in London as a photojournalist. The photographs he produced on his return to Australia in the 1960s form an indispensable record of the era. Certain of his images, like this deeply affecting shot of migrants arriving in Sydney by boat, have attained iconic status in Australian art and popular culture. Originally a colour shot, Moore decided the photograph worked best in black and white. This had the effect of flattening the group of figures, lending the image the quality of an epic frieze. Emerging out of the darkness of the boat, the migrants gesture above and beyond the photographer, towards the new land.

Carol Jerrems
Australia, 1949–1980
Vale Street #2 1975
gelatin silver photograph
20.1 x 30.4
Purchased 1979
46.1979

A quintessential image
of the 1970s, *Vale
Street #2* has lost none
of its capacity to
enchant and disturb in
the intervening years.
In one sense it can be read as a sociological document; in another as a wholly
subjective work of art. Like the mediumistic spirit-photographs of the
nineteenth century, Jerrems's photo seems to disclose the very souls of its
subjects. As they respond, each in their individual fashion, to the regarding
presence of the camera lens, the figures compose themselves, without theatrics,
into telling attitudes. The prominence and bodily confidence of the open-faced
young woman is set against the reticence of her boyish companions. As a
portrait of relationships as well as individuals, *Vale Street* speaks of gender
relations, adolescent sexuality, suburban mores and the photographer's own
subtly partisan demeanour in regard to these themes.

Bill Henson
Australia, b. 1955
*Untitled image
no. 31* 1979
from the series
'Untitled sequence
(European crowds)'
gelatin silver
photograph
23 x 42.1
Purchased 1981
183.1981.31

Oscillating between observation and participation, Bill Henson's authorial
stance is complex, if not contradictory. Beginning with a meticulous attention to
technique, to the protocols of 'good' photography, Henson then supersedes all
the usual standards by which the medium is judged. He does this consciously,
seeking to penetrate to a mythic space he knows the camera cannot, of itself,
record. Call this the psyche, the heart, what you will: it is Henson's special
territory. Whether focusing on a single face isolated within a crowd, or capturing
the atavistic character of the crowd itself, Henson is attentive to the slightest
intake of breath, the most secret motivation or thought. The monochromatic
tendency and modest proportions of his earliest exhibited work have lately
given way to ambitious *mise-en-scènes* cinematic in their colour and scale.

Tracey Moffatt
Australia, b. 1960
Untitled (Woman in shed) 1989
from the series 'Something more'
cibachrome photograph, 103 x 133
Hallmark Cards Australian Photography Collection Fund 1989
334.1989

This brilliantly conceived photograph and the epic series to which it belongs
have achieved wide circulation in both high and popular cultural contexts.
Right from the start *Untitled (Woman in shed)* gave evidence of being a classic
that touched upon a dizzying but well-articulated number of social, political
and artistic questions. Borrowing the overblown form of a B-grade film to
reference themes of race and gender relations, it is a complex work that also
critiques Australian art history and abiding clichés concerning the land and
its occupation. Moffatt pulls no punches. Though self-evidently, indeed self-
consciously, a studio tableau, the image transcends any such limiting category
to become a disconcertingly real, human drama. This is made more resonant
by Moffatt's inclusion of herself as the central figure: a misfit in red yearning
for deliverance from history.

Aboriginal and Torres Strait Islander Art

Laurie Nelson Tukilalila b. c. 1923–dec.
Bob One Galadingwama 1925–1976
Big Jack Yarunga c. 1910–1973
Don Burak-Madjua b. c. 1925
Charlie Quiet Kwangdini b. c. 1905–dec.
and unknown artist
Melville Island, Northern Territory
Language group: Tiwi
Pukumani grave posts 1958
natural pigments on ironwood, 147.3 to 274.2 height
Gift of Dr Stuart Scougall 1959
P1–P17.1959

These ceremonial sculptures are central to the collection of the Art Gallery
of New South Wales, marking a breakthrough in the display of Aboriginal
cultural objects in an Australian museum of fine art, as well as testifying to the
spiritual vitality of a particular indigenous group – the Tiwi people of Melville
and Bathurst Islands, north of Darwin. Instrumental in their accession to the
collection was the late assistant director and artist Tony Tuckson, a champion
of Aboriginal art. Commissioned with the assistance of Dr Stuart Scougall, the
Pukumani poles or grave-posts (individually known as *tutini*) were fashioned
by six senior Tiwi artists in accordance with the conventions governing the
ritual of Pukumani. Within this traditional framework, however, each artist has
expressed an individual sensibility. The tutini, showing clan and territory
markings, are stationed like ancestral guardians around a grave site. In purely
formal terms, quite apart from the ritual significance it embodies, the group is
a masterpiece of Australian sculpture.

Artist unknown
La Perouse, New South Wales
Sydney Harbour Bridge c. 1939
assorted shells, blue velvet, cardboard, 9 x 17.5 x 5
Gift of Alan Lloyd 1995
21.1995

Drawing on the traditional practices of the Aboriginal people of the La Perouse community, this unassuming object is a moving demonstration of the cultural collisions set in motion by the European colonisation of Australia in 1788. These collisions are as current today as they were in the 1930s when an unknown Aboriginal woman crafted this collage of cardboard, cloth and shell. It is instantly recognisable as the Sydney Harbour Bridge, an icon of modernity. Completed in 1930, the bridge was celebrated in the production of countless souvenirs and trinkets, as well as inspiring a succession of Australian artists from Grace Cossington Smith to Brett Whiteley. This item belongs to that celebratory outpouring, yet other associations arise unmistakably from it. Shellfish were a dietary staple of the traditional inhabitants of the La Perouse area, the shells also having significance in their rituals. La Perouse itself was one of the earliest sites of black–white contact. The heaping of shell upon fragmentary shell in *Sydney Harbour Bridge* evokes as well the middens of coastal Australia, the evidence of immemorial Aboriginal occupation and ownership of the land. The 'white' bridge, in this sense, wears an indigenous overlay.

Albert Namatjira
Ntaria, Northern Territory, 1902–1959
Language group: Arrernte
Palm Valley 1940s
watercolour, 37 x 54
Purchased 1986
© Legend Press
93.1986

Albert Namatjira was of the western Arrernte people, growing up on the Lutheran Mission at Ntaria (Hermannsburg) near Alice Springs. While not the first Aboriginal artist to work in a European style, he is certainly the most famous. Once viewed as images that acquiesced all too completely to European pictorial conventions – and indeed to a notion of European ascendancy over the land – Namatjira's landscapes are latterly seen as coded meditations on traditional sites and sacred knowledge. In this way, his work has a symbolic quality comparable to the paintings of the nearby Papunya Tula artists. Palm Valley the place and *Palm Valley* the painting intersect at the level of a map, detailing Namatjira's artistic, ritual and proprietorial interest in the land. Despite his fame, Namatjira was denied 'privileges' such as owning land, in keeping with government policy for Aboriginal people at the time.

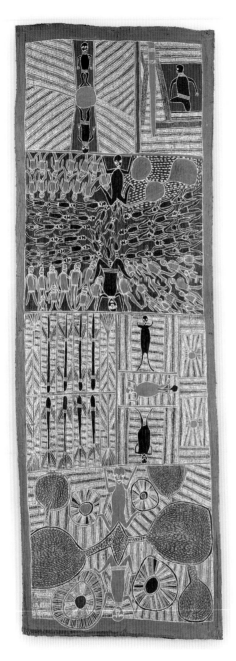

Mawalan Marika
Yirrkala, Arnhem Land,
Northern Territory, 1908–1967
Language group: Rirratjingu
Djang'kawu creation story
1959
natural pigments on eucalyptus
bark, 188 x 64.8
Gift of Dr Stuart Scougall 1959
© Aboriginal Artists Agency Ltd.
P68.1959

Mawalan's extraordinary gifts
as a painter are obvious in this
large, important, and partly
collaborative bark. It represents
elements of the story of the
Djang'kawu Sisters, who spread
fertility and increase as they
moved across the land. Plunging
their digging-sticks into the
earth, they created life-giving
waterholes as well as flora and
fauna. In their travels they were
accompanied by their brother,
shown here as the artist sitting
before his sacred goanna tail and
singing. In the panel below – a
striking example of pictorial
concision – the sisters give birth
to the original Dhuwa people.
Male children are shown as
yellow, female as black.
Prominent in the next panel, the
eight digging-sticks turn into
shade trees to protect the
Dhuwa progeny.

Mawalan Marika

Yirrkala, Arnhem Land,
Northern Territory, 1908–1967
Language group: Rirratjingu
Figure of an ancestral being of the Dhuwa moiety
1960
wood, human hair, bark fibre, parakeet feathers,
white feathers, natural pigments, 74.3 height
Gift of Dr Stuart Scougall 1960

© Aboriginal Artists Agency Ltd.
P7.1960

Creation stories, or dreamings, are central to the beliefs
that form the basis of Aboriginal cultures across the
Australian continent. For the people of central and
north-east Arnhem Land, the world is divided into two
principal categories or moieties: Yirritja and Dhuwa.
Mawalan Marika was an affiliate of the latter, entitled
by tradition, and through his role as a ceremonial leader,
to depict aspects of the Dhuwa cosmology. In this masterly representation of an
ancestral being, sculptural and painterly qualities are impressively reconciled.
The figure represents one of three founding ancestors, two sisters and a brother,
who migrated east to west giving birth to all the Dhuwa clans of the region.
Mawalan himself fathered and taught the well-known artists Wandjuk, Banduk,
Bayngul and Dhuwarrwarr, ensuring the preservation and continuity of his
immense ritual knowledge through familial descent.

Munggurrawuy Yunupingu

Yirrkala, Arnhem Land,
Northern Territory, 1907–1979
Language group: Gumatj
Figure of Lany'tjung, ancestral being of
the Yirritja moiety 1960
wood, human hair, bark fibre, parakeet feathers,
white feathers, natural pigments, 87.6 height
Gift of Dr Stuart Scougall 1960

P80.1960

This majestic and marvellously crafted object is one
of an important group of sculptural figures collected
at Yirrkala, a Christian mission in north-east Arnhem
Land, during the 1959 and 1960 excursions of the
Scougall–Tuckson team. Though it depicts Lany'tjung,
an ancestral being, the work has an unmistakably
human demeanour. The clearly carved facial features
would suggest repose, but for the characteristically
open-eyed expression. Tufts of real hair serve to further
humanise the image of the ancestor. Delicately trailing
feathers, a skirt of fibres and the exquisitely cross-hatched body markings also
contribute to the figure's majesty. Lany'tjung belongs, with his fellow ancestor
Barama, to the Yirritja moiety. It was their responsibility to introduce tribal law
and social organisation to the people of the region.

Dawidi Djulwarak
Milingimbi, Arnhem Land,
Northern Territory, c. 1921–1970
Language group: Liyagalawumirri
Wagilag Sisters story 1960
natural pigments on eucalyptus bark
95.3 x 49.5
Gift of Dr Stuart Scougall 1960
P43.1960

While the Djang'kawu Sisters are associated with the salt-water stories of the Dhuwa moiety, their fresh-water equivalents are the Wagilag Sisters. Dawidi was the traditional custodian of the Wagilag story, having inherited the role from his predecessor and uncle, Yilkarri Kitani, in 1956. It was not until 1963, however, that Dawidi gained full ritual entitlement to the Wagilag repertoire. His style is often referred to as 'classical'. It involves a characteristically angular system of cross-hatching, or *rarrk*, that is immediately identifiable in terms of clan and moiety grouping. In this bark, the Wagilag Sisters and their offspring travel north to a waterhole. They enrage a resident serpent, the great olive python, Wititj. He assails them with storms and water-spouts before swallowing them whole. Questioned by other ancestral serpents, he admits to consuming members of his own moiety. The cycle of regurgitation ends when Wititj vomits the sisters as boulders at the Mirrarrmina waterhole.

Gurruwiwi Midinari
Yirrkala, Arnhem Land,
Northern Territory, 1929–1976
Language group: Galpu
Djaykung – File snakes c. 1960
natural pigments on eucalyptus bark
280 x 70
Gift of Professor Harry Messel 1987
392.1987

Gurruwiwi Midinari was an exceptional and prolific artist from the Blue Mud Bay area of north-east Arnhem Land. His powerful, and in this case monumental, bark paintings represent an invaluable archive of clan and moiety markings of the area. They are also bravura examples of bark-painting technique. The shimmering effect in this work is produced by a complex skein of painted marks: lines, stripes, serial dots, *rarrk* or cross-hatching, and even areas of pure colour. The initial impact is dazzling, almost in the manner of op art, but this rapidly gives way to a sense of the patterns of time and motion addressed in the narrative. Treating the familiar encounter of the Wagilag Sisters with the Great Python, the story opens to the wider context of food-gathering and the artist's own personal totems: the star-shaped waterholes fringed with lilies, for example, and the plump and plentiful file snakes which are regarded as a succulent dietary staple.

Nym Bunduk
1900–1974
Kevin Bunduk
1942–1994
Wadeye (Port Keats),
Northern Territory
Language group:
Murrinpatha
Emus feeding 1961
natural pigments
on eucalyptus bark
179 x 78.8
Gift of Dr Stuart Scougall
1961
P22.1961

Combining figural and
abstract elements, this bark
is typical of the Wadeye
(Port Keats) region,
having been produced in
a decade when local artists
reinvigorated the repertoire
of traditional forms.
Experimental motifs and
procedures were intro-
duced, resulting in an
artistic and ritual renaissance. Unlike the isolated practices of the Tiwi, Wadeye
art was open to influence, converging with that of the nearby community at
Kimul. The basic palette of colours used elsewhere in the Northern Territory –
white, black, red and yellow – was extended in these communities to include
green, purple and pink. Nym Bunduk, a major ceremonial leader in his
community, painted this sensitive rendition of hungry emus in a desiccated and
fire-blackened landscape with the assistance of his son.

Munggurrawuy Yunupingu
Yirrkala, Arnhem Land,
Northern Territory, 1907–1979
Language group: Gumatj
*Birimbira (The thunder
spirits)* 1961
natural pigments on eucalyptus
bark, 150.2 x 60.4
Gift of Dr Stuart Scougall 1961
P19.1961

Yirrkala was originally a
Christian mission at the tip of
north-east Arnhem land. In the
creation cycles of the Yirritja
moiety, Yirrkala is also the
place where the ancestral being,
Lany'tjung, transgressed tribal
law by revealing rituals and
rangga (sacred objects) to
women and children. This well-
known and much-exhibited
bark is part of an historic group
of works gifted to the Gallery
by Dr Stuart Scougall between
1957 and 1964. Its painter,
Munggurrawuy Yunupingu,
was a senior master adept in the
shimmering geometries and
naturalistic designs that
combine to form the Yirrkala
style. Naturalism was used by Aboriginal artists as a means to conceal, or
acceptably present, sensitive and secret imagery. Marine creatures such as
dugongs, turtles, water snakes, stingrays and estuarine crocodiles are prominent
in this work, and representative of the artist's totemic agenda. His slightly
earlier bark, *Lany'tjung story 2 – crocodile and bandicoot* (1959), is also in
the collection.

Unknown artist
Kimberleys, Western Australia
Wandjina figure with turtles 1962
natural pigments on eucalyptus bark, 99.1 x 55.9
Gift of Dr Stuart Scougall 1962
P165.1962

Among the most mysterious presences in Aboriginal history, the Wandjina
are a group of ancestral beings who emerged from the sea and the sky.
Although often benign, their association with water encompasses its life-giving
properties as well as the destructive potential of flood and drought. While
specific to the Kimberley region, their influence has spread widely in more
recent times, to the extent that Wandjina have the same national currency in
Aboriginal culture as the Mimi figures of western Arnhem Land. The rayed
headdress, or aureole, is a typical and much-debated feature of Wandjina,
a merging of ceremonial form and supernatural symbol. The earliest versions
found in the caves and rock shelters of the Kimberley are traditionally believed
to have been made by the Wandjinas themselves. Repainting such images is
a ritual obligation of their human descendants, ensuring the continuity of the
great cycles of nature.

Yangarriny Wunungmurra
Yirrkala, Arnhem Land,
Northern Territory, b. 1932
Language group:
Dhalwangu-Narrkala
*Barama and Lany'tjung:
Yirritja creation story* c. 1966
natural pigments on eucalyptus bark
275.6 x 80.8
Gift of Dr Stuart Scougall 1964
P1.1964

The ancestral beings so vividly
evoked in this bark, Barama and
Lany'tjung, belong to a major
Yirritja creation narrative from
north-east Arnhem Land. The
story represented here has crucial
implications for the social and
ceremonial conduct of members
of the Yirritja moiety. Barama is
shown emerging from the depths
near Blue Mud Bay. His arms,
chest and thighs are draped in
weeds, accentuated by patterns
left by the draining water. These
form the basis of a symbolic
system which Barama discusses
with his companion Lany'tjung,
whom he subsequently appoints
to instruct Yirritja men in their
rituals and *rangga* (sacred
objects). Against Barama's
interdiction, Lany'tjung reveals
these secret matters to women
and children. Barama orders his
death, which is solemnised by the
burning of the ceremonial ground.

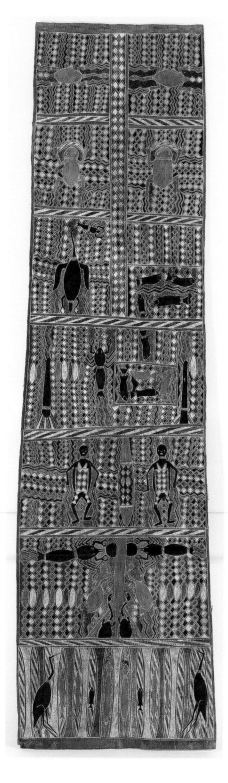

Kevin Gilbert

Canberra, Australian Capital
Territory, 1933–1993
Language group: Wiradjuri
*Christmas Eve in the land
of the dispossessed* 1968
(printed 1990)
linocut, 45.2 x 63.4
Purchased 1993
310.1993

Kevin Gilbert, who has the
distinction of being the first Koori printmaker, was instrumental in the
movement that awakened the Australian public to the richness and continuity
of Aboriginal culture. In fact, Gilbert is better known as a playwright, poet and
social polemicist than a visual artist. It is on the basis of a quite extraordinary
and unprecedented body of linocuts he produced between 1965 and 1969 that
his artistic reputation rests. Reprinted in 1990, this series has subsequently
achieved wider public recognition. Much of the stylistic repertoire and subject
matter found in the work of later Koori artists is foretold in Gilbert's grim and
graphic prints. Typically in monochrome, these images detail ancestral totems
and narratives as well as recording the condition of contemporary Aboriginal
people, especially Gilbert's own family. *Christmas Eve in the land of the
dispossessed* is an acerbic yet defiant representation of a bitter reality, since
addressed by a new generation of painters and printmakers.

Mervyn Bishop

Brewarrina, New South Wales, b. 1945
*Prime Minister Gough Whitlam pours
soil into the hands of traditional land
owner Vincent Lingiari* 1975
cibachrome photograph, 30.6 x 30.5
Hallmark Cards Australian Photography
Collection Fund 1991
169.1991

The political struggle that led to the
affirmation of native title enshrined
in the Mabo and Wik decisions is the
subject of this momentous photograph.
Appropriately, it was taken by Mervyn Bishop, Australia's first Aboriginal
press photographer and a noted recorder of customary and contemporary life
in Aboriginal communities. Bishop caught the human as well as the historical
significance of the transferral of soil from the hand of a white prime minister,
the reformist Gough Whitlam, to that of a Gurindji elder, Vincent Lingiari. Both
men seem awed, even humbled, by the power of their own gesture, enacted
against a brilliant blue Australian sky. Land at the Vestey-operated Wave Hill
Station was handed back to its traditional owners, the Gurindji people, in
August 1975, after decades of servitude and a nine-year walkout. The centrality
of the concept of land, or more properly of place, in Aboriginal culture and
consciousness is here given expression in a modern medium.

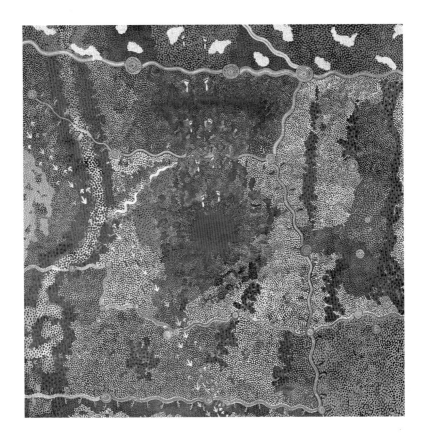

Clifford Possum Tjapaltjarri
Napperby, Northern Territory, b. c. 1932
Tim Leura Tjapaltjarri
Napperby, Northern Territory, c. 1929–1984
Language group: Anmatyerre/Arrernte
Warlugulong 1976
synthetic polymer paint on canvas, 168.5 x 170.5
Purchased 1981

This painting possesses all the formal qualities of a masterpiece of modern art. It is also a compendium of the artists' customary law and dreamings of the Central Desert region. Clifford Possum Tjapaltjarri was born about 200 kilometres north-west of Alice Springs, growing up in the 1930s and 1940s during the heyday of the cattle industry around Napperby Station. With his older brother, Tim Leura Tjapaltjarri, he was among the first to experiment with the transposition of ceremonial body- and ground-painting designs to an acrylic-on-canvas medium in the early 1970s: a cultural development of lasting significance to Aboriginal art. The main incident in the composition involves the fiery doom of the sons of Lungkata, the Blue Tongue Lizard Man. To punish these sons for transgression of dietary and ritual codes, their father ignites the terrible bushfire seen at the centre of the image. Their ashen footprints show the sons' attempt to flee. The ancestral stories of carpet snakes, emus and emu men, possums, wedge-tailed eagles, many varieties of flora and entire landscapes are embraced in this encyclopaedic work.

Tim Leura Tjapaltjarri
Napperby, Northern Territory, c. 1939–1984
Language group: Anmatyerre/Arrernte
Kooralia 1980
synthetic polymer paint on canvas, 183 x 152.5
Gift of the Art Gallery Society of New South Wales 1995
© Aboriginal Artists Agency Ltd.
482.1995

The younger brother of Clifford Possum Tjapaltjarri, Tim Leura Tjapaltjarri was a senior artist in his own right and the creator of an exceptional body of acrylic paintings in the desert style. His independent work is somewhat darker in colour than his brother's, and has been interpreted as more melancholy in mood. He was especially aware of the destructive incursions European culture had made upon the traditions of his people and took great care to reference it in his work. Much of his painting is concerned with recording important clan ceremonials and symbols, especially those centred on aspects of the secret rituals of 'men's business'. His *Men's camp at Lyrrpurrung Ngurra* (1979), in the National Gallery of Australia, is a sparse and ruminative rendition of a major ritual camp. *Kooralia* addresses similar concerns, but deals instead with details of the Seven Sisters dreaming, evoking the topography of the area around the Napperby creek bed.

David Malangi
Ramingining, Arnhem Land, Northern Territory, b. 1927
Language group: Manharrngu
Gunmirringu funeral scene 1983
natural pigments on eucalyptus bark, 156.5 x 74
Purchased 1984
126.1984

The word *gunmirringu* means 'the first people', and also refers to the great ancestral hunter of the same name. The cycle of stories around the life and death of Gunmirringu is crucially significant in the mourning and mortuary traditions of Malangi's people, the Manharrngu. A sacred song cycle, initiated by the death of Gunmirringu, is performed when a member of this clan grouping dies. As a major guardian figure, Gunmirringu is identified with a prominent rock visible in the sea off the mouth of the Glyde River. Malangi is the traditional custodian of three tracts of land along the river, near Ramingining in central Arnhem Land. His title to this land has been demonstrated through a series of paintings and sculptures to which this work relates. The dark ochre, rarely used by other artists in the area, is a distinctive feature of his style, as is his preference for bold and graphic imagery. The design on the first Australian dollar note, issued with the introduction of decimal currency in 1966, was based – without accreditation at the time – on one of Malangi's works.

Crusoe Kurddal
Maningrida, Arnhem Land,
Northern Territory, b. 1964
Language group: Kuninjku
Mimi spirits c. 1985
natural pigments on wood
70 to 272 height
Purchased 1985
80.1985, 81.1985, 180.1985

Crusoe Kurddal's father, Crusoe
Kuningbal, was a prodigious
carver of Mimi figures, passing
on to his son the sole right to
produce them for ritual purposes
and for commercial sale. The
carvings relate to the wealth
of Mimi representations painted
on the natural rock walls of
Kakadu and the Arnhem Land
escarpment, as well as to the
countless bark paintings
depicting the mysterious, slender
and famously reticent beings.
Here, in their sculpted form,
they are more static and stately.
Kurddal lives and works in
Maningrida, an important
Aboriginal settlement and
artistic centre at the mouth of
the Liverpool River on the coast
of central Arnhem Land. Believed to be the originators of human cultural
and social organisation, the Mimi also have their own clan and language
system. Wary of direct human contact, the Mimi open rocks with their breath
and disappear into them at the approach of people. Susceptible to breezes,
they hunt on windless days and nights. Mimi can be dangerous to humans,
but more through mischief than malice. These sculpted versions are used in
mamurrng – exchange ceremonies – associated with the birth of male children.

Jimmy Njiminjuma
Oenpelli, Arnhem Land,
Northern Territory,
b. 1945
Language group: Kunwinjku
*Ngalyod – The Rainbow
Serpent* c. 1985
natural pigments on
eucalyptus bark
148.5 x 55
Purchased 1989
238.1989

Common to both the
Dhuwa and Yirritja moiety
groupings of the western
Arnhem Land region, the
Rainbow Serpent is really
a generic name for several
ancestral beings in their
manifestation as snakes.
They can be simultaneously
male and female, and are fundamental to the creation cycles and ancestral
narratives that form the core of many Aboriginal cultures. They have different,
indeed seemingly infinite, aspects depending on their appearance and function
in any given story or place. Yingarna is the mother of other rainbow serpents,
or Ngalyod as they are called in the language group of this artist, Jimmy
Njiminjuma. The Ngalyod themselves are creator spirits, associated with watery
environments like billabongs and lagoons. In the wet season, a period of
remarkable climatological activity and natural growth, they can appear in the
sky as rainbows, hence their description by that name. Masters of disguise,
Ngalyod are only ever seen by the canniest or most unfortunate mortals.
Njiminjuma's style exploits the rarrk patterning typical of the area, pushing his
design to the very edges of this impressive bark and implying the physical size
and power of Ngalyod.

Darby Jampijinpa Ross
Yuendumu, Northern Territory, b. c. 1910
Jimija Jungarrayi
Yuendumu, Northern Territory, 1908–1989
Language group: Warlpiri
Yankiri Jukurrpa (Emu dreaming) 1986
synthetic polymer paint on cotton duck
92 x 173
Gift of the Art Gallery Society of New South Wales 1995
480.1985

Some of the artistic communities that contributed to the stylistic category
generally known as Western Desert art include Papunya, Yuendumu and
Kintore. Papunya was the site of the first extraordinary transpositions of
traditional sand 'paintings' into contemporary media. These works, rich in
the rusty splendour of their desert colouring and dramatic patterning, have
remained a self-renewing source of cultural pride for the people of the area,
as well as serving to spearhead the dissemination of contemporary Aboriginal
art both nationally and internationally. From Yuendumu comes this large
and dynamic composition by the Warlpiri artists Darby Jampijinpa Ross and
Jimija Jungurrayi. A more eloquent embodiment of the concept of Aboriginal
painting as a form of land title would be hard to imagine. *Yankiri Jukurrpa*
is the Warlpiri language term designating Emu dreaming. The movements of
these flightless birds – a dietary staple and an important creature in ancestral
stories – are depicted against a symbolic, yet highly specific representation of
the desert landscape.

Willy Tjungurrayi
Kintore, Northern Territory, b. c. 1936
Language group: Pintupi
Tingari Story 1986
synthetic polymer paint on linen, 240 x 360
Mollie Gowing Acquisition Fund for Contemporary Aboriginal Art 1993
© Aboriginal Artists Agency Ltd.
548.1993

An elder of the Pintupi people, Willy Tjungurrayi began painting in acrylic-on-canvas for the Papunya Tula artists' collective in 1976. In the early 1980s, Tjungurrayi joined the Pintupi in their historic return to ancestral lands around Kintore, sparking a period of prolific artistic production for him and his colleagues. On this, one of his largest works, he was assisted by John and Simon Tjakamara, whose different techniques can be distinguished from his. The site represented is most likely around Lake McDonald, where the mythic Tingari men made camp on their journey from Peterman Range towards Kintore. The paths which so dynamically interconnect in the composition were made as the Tingari travelled across the land, typically east to west, bringing law, ritual and the fundamentals of culture to the people of the Western Desert. Often accompanied by novices, the Tingari played a special role in the secret, post-initiatory instruction of young men, and do so today. As a result, much of the ultimate meaning of this pictorial *tour de force* is intentionally veiled.

Judy Watson
Brisbane, Queensland, b. 1959
Language group: Waanyi
The guardians 1986–87
powder pigment on plywood, 180 x 58 each figure
Purchased 1990

The suppleness of Aboriginal artistic convention is one of its most remarkable
features. The ease with which designs once created in the ephemeral medium
of sand, or on the body, became durable acrylic paintings is a case in point.
So too is the consequent blossoming of ever-new regional schools of painting
across Australia. Judy Watson's work is representative of this dynamic relationship between tradition and innovation, conveying the artist's connectedness to
her Waanyi origins (in the south-west Gulf of Carpentaria) into a wider realm.
These ominous yet reassuring presences, striated by the artist's hands, are
reminiscent of the anthills believed by some Aboriginal groups to contain the
watchful dead. Above them hangs a ghostly print taken from the inked surface
of the central guardian.

Rover Thomas (Joolama)
Warmun (Turkey Creek), Western Australia, 1926–1998
Language group: Wangkatjungka/Kukatja
Ngarin Janu Country 1988
earth pigments in synthetic polymer resin on canvas, 100 x 140
Purchased 1988
512.1988

The late Rover Thomas was born on the Canning Stock Route in Western Australia. His distinctive Aboriginal vision of this country is informed by his experience of working in the pastoral industry and its violent history, as well as his ceremonial life. Following a prophetic dream, where Thomas's mother revealed songs and stories relating to her spiritual journey to sacred sites in the Kimberley, Thomas became the catalyst for a cultural revival in the east Kimberley. In 1990 Thomas represented Australia at the 1990 Venice Biennale in company with another Aboriginal artist, Trevor Nickolls. *Ngarin Janu Country* represents the tragic ancestral flooding of lake Ngarin Janu, when the people living there were drowned attempting to escape the rising waters by crossing the channel from Dalidali (the sandbar) to Miwuda (the big hill). The different planes of ochred colour, edged by Thomas's distinctive white dots, suggest the major features of the landscape; the black representing the lake with the channel dissecting the sandbar and the hills. This stark depiction characterises the potency of Thomas's vision.

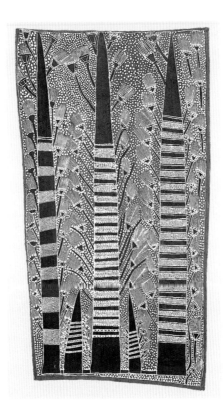

Paddy Lilipiyana
Ramingining, Arnhem Land, Northern Territory, 1920–1993
Dorothy Djukulul
Ramingining, Arnhem Land, Northern Territory, b. 1942
Language group: Ganalbingu
Wagilag Sisters story: Wurrutjurra (sand palm) 1989
natural pigments and synthetic polymer paint on eucalyptus bark, 108 x 63
Purchased 1989
350.1989

Of the small group of women artists working in the bark-painting technique,
Dorothy Djukulul is perhaps the best known and one of the most accomplished.
She was taught by her father, the senior master and chief custodian of the
Wagilag Sisters story, Dawidi Djulwarak, as well as her uncle, the noted
Lilipiyana, with whom she collaborated on this exquisite and unusually
abstracted image. Dorothy's brother, the late George Milpurrurru, was another
celebrated painter of the region. The three immense verticals represent
Mirrarrmina, the sacred waterhole where the great Python, Wititj, rose up and
swallowed the Wagilag Sisters before regurgitating them, thereby instituting
seasonal cycles and social codes. Sprouting from the sides of the waterhole are
fan-shaped Wurrutjurra palm trees, the stylisation of which has an almost
Egyptian formality. The vibratory effect of silvery white dots and *rarrk* over
dense black underpainting is a conscious approximation of the unutterable
spirituality of the subject.

Lin Onus
Melbourne, Victoria, 1948–1996
Language group: Yorta Yorta
Fruit bats 1991
polychromed fibreglass sculptures, polychromed wooden disks,
Hill's Hoist clothesline, 250 height
Purchased 1993

A pioneer among Aboriginal artists working in and with a modern urban
milieu, Lin Onus was nonetheless deeply concerned with traditional themes
and forms in his work. He expressed his Aboriginality with dazzling technical
skill and variety, being an accomplished painter in a photo-realist manner as
well as a sculptor of great virtuosity. This show-stopping work features an
installation of ninety-nine fibreglass fruit bats, painted in the *rarrk* patterning of
Arnhem Land, and suspended from a commercially produced Hill's Hoist – an
icon of white suburbia. Onus's work was always infused with humour, but *Fruit
bats* is also a serious statement about race relations in Australia. It is as though
the racist sins of the colonial past had come home to roost in the backyards of
Australia.

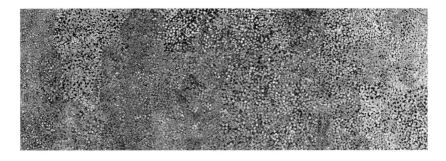

Emily Kame Kngwarreye
Utopia, Northern Territory, c. 1910–1996
Language group: Anmatyerre
Untitled (Alhalkere) 1992
synthetic polymer paint on canvas, 165.0 x 480.0
Mollie Gowing Acquisition Fund for Contemporary Aboriginal Art 1992

This painting matches the greatest religious images of Western art in the sheer moral conviction of its making. Quite apart from the unfettered painterliness and gestural animation which ally it to abstract expressionism, the image is imbued with the life experience of a mature artist who brought to it the traditions and textures of her spiritual and cultural heritage. A member of the Utopia community at Soakage Bore, located some 400 kilometres north-east of Alice Springs, Kngwarreye was a leading figure in eastern Anmatyerre ceremony and ritual. In her final decades, during which she adapted traditional body- and sand-painting techniques to modern media such as batik and acrylic-on-canvas, she became one of the most celebrated and sought-after Aboriginal

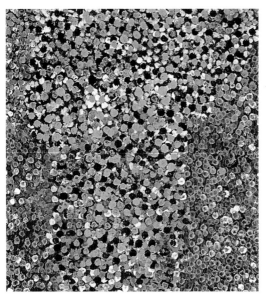

artists. Characteristic of its period, and exploited to the full in this painting, is the near-concealment of sacred signs beneath a surface patterning of slurried dots evocative of dust, dance, song, heat, light and landscape. Kngwarreye's final works were pared back to purely linear motifs, suggestive of the spindly yam roots that were her principal totemic device.

Ginger Riley Munduwalawala
South-east Arnhem Land, Northern Territory, b. c. 1937
Language group: Mara
Limmen Bight River country 1992
synthetic polymer paint on canvas, 244.0 x 244.0
Mollie Gowing Acquisition Fund for Contemporary Aboriginal Art 1992

Reproduced courtesy of Alcaston Gallery, Melbourne
291.1992

Traditional in subject matter and experimental in style, the paintings of Ginger
Riley Munduwalawala are impressive pictorial presences, not least because of
their scale and dramatic colour schemes. As an elder of his community, the
artist is entrusted with the preservation of aspects of the stories of his mother's
people at Four Arches, 45 kilometres inland from Limmen Bight in the Gulf
of Carpentaria. Limmen Bight country is the landscape depicted in this stately
retelling of the story of the first being, a kangaroo, shown in solitary grandeur
at the bottom of Riley's successively layered composition. In order to populate
the world, it was the task of this being to find himself a mate. Garimala, an
ancestral snake, recommended he seek out a young girl, a quest which leads
the kangaroo into many deprivations and dangers. The near-fatal spearing
shown in the second register was probably in punishment for his trespass on
the territory of another clan. The hump-like landforms which characterise the
work, and Limmen Bight itself, are believed to have resulted from the writhings
of the great serpents whose appearance in this painting, and elsewhere in
Aboriginal art, is significantly hieratic.

Gordon Bennett
Brisbane, Queensland, b. 1955
Myth of the Western man (White man's burden) 1992
synthetic polymer paint on canvas, 175.0 x 304.0
Purchased 1993
390.1993

A Victorian pioneer grapples pathetically but determinedly with a central pole,
cast adrift in a cosmic tempest of temporality. The dates scattered like wreckage
in the maelstrom are significant moments in the Aboriginal diaspora – including
the first legally sanctioned massacre of indigenous people in 1795 – while the
figure itself is taken from a school primer illustrating the saga of explorers
Burke and Wills. In Bennett's imaginative reversal of art-historical conventions,
this saga assumes the status of a white myth investigated by a black ethnologist.
The painting's studied organisation of drips and dots suggests both abstract
expressionism – one is reminded of Jackson Pollock's *Blue poles* – and Western
Desert art. Bennett gives these dots the mechanical character of commercially
screened images, enhancing their cross-cultural, indeed subversive, complexity.
He is an artist of unflagging vision, whose deeply held political beliefs inform
his entire project, which might be described as an attempt to inscribe reality into
legend and truth into misconception.

Pantjiti Mary Mclean
Kalgoorlie, Western Australia, b. c. 1935
Language group: Ngaatjatarra
Hunting grounds 1993
synthetic polymer paint, charcoal, ochres on paper, 138.5 x 261 (irregular)
Mollie Gowing Acquisition Fund for Contemporary Aboriginal Art 1993
© Pantjiti Mary Mclean and Nalda May Searles
547.1993

Though an experienced carver, Pantjiti Mary Mclean came late to the
Western painterly technique she now adroitly exercises. Her paintings are,
generally speaking, rumbustious arrangements of floral, animal and human
life; colourful and teeming Edens in which Aboriginal communities can be
observed participating in their traditional practices. Pantjiti, a matriarchal
figure, offers a vision of the way things were, and might be again, though
her own early years were marred by forced removal to a mission station.
Unlike many other desert artists, Pantjiti restricts the use of both dot-painting
and clan-marking in her painterly system, feeling free to produce improvised
images of great vitality and naturalism. *Hunting grounds* perfectly captures the
excitement of the hunt and related communal events remembered by the artist
from her childhood.

H. J. Wedge
Cowra, New South Wales,
b. 1957
Language group: Wiradjuri
Stop and think 1993
(detail)
5 panels: synthetic polymer
paint on canvas
76 x 91.2 each panel
Purchased 1994
217.1994.1–5

The traditional figure most identified with the marvellous paintings of H. J. Wedge is the spirit seen hovering in the upper left of this panel. Constantly metamorphosing as it goes, the spirit figure combines aspects of both genders, seemingly integrating animal and human capabilities. Its most startling feature is the radial halo of hair that produces a charged, almost electric sense of energy around it, an energy that is condoning and benign. Wedge grew up at Erambie Mission near Cowra. As someone who neither reads nor writes, his gift for visual story-telling is acutely developed, accounting in no small part for the immediacy and clarity of *Stop and think*. The incident portrayed in this image is didactic in tone. This is often the case with Wedge, whose desire to instruct and admonish links directly to the conventions of traditional narrative. Here, in a parody of Red Riding Hood, an emu-child is offered a bag of sweets – which could be drugs – by a charismatic wolf: a species introduced from Europe.

Thancoupie
Weipa, Queensland, b. 1937
Mosquito corroboree 1994
stoneware, 30.0 x 31.5
Mollie Gowing Acquisition Fund for
Contemporary Aboriginal Art 1995
94.1995

The town of Weipa in Queensland is the birthplace of Thancoupie, one of Australia's premier potters and pottery teachers. She was in the first wave of Aboriginal artists to receive international recognition, coming to attention as early as the 1970s. Although fired ceramic utensils are not a feature of traditional Aboriginal domestic or ritual practice, clay itself has always been extensively used in ceremonial activity and artistic production. Thancoupie's people, the Thanaquith of Cape York, baked clay balls, easily stored sources of the ochreous pigments used in their rituals. This traditional association has been continued in the dramatic spherical pots which are Thancoupie's signature. These gourd-like vessels seem to take form from the very mud. Symbolising unity, fire and earth, they typically bear incised decorations based on traditional stories of the Thanaquith – in this case a totemic mosquito corroboree.

Rea

Sydney, New South Wales, b. 1962
Language group: Gamileroi
Highly coloured: my life is coloured by my colour 1994 (detail)
6 panels: computer-generated photographs, 185 x 58.5 each panel
Purchased with funds provided by the Young Friends of the Art Gallery Society
of New South Wales 1994

573.1994.1–6

Although the panels in this life-size set of self-portraits recall Aboriginal bark
painting in their verticality and visual layering, Rea's methods are entirely
contemporary. State-of-the-art computer-generation is used to produce flawless
compositions and seamless surfaces. Rea, the artist's professional name, is a
Gamileroi woman from western New South Wales. The subject matter of her
work is Aboriginality, viewed through a mesh of personal narrative and private
memory in which gender, sexuality and society are intertwined. The *Yellow*
image, for instance, refers to her experience of a death in custody. Here, the
artist's face – and by extension her identity – is literally embedded in the work.
She reveals herself, yet resists being seen, turning the camera's gaze back upon
the spectator.

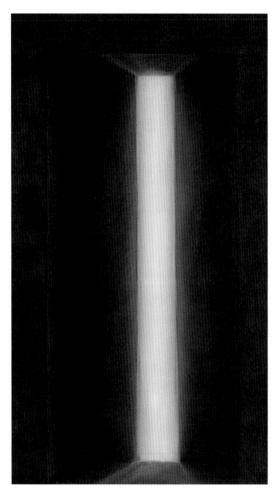

Karen Casey
Hobart, Tasmania, b. 1956
Gateway 1994
oil and mixed media on
linen, 213.0 x 121.0
Mollie Gowing Acquisition
Fund for Contemporary
Aboriginal Art 1995
268.1995

Karen Casey was born in
Tasmania, an island state
infamous in the history
of European settlement
for its violence against the
indigenous inhabitants.
The original Aboriginal
population was believed
to have been exterminated
by about 1876, although
a number in fact survived.
Casey first came to prominence with a series of
figurative paintings that
addressed this institutionalised attempt at genocide through the metaphor of the
great white hunter, a hideous buffoon who gloats as he kills, wiping out species
with neither remorse nor self-awareness. *Gateway* represents a shift towards a
more abstract treatment of Australian history, presenting a poetic but still
potent translation of issues and feelings around Aboriginality. One such concern
is the ongoing tragedy of black deaths in custody. This image might, after all, be
the light-emitting slit in a cell wall, the last thing the suiciding prisoner sees; or,
more generally, a symbol of psychic release.

Ian Abdulla
Gerard, South Australia, b. 1943
Language group: Ngarrindjeri
Swimming before school 1995
synthetic polymer paint on canvas, 160 x 240
Mollie Gowing Acquisition Fund for Contemporary Aboriginal Art 1996
219.1996

The Coorong is a famously fertile area on the lower Murray River near
Adelaide in South Australia. It has long been a site of traditional Aboriginal
activity as well as, more recently, an important agricultural centre. Ian Abdulla's
rural upbringing in the Riverland is reflected in many of his paintings, as it is in
his written reminiscences of life on the fringe of settler society. His works are
personal in content, but wider in their connotation. In this painting, what at
first appears a simple and blissfully bucolic record of country life – going
swimming before school – turns out to reference matters of social alienation,
poverty and hardship. The swimming served as a necessary bath, the warming
fire as a means to make a rudimentary breakfast of toast, and the whole thing
a prelude to a sixteen-kilometre trek to, and back from, a distant government
schoolhouse. Nonetheless, Abdulla's fond attachment to this moment of
childhood happiness is told in the flawless blue sky and verdant landscape.

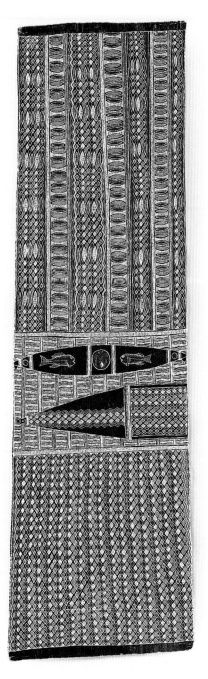

Nawurapu Wunungmurra
Yirrkala, Arnhem Land,
Northern Territory, b. 1952
Language group: Dhalwangu
Dhalwangu miny'tji 1996
natural pigments on eucalyptus bark,
294.0 x 93.0
Mollie Gowing Acquisition Fund for
Contemporary Aboriginal Art 1996
487.1996

Monumental in scale and mes-
merising in its visual power,
this austerely patterned bark
was painted by Nawurapu
Wunungmurra, son of the senior
artist Yanggarriny Wunungmurra.
It evinces an uncompromising
clarity of pictorial organisation,
encapsulating many of the qualities
of contemporary Aboriginal art.
Without the least knowledge of its
ceremonial and spiritual content,
an uninstructed viewer would still
be overwhelmed by its formal
power, its pristine application, its
elegance. The Dhalwangu word
miny'tji refers to the sacred designs
painted on the body for certain
ceremonies. According to the
conventions of the Yirritja moiety,
to which the Wunungmurra family
belong, these designs were given to
the clans by the ancestral being
Barama. The bark is characterised
by large, unbroken masses of
miny'tji; a regular diamond pattern
at one end, denoting fresh-water;
and a mixture of *miny'tji* at the other signifying the fertile stirring of estuarine
silts where salt-water and fresh-water mingle. The striking elliptical shape at the
centre is the Yingapungapu, a sand sculpture constructed on the coastal ground
where mortuary ceremonies are held. The ancestral Parrot Fish skeleton is a
totem typically associated with this form.

Gloria Tamerre Petyarre

Utopia, Northern Territory, b. c. 1945
Language group: Anmatyerre
*Awelye for the mountain devil lizard:
twenty-one women* 1996 (detail)
21 panels: synthetic polymer paint on canvas
98 x 70 each panel, 294 x 490 overall
Gift of Yuana and Stephen Hesketh 1997
376.1997.a–v

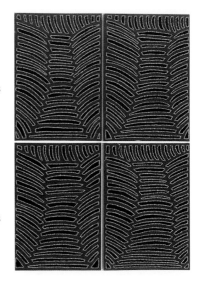

To experience this work in all its multi-panelled complexity and scale is to understand the majesty of modern Aboriginal art. *Awelye* is at once an affirmation of undeviating visual traditions and an extraordinary departure into the realm of seriality and high abstraction. There is an aural dimension to the work. One can almost hear, or feel like a shudder, the heavy, chanted rhythms of the *awelye* emanating from each panel. *Awelye* is an Anmatyerre term signifying both the ritual designs and the ceremony of women's business. The mountain devil lizard, or Arnkerthe, is totemic to this artist and her family. Gloria Tamerre Petyarre is a senior painter of the Utopia community at Mosquito Bore, related to Ada Bird Petyarre and the great Kngwarreye.

Ken Thaiday

Erub Island, Eastern Islands of
the Torres Strait, b. 1950
Language group: Meriam Mer
Beizam (shark) dance mask 1996
plywood, black bamboo, string, plastic,
paint, glass, feathers, 86.7 x 106.0 x 71.0
Mollie Gowing Acquisition Fund for
Contemporary Aboriginal Art 1997
4.1997

The art of the few settled islands of the Torres Strait, which once connected the land masses of Aboriginal Cape York and Papua New Guinea, reflects many influences. Masks, articulated headdresses and dance accessories such as drums and woven objects are characteristic of the region, drawing on the visual traditions of both Aboriginal and Papuan cultures and attesting to a significant tendency to the sculptural arts. European contact with the area was limited until 1871, when the London Missionary Society established a presence on Erub (Darnley) Island. Christian imperatives, however, did not entirely override the oral traditions of the Islanders, thereby ensuring the continuity of their material culture. Erub is the traditional home of Ken Thaiday, among the most well known of Islander artists and a specialist exponent of the dance mask. In this case, he represents his preferred *Beizam* (shark) totem, inventively mixing modern products such as plywood and plastic with traditional materials.

Asian Collection

Asian Collection

Crossing the threshold to the Asian Gallery, visitors are made to feel transported to another place and time. The range of art works is an expression of a rich variety of traditions spanning the centuries and also of the links between the differing cultures of the Asian region. Buddhism, for example, spread from India across Central Asia to China and Japan and southward through South-east Asia. Buddhist iconography and artistic styles were absorbed and adapted by local cultures.

The genesis of the Asian collection was the gift of a large group of ceramics and bronzes from the Government of Japan following the Sydney International Exhibition in 1879. Since that time acquisitions were sporadic until the establishment of the Asian Department in 1979 and the subsequent opening, in 1990, of the new Asian Gallery with its distinctive and contemplative atmosphere.

The collection has particular strengths in Chinese ceramics and Japanese paintings and screens, but recent acquisitions have greatly enhanced the representation of Chinese Buddhist sculptures, and Indian and South-east Asian works of art. The works in the Asian Gallery represent some of the finest moments in art in the region's history and also reflect the passions of the individual collectors and patrons who have contributed to the collection. The Asian collection is a powerful symbol of the importance the Gallery places on the research and display of the cultural and artistic traditions of Australia's Asian neighbours.

Shang dynasty
China, c. 1600–1027 BCE
Ritual vessel: ding 12th–11th century BCE
bronze, 21.5 height
Bequest of Kenneth Myer 1993
574.1993

China's first great dynastic era is characterised by the extraordinary achievements of its bronzesmiths. Vessels such as this circular *ding* were made for the complex rituals and ceremonies associated with ancestor worship and burials of the early Bronze Age rulers and aristocracy of ancient China. They are highly esteemed for their technical excellence as well as their decorative quality. Although symbolic in nature, the decoration typically retains elements of realistic inspiration. In this instance the vessel is ringed by a band of stylised cicada motifs, while around the rim there is an alternating pattern of circular designs and animal-like heads based on the *taotie* mask. The latter is the single most pervasive symbolic feature of ancient Chinese bronze vessel design, serving to ward off evil spirits. Among the extensive repertoire of ritual food and wine vessels the *ding*, used for heating and containing food, was the most popular. In addition to this circular example, *ding* may be square or rectangular, and sometimes of exceptionally large size.

Han dynasty

China, 206 BCE – 220 CE
Architectural tower: tomb model
1st–2nd century
earthenware with green glaze
144.8 height
Edward and Goldie Sternberg Chinese
Art Purchase Fund 1992
308.1992

Pottery models of buildings, horses
and other animals, military personnel,
servants and courtiers were made to
furnish the tombs of rulers and royalty
in early China. Thus endowed, the
tomb became a replica of the deceased's
life on earth. Pottery facsimiles or
mingqi have become the most illustrative and evocative images of life in
ancient China, as well as a poignant
demonstration of the Chinese belief in
the afterlife. The production of these
pottery models stimulated one of
China's most distinctive and unique
artistic traditions, which flourished
during the Han and Tang dynasties.
This unusually large model of a four-
storey watchtower is manned by guards

holding crossbows on the lower level, and by alert and watchful sentinels above.
Every architectural detail is observed: in the circular roof tile ends, the ornate
quatrefoil ornaments on the corners, the door and gate fittings and the overall
construction methods. Since most Han dynasty buildings were constructed from
wood and have not therefore survived, such models are the most accurate
records of architecture in early dynastic China.

Northern Wei dynasty
China, 386–534
Buddhist stele c. 525–530
sandstone, 143 height
Purchased with assistance
from the Art Gallery Society
of New South Wales and the
Edward and Goldie Sternberg
Chinese Art Purchase Fund
1995
202.1995

The front side of this stele
is carved with a principal
image of Sakyamuni Buddha
seated in a niche, while the
reverse features a principal
image of the Future Buddha,
Maitreya, sitting cross-legged.
The Sakyamuni Buddha sits
beneath a flame-ornamented
canopy and is flanked by a
pair of Bodhisattvas: those
most human of beings in the
vast pantheon of Buddhist
deities who, having achieved
Buddhahood, elect to remain
on earth out of compassion.
The figure of Maitreya sits
beneath an ornately decorated
canopy and is also flanked
by a pair of small Bodhisattva images. Above both the principal images the stele
is carved with miniature Buddhas. A dedicatory inscription on the upper right
bears the now partially damaged reign date, which reads: '*chang yuan nian...*'.
The absence of the first character precludes a precise date, but indicates either
512, 525 or 532. Further inscriptions on all sides of the stele give the names of
donors who contributed to its construction as an act of Buddhist devotion.

Sui dynasty
China, 581–618
Figure of Buddha
marble, 210 height
Art Gallery of New South
Wales Foundation Purchase
1997
432.1997

This massive and imposing
image of the Buddha con-
veys spiritual power and
presence with emphatic
simplicity. The separately
carved head and hands are
now missing. From the
position of the arms, the
right hand was probably
held in the gesture of
assurance, the *abhaya
mudra*, and the left in the
pendant *varada mudra*,
the gesture of granting a
wish. The date of the sculpture, along with its probable hand gestures and
drapery – including the decorative gathering of the suspended robe around the
left shoulder – indicate the Buddha to be Amitabha, the Buddha of the Western
Paradise. The figure is characterised by the elegant fall of the robes, suggested
by a few simple, fluent lines, and the eloquent economy of the carving. From the
back, sweeping folds define the clinging draperies around an anatomically
credible body.

Tang dynasty
China, 618–906
A pair of tomb guardian figures late 6th–early 7th century
earthenware with traces of red and orange pigment over white slip
93 and 92 heights
Art Gallery of New South Wales Foundation Purchase 1990
249.1990.1-2

Benign but fearsome, this pair of unusually large and meticulously detailed
figures exemplifies ceramic technique in Tang China. The facial features and
elaborate costumes of these tomb guardians are realised with a convincing
naturalism combined with iconographic stylisation. Their dynamic and dramatic
poses are characteristic of figures that were placed in the four corners of the
tomb to ward off evil spirits. Guardian figures such as these, termed *lokapalas*
or guardian kings, became assimilated into the popular concept of the Four
Heavenly Kings of Buddhism, or *tian wang*. The demonic appearance of this
pair is heightened by their flamboyant armour with its flaring epaulettes and
prominent breastplates. Also typical is their heroic pose: by standing on or
trampling a demon or animal the guardians demonstrate their power over
natural elements and evil forces.

Yuan dynasty
China, 1279–1368
Figure of Maitreya 14th century
gilt bronze, 69 height
Purchased 1996
566.1996

In the Buddhist art of China and North Asia, Maitreya is represented as both a Buddha and a Bodhisattva. The Historical Buddha, Sakyamuni, is said to have visited Maitreya in the Tushita heaven when he appointed him to be his successor. For this reason Maitreya is also known as the 'Future Buddha'. In later times and in yet another form, Maitreya became one of the most popular of Buddhist images as Budai, the manifestation of the Future Buddha: always represented as a fat jolly fellow commonly referred to as the 'laughing Buddha'. Here Maitreya is represented as a Bodhisattva, identified by the hands held in the *dharmachakra* (teaching or turning the wheel of the law) *mudra*, with the legs pendant: the only deity in the vast pantheon of Buddhist gods to be shown seated in the European manner. Also visible are the now broken stems of the lotus flower traditionally held by Maitreya. The ornate *dhoti* tied at the waist and elaborate necklaces, headdress and jewellery are all characteristic of Bodhisattva images of this time, when the influence of the Tibetan style was being felt.

Ming dynasty, Yongle period
China, 1403–1424
Dish with bouquet design
porcelain with underglaze blue decoration, 40.9 diameter
Bequest of Kenneth Myer 1993
575.1993

The technical and artistic excellence of Ming dynasty porcelain is without parallel. Although a tremendous variety of wares was produced, the great tradition of blue and white porcelains most confidently expresses the imperial style. The Yongle period at the beginning of the fifteenth century was one of the most glorious and productive eras in the history of Chinese art. Under the inspired patronage of the Yongle emperor all the arts flourished; none more so than the ceramic arts centred on the imperial kilns at Jingdezhen in Jiangxi province. There the characteristics of the local clay had been mastered in the production of translucent high-fired white-bodied porcelain. The technique of painting on the body of the ceramic vessel with cobalt blue had been introduced to China during the preceding Yuan dynasty, probably from Persia. By the late Yuan dynasty (in the second half of the fourteenth century), blue and white porcelain was the hallmark product of Chinese kilns, paving the way for massive expansion and artistic fulfilment in the Ming. This large dish is a classic example of the Ming potters' art. Perfectly shaped, it is covered with a glaze rich in texture, and painted with a flourishing design of a bouquet of lotus and water plantain, with a continuous scroll of lotus blooms around the rim. Characteristic of Ming imperial wares, the shape of the vessel is in perfect harmony with the rhythms of the decoration.

Ming dynasty, mark of Xuande

China
Bowl mid-15th century
porcelain painted in underglaze blue
21.3 diameter
Purchased 1975
56.1975

Exemplifying the mature refinement of
the classic Ming aesthetic, this bowl from
the imperial kilns at Jingdezhen embodies
the ideals of serenity and harmony.
Although its eloquent form with a gently
curled lip attests to the technical supremacy of the Ming potter, the real
hallmark of the imperial Ming style is expressed in the harmony of form and
decoration: the manner in which the lotus scrolls on the exterior – and the six
lotus blooms around a peony spray on the inside of the bowl – flow seamlessly
around the vessel. On the deeply recessed base the bowl carries the six-character
mark of the Xuande reign drawn in underglaze blue. In spite of this mark, the
undisputed quality of the bowl, and the characteristic bluish clear glaze with its
'orange skin' surface, a slightly later date of c. 1450–65 is suggested by a few
anomalies: notably the specific design of the lotus scroll and the weight of the
bowl relative to its size.

Ming dynasty, Hongzhi period

China, 1488–1505
Dish with hibiscus spray design
porcelain decorated in
underglaze blue and overglaze
yellow, 26.7 diameter
Edward and Goldie Sternberg
Chinese Art Purchase Fund 1989
366.1989

The imperial porcelains of the
relatively brief Hongzhi period
of the Ming dynasty have
always been among the most
admired. Dishes like this one
with overglaze yellow enamel were especially regarded, not only for their
imperial associations, but also for the refinements and nuances that could be
achieved in the handling of the yellow. Chinese connoisseurs were particularly
sensitive to the tone of the yellow, which was praised if it was the colour of
steamed chestnuts or the brightness of sunflowers. In this example the almost
lyrical modulations of the overglaze enliven the surface without distracting from
the overall harmony. The central design of the hibiscus spray is rendered with
elegant boldness and compositional sophistication. Around the rim are four
further sprays of lotus, grapevine, persimmon and pomegranate.

Wang Jianzhang
China, active c. 1620–50
*Returning home
from gathering fungus*
dated 1628
hanging scroll; ink and
slight colours on paper,
85.4 x 51.2 image
Purchased with funds
provided by Edward
Sternberg 1991
265.1991

The landscape theme
is the hallmark of the
great Chinese painting
tradition. The Chinese
landscape is not an
exercise in verisimilitude,
but an expression of
nature's cyclical, regen-
erative powers and of humankind's profound dependence upon them. This
painting unites the rationalism of Confucianism with the mysticism of Daoism.
In its human detail it conveys the practicalities of daily life. At the same time,
the magical, almost convulsive landscape evokes the ineffable forces of nature.
Wang Jianzhang was a Nanjing artist of the late Ming dynasty, a time when
China was plagued by uncertainty, corruption and social and political distur-
bances. In such troubled times the literati artists sought solace in nature and the
long-established tradition of landscape painting. The isolation of the artist and
the scholar–gentleman class is symbolised by the lone figure in the lower left of
the scroll, returning to his garden studio after searching for the magic *lingzhi*
fungus of immortality. The poem reads:

> *Trees on the cliff cage clouds, half moist.*
> *The brushwood gate beside a stream is newly opened.*
> *Facing the dawn, I seek for a poem, all alone;*
> *As I gather fungus the sun sets, and I return.*

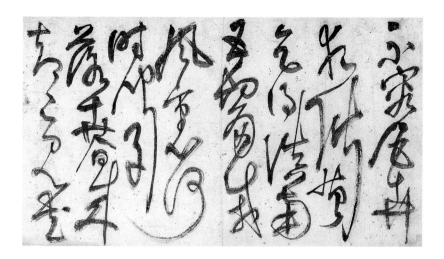

Yu Shaozhi
China, b. early 17th century
Constantly changing clouds (detail)
handscroll: ink on paper, 31 x 318
Edward and Goldie Sternberg Chinese Art Purchase Fund 1991
367.1991

Of all the arts of China calligraphy is the most esteemed. It embodies the
highest visual, philosophic and aesthetic ideals of the scholar for whom
proficiency in the Four Accomplishments – painting, calligraphy, poetry and
chess – was a fundamental objective, indeed a necessity. Of equal significance
are the Three Perfections: painting, poetry and calligraphy, with calligraphy
again deemed to be the highest achievement because it combined the beauty
and morality of ideas and poetry with the visual eloquence of writing. In
consequence, as much emphasis was placed on the expressiveness and aesthetic
fluency of calligraphy as on its meaning. Of the many groups and styles of
calligraphy, the cursive or *caoshu* – literally 'grass script' – style is among the
most expressive. It is distinguished by its spontaneity, speed and dynamic
energy, but always without compromising the legibility of the characters.
The scroll comprises three poems composed by the artist, under the overall
title 'Constantly changing clouds', which is written in four large characters
at the beginning. While little is known of Yu Shaozhi, except that he came
from Wuyuan in Anhui province, the status of this work is confirmed in a
poetic inscription dated 1916 by the great late Qing dynasty master Wu
Changshuo (1844–1927) which praises the quality of this calligraphy.

Hua Yan
China, 1682–1756
*Landscape in the style
of Mi Fu*
hanging scroll: ink on paper
129.5 x 61 image
Purchased with funds provided
by the Art Gallery Society of
New South Wales 1993
570.1993

Hua Yan was one of the
'Eight Eccentrics of
Yangzhou', an evocative
epithet coined to describe a
group of eighteenth-century
artists who challenged the
traditions of orthodoxy in
Chinese painting. Wang
Yuanqi (1642–1715), one
of the great masters of
early Qing painting and an
advocate of the true literati
tradition, bemoaned 'the
corrupt practices of the
Yangzhou artists…'. Hua Yan
was recognised as the most
versatile and technically accomplished of this group. In his time he was known
more for his bird and flower paintings than his landscapes, a contemporary
noting that 'he left out too much'. In terms of the real eccentricities of which
the artist was capable in his various styles, this scroll is a more substantial and
traditional painting, echoing the literati ideal of the great eleventh-century Song
painter, Mi Fu. Mi's style is distinguished by its wet-brush technique in which
there is an almost arbitrary definition of the landscape and its elements through
the chance configuration of splashed ink. It was a manner well suited to express
the literati ideal of the landscape as a metaphor for personal experience and
expression. Hua Yan, some six centuries later, demonstrates powerfully the
sense of continuity flowing through Chinese painting traditions, even in their
more radical forms.

Qing dynasty, Kangxi period

China, 1662–1722
Pair of vases c. 1680–1700
porcelain with *famille verte* decoration
27.5 and 28.5 heights
Purchased 1965
EC2.1965.1–2

The most celebrated product of the
great reigns of the early Qing dynasty
emperors was porcelain: vast amounts
were produced in the imperial kilns at
Jingdezhen. Porcelains such as these
were distinguished by their infinite
variety and supreme technical dexterity.
The term *famille verte*, coined by the nineteenth-century French collector Jules
Jacquemart, acknowledges the impact of shades of green in the painted enamel
decoration. Such wares – developed from the *wucai* or 'five-colour' painted
enamel porcelain of the previous Ming dynasty – rapidly became popular in the
early Qing, particularly during the reign of the Kangxi emperor. Not only were
they produced for the Manchu imperial court in Beijing; their ready appeal and
highly coloured exotic decoration made *famille verte* porcelains popular in the
courts of European nobility. These vases – decorated with patterns of a singing
bird perched on a prunus tree, surrounded by fantastic rock formations – are
very much in the Chinese style. The bases are painted in manganese and black
to simulate wood.

Qing dynasty, Yongzheng-Qianlong period

China, 1723–1795
Wine cup decorated in doucai *colours*
1725–1750
porcelain decorated in underglaze blue and
overglaze enamel colours, 3.9 x 8.1
Gift of J. Hepburn Myrtle 1992
193.1992

Reference to and reverence for the past are enshrined in the Chinese artistic
tradition. Just as painters sought to achieve the lofty ideals of earlier masters, so
potters sought to emulate the refined achievements of their predecessors. This
exquisite wine cup demonstrates that the extraordinarily fine porcelains of the
Chenghua period (1467–87) of the Ming dynasty were a natural source of
inspiration for the technically accomplished potters of the early Qing. In all
respects the vessel emulates its Chenghua precursors. The perfection of the
almost miniature form is matched by the quiet refinement of the underglaze blue
decoration and the subtle exuberance of the overglaze enamels. The *doucai*
technique, meaning 'contending' or 'contrasting colours', juxtaposes the bright
but transparent enamel colours – in this case red, green, yellow, turquoise and
pale aubergine – with the softer tone of the underglaze blue.

Qing dynasty, Qianlong period

China, 1736–1795
Moonflask with a design on each side of a dragon and a flaming pearl
porcelain decorated in underglaze blue and underglaze red, 30.5 height
Purchased 1964
EC1.1964

The Qianlong reign is regarded as one of the most significant in the history
of the ceramic art of China, largely because of the massive production at the
imperial kilns under the relentless patronage of the emperor. Renowned for his
culturally gregarious nature, the Qianlong emperor enormously enriched the
imperial art collections in the Forbidden City. This moonflask, with waves and
clouds painted in underglaze blue and a rampant dragon in underglaze red, is
a product of the imperial kilns. It is also a testimony to the faultless technical
standards that were achieved, particularly in the handling of the volatile
underglaze red. On the base of the flask the six-character mark of the Qianlong
emperor is painted in underglaze blue. His domain is described in abbreviated
form in the decoration. The benevolent rain-bearing dragon represents the
authority and power of the imperial throne; the clouds and the waves two basic
elements of the universe.

Ren Bonian
China, 1840–1896
Figure in a boat under a wintry tree dated 1893
hanging scroll; colours and ink on paper, 114.3 x 48.2
Purchased 1988
395.1988

Orphaned in his early teens Ren Bonian, also known as Ren Yi, was apprenticed to a fan shop in Shanghai where he learned to paint and to forge the work of the then well-known and established artist Ren Xiung (1820–57). He subsequently became Ren Xiung's pupil. Ren Bonian gained his fame as a portrait and figure painter but is equally well known for his bird and flower subjects. This example is fully characteristic of his style: eloquent, sparse, delicate, with the brush strokes echoing against the empty space of the background. The inscription, also written by Ren Bonian, reads: 'Painted by Ren Yi Bonian in his studio in Shanghai in the third month of the *guizi* year of the Guangxu reign' (1893).

Wu Changshuo

China, 1844–1927
Loquats 1918
hanging scroll: ink and colour
on paper, 181.5 x 82
Purchased 1987
460.1987

Wu was one of the leading
artists of the Shanghai school
of painting, distinguished by
its qualities of immediacy
and directness, as well as its
strong colours. The part
played by the artists of the
Shanghai school in the
renaissance of Chinese
painting traditions at the end
of the nineteenth century is
well recognised. Painted by
the master in his seventy-
fifth year, this scroll typifies
Wu's energetic style marked
by a graphic bravura, both
in the painting and in the
calligraphy. Indeed Wu is
recognised not only as a painter, but as a calligrapher, seal-carver and poet. The
subject of the mature and ripening loquats combined with the energy of the
brushwork seems to echo a sense of regeneration in the elderly artist. The poem
is also written by Wu:

> *During the May 5th festival,*
> *the good food ripens with the warm wind,*
> *though its colour is like yellow gold*
> *that hardly relieves poverty.*
> *Placed with pomegranate flowers on the table for appreciation.*
> *In the* wuwu *year four days before the ninth day of September,*
> *a guest in the Qu Zhi Sui Yuan studio,*
> *Wu Changshuo at the age of seventy-five.*
>
> *Hanging on the wall,*
> *resembling Li Futang's old brushwork.*
>
> *Written by a Fu-Daoist at Chan Bi Xian studio.*

Wang Zhen
China, 1867–1938
Nine years facing the wall
hanging scroll: ink and colour on
paper, 148.3 x 80.5
Purchased 1989
338.1989

This endearing and robust image
of the Buddhist deity Bodhidharma
is a testament to the imaginative
combination of tradition and
modernity in late nineteenth and
early twentieth century painting.
It also testifies to the enduring
tradition of the 'amateur' in the
scholar–artist tradition, for Wang
Zhen took to painting relatively
late in life, having previously been a successful and wealthy Shanghai
businessman. As a pupil of Wu Changshuo, Wang was known initially for his
bird and flower paintings but is now more often associated with his images
of Buddhist subjects. Bodhidharma was the chief patriarch of Zen Buddhism,
a popular figure owing to his eccentric life and traditionally slightly wild and
unkempt appearance. According to legend Bodhidharma achieved enlightenment
after spending nine years staring at a blank wall. This empathy with the
Buddhist ideal is alluded to in the inscription on the right by the well-known
Beijing intellectual of the time, Cai Yuanpei. The poem, by Wang, is an ode to
Bodhidharma:

> *Nine years facing the wall,*
> *shadow impressed on stone;*
> *to move is not as good*
> *as it is to remain stationary.*

The scroll is then signed *Bailong Shanren* (white dragon hermit).

Qi Baishi

China, 1863–1957
Gourds on a trellis 1945–47
hanging scroll: ink and colour on
paper, 137 x 61
Purchased 1986
96.1986

Qi Baishi is the quintessential
master of contemporary Chinese
painting. His work embodies
the qualities of freshness, colour
and audacious brushwork that
characterised traditional
painting in China around the
turn of the nineteenth century.
Born in Hunan province, Qi was
plagued by illness in his youth
and learnt carpentry in an
attempt to improve his health.
Although always interested in
painting, it was not until his
late thirties that Qi began to
formally study painting and
poetry, initially with the great
scholar Wang Xiangyi. As his
career progressed Qi became the
most established Chinese artist
of the twentieth century. Later in
life, following the foundation of
the People's Republic in 1949,
his achievement was recognised
in a number of positions and
honours, including his 1953
appointment by the Chinese
government as 'People's Artist'.

This is a classic work by Qi, brimming with a vitality and optimism that belies
his eighty-plus years. Always the master of the *xieyi* – the 'spontaneous' manner
of writing or defining – this scroll demonstrates the artist's delight in his subject
and in the experience of painting. Gourds are commonly seen as symbols of
immortality. Qi is equally well known for his often eccentric insect, bird, flower
and fish paintings, accomplished in the typical *xieyi* style with a few evocative
and spontaneous flourishes of the brush. The inscription, also by Qi, reads:

> *Presented to Lo Shan*
> *in the third month of the yiyou year (1945) on a fine day.*
> *I made this large painting*
> *which made me very happy and not a bit tired,*
> *and I dedicate the painting with this calligraphy.*
> *Baishi at the age of eighty-three years.*

Wu Zuoren
China, b. 1908
Camels in the Gobi desert dated 1977
hanging scroll: ink on paper, 69.8 x 45.7
Gift of Graham Fraser 1993
591.1993

The work of Wu Zuoren is a wonderful example of the timeless quality in the art of Chinese painting. The great tradition of ink painting in which his style is so steeped is centuries old, and yet here it is expressed in an entirely modern idiom. In his early years Wu studied with another master of modern Chinese painting, Xu Beihong, and then from 1930 to 1935 he studied and worked in France and Belgium. His distinctive use of broad wet brush strokes in the *mogu-hua* or 'boneless' manner, used here to infer the volumes and mass of the camels, hints at the Western tradition that he sought to imbue into the Chinese style. Wu is renowned for his evocative images of camels, yaks, oxen and pandas. The title reads *damo*, 'great desert', and is signed and dated 1977.

Li Shaoyan
China, b. 1918
Struggle 1942
woodcut, 29.3 x 27.5
Purchased 1993
515.1993

The pioneers of the modern woodcut in China were those adventurous young artists who went abroad to study Western art in the early twentieth century, bringing back new ideas and techniques. During the 1930s and 1940s the turmoil of protest and civil war gave rise to a new woodcut movement influenced by the potent prints of Western artists such as Käthe Kollwitz. Unlike the traditional woodblock prints with their expressions of harmony and propriety, these works graphically convey feelings of suffering and struggle as vividly illustrated in this violent image of individual resistance against the Japanese invasion, in which a small, feeble Chinese woman viciously bites the enemy soldier. Li Shaoyan, a native of Shandong, was a member of the Eighth Route Army during the resistance against the Japanese invasion.

Xu Kuang and Age
China, b. 1938 and 1948
Master 1978
woodcut, 58 x 58
Purchased 1993
522.1993

After turbulent years of social, political and economic turmoil, Chinese graphic art again enjoyed a vigorous revival in the late 1970s. As a potent example of this first harvest, *Master* harks back to the spirited realism of the woodcut movement of the 1930s and 1940s, but embraces photographic naturalism in its close observation of a real person, wrinkled by the sun and dirty from tilling the soil. It encapsulates the idea that following liberation the people were masters of their own country. After graduating from the middle school attached to the Central Academy of Fine Arts in Beijing, Xu Kuang concentrated on the woodcut at Chongqing in Sichuan. In collaboration with Age, a graduate of the Sichuan Academy of Fine Arts, he created some outstanding graphic works, including *Master*, which was awarded the gold medal at the Fifth Chinese National Art Exhibition in 1979. It also won an honorary award at the Fifth International Graphic Arts Competition held in Norway.

Su Xinping
China, b. 1960
The open grasslands 1991
lithograph, 56.5 x 79
Purchased 1992
181.1992

By the beginning of the 1990s Chinese artists were confidently experimenting
with the various options available through the adaptation of Western styles to
Chinese idioms, as can be seen in this lithograph by Su Xinping. Surrealism and
photo-realism have been absorbed into the artist's repertoire, resulting in this
disturbing and enigmatic evocation of an unspecified place in remote Inner-
Mongolia. While the four figures are precisely drawn and modelled, their actions
remain cryptic and the sharp spotlight from the viewer's right (traditionally the
East) creates an ambiguous stage-like setting. Su Xinping's formal training in
the arts began in 1979 at the painting department of the Tianjin Institute of
Fine Arts. He worked as an art teacher in Inner Mongolia before resuming his
studies and graduating from the printmaking department of the Central
Academy of Fine Arts where he is now a lecturer.

Xu Lele
China, b. 1955
Teaching the classical canon 1997
album leaf: ink and colour on paper, 37 x 58
Purchased 1997
365.1997

Xu Lele is a young female artist from Nanjing who brings the great tradition of literati painting in China into a humorous, almost satirical, contemporary idiom. The scene of the scholar seated, in his long flowing robes, on the dais and beside him the young acolyte reading the text, surrounded by the scholar's accoutrements of scrolls, inkstone and brush, is a typical composition of the Ming dynasty (1368–1644). But here the amusingly droll expressions on the faces of scholar and acolyte, and the eloquent modelling of the brush washes, betray a late twentieth-century modernity. Xu belongs to a group of artists living and working in Nanjing, many of whom have received some 'Western' art training, and who are committed to instilling Chinese painting traditions with the spirit and imagination of the modern age.

Koryŏ period

Korea, 918–1392
Cup stand of lotus form with five-petalled flange early 12th century
stoneware with celadon glaze
6 height, 14.5 overall diameter
Gift of J. Hepburn Myrtle 1989
253.1989

Celadons of the Koryŏ period are
among the most celebrated works of
Korean art. In this piece the combination of the naturalistically inspired lotus
petal form with the abstract qualities of the glaze and texture have produced an
object of the highest artistry and sophistication. Like the majority of the Koryŏ
celadon repertoire, the cup stand derives from Song dynasty Chinese prototypes:
wares distinguished by their simple and refined forms and the exquisite lustre
of their glazes. The unusual shape of this cup stand harks back to the silver
and lacquer types of Tang dynasty China (eighth century), which combined the
offering cup and separate stand into a single unit. The ceramic version was
refined in the Song dynasty, most especially by potters at the rarefied imperial
Ru ware kilns in Henan province.

Yoon Kwang-Cho

Korea, b. 1946
Punch'ŏng ware jar c. 1990
stoneware, 39 height
Purchased with assistance from
an anonymous donor 1992
198.1992

In a seeming contradiction of its
substance as an object, this unusual
jar carries inscriptions from a
Buddhist text on nothingness. The
potter, a Buddhist who lives in the
mountains of Kwangju, believes that
dedication and painstaking effort are
an essential part of the creative
process. His work is praised for its
individuality and for its imaginative
embrace of antiquity, particularly the
austere but beautiful aesthetic of the uniquely Korean *punch'ŏng* (literally
'powder green') ceramics of the fifteenth and sixteenth centuries. In this
engaging object the artist has employed the *sgraffito* technique in which the
vessel, made in this case by the coiling method, is then beaten and its surface
scoured in an instant 'maturing' process before being covered with a white
slip. The characters have then been scratched through the thin slip. This rich
combination of contemporary individuality with a spirit of antiquity expresses
the ideals of purity, honesty and humble sparseness so admired by the
connoisseurs and tea masters of modern Japan.

Heian period
Japan, 794–1185
Figure of Amida Buddha 11th–12th century
nutmeg wood with black lacquer and some gilding, 53.5 height excluding pedestal
Purchased with assistance from the W. H. Nolan Bequest 1984
119.1984

This classic image of the Amida Buddha echoes the qualities of formality and spiritual serenity so characteristic of the Buddhist art of Japan. The personification of eternal life, compassion and boundless light, Amida is the Buddha who reigns over the Western Paradise. He is the central deity of the Pure Land sect of Buddhism that had its foundations in the teachings of the fourth-century Chinese monk Hui Yuan, and grew to become the most popular sect of the faith in East Asia. Central to its teachings is the doctrine that for rebirth in the Pure Land nothing more than the constant invocation of the name of Amida is required. In Japan, under the inspiration of the Heian period monk Genshin (942–1017), the sect gained immense influence: not only through its promise of a passage to the Paradise, but also through Genshin's colourful descriptions of the Western Paradise and the beguiling imagery and art they stimulated. Carved from a hard, dense nutmeg wood – with that inherent feeling for the qualities of the material for which the Japanese artist and craftsman are so admired – the image conveys the peace, harmony and spiritual certainty that is the promise of the Western Paradise of Amida.

Kamakura period

Japan, 1185–1332
Taima mandala early 14th century (detail)
hanging scroll: ink and colour with gold on silk, 146 x 138
Art Gallery of New South Wales Foundation Purchase 1991
369.1991

The *Taima mandala* is one of the most celebrated of the group of works of
early Japanese Buddhist art known as the Pure Land mandalas. The prototypes
for these mandalas, sacred diagrams of the cosmos, were established in eighth-
century China when the Paradise sutras and the realms of Amitabha (Amida)
Buddha were gaining widespread popularity. The Chinese sense of order and
design is pervasive in the complex layout of gardens, landscape, temples and
architecture, all occupied by numerous Bodhisattvas, deities and divine attendants.
This painted version of the *Taima mandala* faithfully replicates the silk original,
which according to legend was woven in the eighth century, and is still housed
in the Taima-dera monastery south of the ancient capital of Nara. The design is
dominated by the central figure of Amida Buddha, attended by his Bodhisattvas
Kannon (Avalokitesvara) and Seishi (Mahasthamaprapta), along with a rich host
of deities, attendants and celestial musicians, all presiding over their Western
Paradise. The borders also follow the original layout. Depicted on the left
side is the story of Prince Ajatasatru. On the right are thirteen of the sixteen
contemplations embodying the essentials of Sakyamuni Buddha's teachings.
These teach the devotee how to visualise and thereby realise within himself the
glories of the Pure Land. Along the lower edge the three remaining contemplations
are divided into the nine possible degrees of rebirth into the Western Paradise.

Momoyama period
Japan, 1568–1615
The arrival of the Portuguese
single six-fold screen: ink and colours on gold-leafed paper, 152 x 369
Purchased 1996
301.1996

The first Westerners to reach the shores of Japan were Portuguese seamen
who, on route to their regular trading posts in South-east Asia, were blown
off course in 1542. Subsequently the Portuguese established trading posts in
Japan (initially in Nagasaki), and the arrival of these strange people with their
odd clothes and seemingly invincible ships naturally caused immense curiosity
among the Japanese. These new and unexpected arrivals were known as
namban, 'southern barbarians', as they always arrived in Japan from the south.
Their presence, and the Japanese fascination with these exotic commercial
itinerants, gave rise to a whole artistic genre. This beautiful and atmospheric
screen was originally one of a pair. It is an exceptional example of this relatively
rare genre, combining the classic Japanese sensitivity to seasonal moods, and the
abstract stylisation of the Japanese decorative instinct. The screen illustrates an
ascending hierarchy from left to right; beginning with the group of three
servants, one of whom is holding a dog on a leash. In the centre is a senior
member of the ship's crew, and on the right the captain-major.

Edo period
Japan, 1615–1868
Rakuchū-rakugai zu (Views in and around Kyoto) c. 1660
left screen of a pair of six-fold screens: colour and gold on paper, 125 x 369.8
Purchased with funds provided by Kenneth Myer 1980
7.1980.1–2

Following a long period of strife and civil wars in the fifteenth century, the ancient political and cultural capital of Kyoto was restored to its earlier splendour in the sixteenth and seventeenth centuries. This reconstruction is documented and lauded in screens such as these which, in their panoramic view, record with accuracy and detail the features of the city. Looking eastwards across the Kamo River towards the Higashimaya hills, the area beyond the river at the top of the screens is *rakugai* (without the city), while the area below is *rakuchū* (within the city). The lower section of each screen illustrates the busy mercantile life of Kyoto, with the townspeople going about their business in stores and workshops. On the far left of the left screen is the Imperial Palace.

Edo period
Japan, 1615–1868
Ko-Kutani ware bottle late 17th century
porcelain painted with coloured enamels
20.1 height
Purchased 1979
212.1979

Ko-Kutani or 'old Kutani' wares are distinguished by their brightly coloured and graphically strong decoration. This square-shaped sake bottle, painted in overglaze enamels, is dominated by four panels of similar but not identical landscape and flower designs. The bright and unexpected green, blue and yellow mountains and rocks; the red trees and green pagodas, set against a brilliant white, are startling in their effect, as are the two panels of flowering *nadeshiko* pinks. Ko-Kutani ware takes its name from the village of Kutani on the west coast of Japan's main island, Honshu, in Kaga prefecture. It was here, reputedly in 1661, that the Maeda clan began producing porcelain that was distinguished by its colourful overglaze enamel decoration. By around 1700 the industry had lost its vitality and the kilns closed. Early in the nineteenth century they were re-established to produce a later variant known as Ao-Kutani, or 'green' Kutani ware.

Edo period
Japan, 1615–1868
Suzuribako (Inkstone case) 17th century
lacquered wood decorated in *nashiji* and gold *takamaki-e*, inlaid with silver and gold foil
4.2 x 33 x 23.1
Gift of Mr Klaus Naumann 1989
346.1989

The care and quality of the craftsmanship lavished on a box such as this is a testament to the high esteem in which the objects and utensils for writing and painting are held in both Japan and China. The practice of using a smooth dark stone moistened with water for rubbing and preparing the solid ink was introduced from China; however the elaborate box with its partitions for brushes, ink sticks and a water dropper is more in keeping with the Japanese tradition. The lid is ornamented with a design of pine tree with pomegranate; the inside with a stylised fishing net and bird pattern. The technique of *nashiji* involves small flakes of gold of irregular shape and varying sizes being set in an almost random pattern in a bed of wet lacquer. *Takamaki-e* is a technique in which the design is built up in relief and modelled in a mixture of lacquer and charcoal or clay dust.

Kanō Einō

Japan, 1631–1697
Three friends 17th century
pair of six-fold screens: colour and gold on paper
each screen 167 x 359.5
Art Gallery of New South Wales Foundation Purchase 1994
638.1994.1–2

Confident, colourful, flamboyant yet at the same time elegant in their
composure and restraint, these screens illustrate the height of achievement in
the golden age of Japanese screen painting, the seventeenth century. The style
so richly expressed here had emerged in the Momoyama period (1568–1615)
when a brash and newly emergent samurai elite sought an ostentatious display
of their new-found wealth. The artists of the Kanō school from Kyoto were
the finest exponents of this new style, characterised by the distillation of the
Chinese tradition into a thoroughly Japanese aesthetic. This relationship is
realised in a series of opposites: monochrome against colour; emotion against
restraint; abstraction against realism. Particularly evident in this instance are
the bold, rich brush strokes characteristic of the Chinese influence, in
conjunction with the clear, bright colours and definitive sense of design that
are so distinctively Japanese. The symbolism too has its origins in the Chinese
tradition: the theme of the pine, bamboo and prunus – the so-called 'three
friends of winter' (known in Japanese as *shōchikubai*) – originated in
thirteenth-century China.

Genroku period
Japan, 1688–1703
Mount Sumiyoshi
single six-fold screen: ink, colour and gold on paper, 151 x 348.8
Purchased 1987
584.1987

A beautiful and classic evocation of the Japanese aesthetic, this screen portrays
the softly contoured hills of Mount Sumiyoshi near Osaka, partially shrouded
in clouds. In the top left the famous Shinto shrine built in honour of the gods
of the sea floats above the clouds, but nonetheless lends an air of material
reality to a scene clearly inspired more by the spirit of place and its poetic
resonances than by any specific resemblance. In some contrast the right section
of the screen illustrates lowly saltmakers on the shore, the figures rendered
with an endearing detail and not without humour. The semi-abstract quality
of the deliberately asymmetrical composition and the sumptuous combination
of greens and gold are characteristic of the native Japanese style of *yamato-e*
painting. This style, based on outline and flat colour, had its origins in the
literary interests of the Heian period, when such themes as the four seasons
and famous scenic places brought a fresh and distinctively Japanese inspiration
to native imagery and creativity.

Edo period

Japan, 1615–1868
Merrymaking in the garden mid-17th century
single six-fold screen: colour and gold leaf on paper, 74 x 201.4
Purchased 1986
41.1986

This rare and exquisitely painted screen, full of detail and sensitive observation,
illustrates the elite at play in the pleasure quarters. It is an early example of
the distinctive *ukiyo-e* tradition. The term *ukiyo-e*, literally translated as the
'floating world', was originally a Buddhist expression used to describe the sadly
irrelevant and transient nature of the material world and our life on earth.
By the seventeenth century Japan's medieval samurai-based culture was being
superseded by a newly emergent mercantile class. *Ukiyo-e* came to define a
whole tradition inspired by the colourful lives and times enjoyed by these
townspeople, *chōnin*, in the pleasure quarters and entertainment districts. Here,
in a series of enchanting vignettes, the picture of the pleasure quarters unfolds:
the activities of drinking, taking tea, playing games, listening to music, reading
and chatting are all illustrated.

Miyagawa Chōshun
Japan, 1683–1753
Portrait of an onnagata
c. 1713
hanging scroll: ink and
colour on paper, 110 x 53
Art Gallery of New South
Wales Foundation Purchase
1987
583.1987

A classic but bold *ukiyo-e* image, this beautifully poised figure conveys a mood of solitude and studied introspection which contrasts with the showy and dramatic costume. It is an image that combines, in that uniquely Japanese way, qualities of reticence and flamboyance. The nature of the dress, the small, tightly fitting cap, the theatricality of the pose, all suggest that this is an image of an *onnagata*, or female impersonator of the kabuki theatre. Kabuki developed in Edo Japan in response to a growing demand among the emergent mercantile class for a type of theatre more entertaining and accessible than the long-established classic noh theatre patronised by the upper classes. The Edo authorities sought to control possible abuse and prostitution in the new world of the kabuki by banning women and young boys from participating. Thus there arose a role for female impersonators and the *onnagata* became a skilled, highly appreciated and sought-after category of actors, known for their subtle and convincing portrayal of every nuance of female demeanour.

Katsukawa Shun'ei
Japan, 1762–1819
*Bijin (Portrait of a
beautiful woman)* 1790s
hanging scroll: ink and colour
on silk, 84 x 33
Purchased 1985
339.1985

A sense of deep sadness pervades
this image of a *bijin*, an idealised
beauty, as she sits in isolation
staring at a letter unrolled before
her, perhaps contemplating a
bleak future. Certainly there is
an air of despair, of rejection and
poignant introspection to the
image. The poem above, written
by the satirical poet and writer
of popular fiction Ōta Nampo
(1749–1823), tells of her plight
in commenting upon the life of
a courtesan:

> *A courtesan, twenty-seven
> years old,
> laments the ten years spent
> on the bitter ocean.
> Looking back,
> her life appears a mirage
> now she is leaving the quarter*

The expression 'bitter ocean' usually refers to life as a prostitute, and twenty-
six or twenty-seven was the usual age at which courtesans were released from
their contracts. Something of the harshness of such a life is subtly echoed in
the sharply outlined folds of the rich red kimono. The strong graphic character
of the image, the subject matter, and the bold colours and rich decorative effect
typify the unashamedly populist *ukiyo-e* style.

Watanabe Shikō
Japan, 1683–1755
Full moon over pine covered mountain
single two-fold screen: ink, gold and silver on paper, 168 x 184
Purchased with funds provided by Kenneth Myer 1990
105.1990

Nothing could be more telling of the unique Japanese aesthetic than the mysterious poetry of this screen, as abbreviated in its delivery as it is fulfilling in its effect. Watanabe Shikō belonged to the very Japanese Rinpa school of painting, named after Ogata Kōrin (1658–1716) with whom Shikō studied. The school's origins go back to the late sixteenth and early seventeenth centuries, when the artists Tawaraya Sōtatsu and Hon'ami Kōetsu sought to re-establish the brilliant style and unique sensitivity of the aristocratic art of Japan's 'golden age', the Heian period (794–1184). Hallmarks of the Rinpa school are a rich but refined decorative effect, achieved through an impeccable compositional balance; a fondness for metallic washes and inlays; and an emphasis on nature. Here the full autumn moon peers out from the mountainside, and pine trees are defined by a few sparse but expressive black ink strokes.

Hakuin Ekaku
Japan, 1685–1768
Three Shinto deities
hanging scroll: ink on silk, 110.2 x 35
Yasuko Myer Bequest Fund 1996
227.1996

The three inscriptions read:

> Centre: *The Shrine of Heaven illuminating great-august-God*
> Left: *Kasuga, the great illuminating God*
> Right: *Hachiman, the great Bodhisattva*

Hakuin is revered as one of the great teachers of the Rinzai sect of Zen Buddhism and is particularly known for his bold and emphatic large characters which reveal great expressive power, reflecting the spontaneous and subjective aspirations that are at the heart of Zen philosophy. The harmony between the complementary ideologies of Buddhism and the native Shinto is perfectly illustrated in this calligraphy, with its synthesis of Buddhist and Shinto messages, written by a Buddhist monk. The central line refers to Amaterasu, the principal female deity of Shinto mythology, deified as the sun goddess. Kasuga is the patron deity of the most powerful clan in Heian Japan, the Fujiwara. Hachiman is another popular Shinto deity, the god of war, who protects warriors and was adopted as the patron god of the Minamoto clan. In this scroll Hakuin has given Hachiman the Buddhist title of Maha-Bodhisattva, the great being of wisdom.

Nagasawa Rosetsu
Japan, 1754–99
Kanzan and Jittoku 1780s
hanging scroll: ink on paper,
157.7 x 81.8
Purchased 1985
338.1985

This eccentric pair were one of the most popular subjects among Zen painters. Kanzan and Jittoku were two monks who lived on Mount Tiantai in Tang dynasty China (618–906), where they were known as Han Shan and Shi De respectively. Kanzan, in the true Zen manner, was a hermit–poet who befriended Jittoku, a kitchen-hand in the nearby Guoqing temple. Jittoku would give his friend leftover food from the temple, and in return Kanzan would read his humble colleague his poems. Here Jittoku, holding a bamboo pail, scrutinises his friend's poem with studied concentration, while Kanzan's expression is one of shy anticipation. There is a rich harmony between the two: the kitchen-hand and the poet are equals. Although Rosetsu has carefully distinguished the two in his handling of the brushwork, Kanzan's sharp definitive lines contrast with Jittoku's more unruly brush strokes and washes. Born into the family of a low-ranking samurai, Rosetsu was a pupil of the great master and founder of the Maruyama school, Maruyama Ōkyo, but was expelled and became a versatile individualist. The characters Kanzan and Jittoku capture something of the artist's own spontaneous independence of spirit.

Tani Bunchō
Japan, 1763–1840
*Mountains in the
early summer rain*
dated 1826
hanging scroll: ink
and colour on paper,
174 x 96
Purchased with
funds provided by
Kenneth Myer 1987
461.1987

A conscious tribute
to the great land-
scape painting
tradition of the Song
and Yuan dynasties of China (eleventh to fourteenth centuries), this majestic
scroll also pays homage to the relentless and regenerative powers of nature.
Characteristically, the composition evolves vertically from the humble village
approached by a lone insignificant fisherman in the foreground, to a middle
ground dominated by soaring peaks and floating clouds, through to a
glimpse of distant peaks in the faintly defined background. Bunchō here
communicates two innately Japanese aesthetic concepts: *yūgen*, an appreciation
of the mysterious and the profound; and *aware*, a poignant reverie of sadness
at the passage of time. The artist is best known for his work, such as this scroll,
in the *nanga* or 'southern painting' style, based on the Chinese literati landscape
tradition. The inscription includes the title, date and signature of the artist.

Itaya Haruhiro
Japan, active 1820s
Parody of the Kasuga procession c. 1820 (detail)
handscroll: ink and colour on paper, 29.5 x 600
Purchased with funds provided by the Asian Collection Benefactors' Scheme 1995
125.1995

This *emakimono* (handscroll) depicts a popular subject known as *Hyakki Yagyō* (the Night Procession of One Hundred Demons). This subject, centring on the ancient Japanese belief that demons and goblins emerge with nightfall to parade until dawn, dates to the Heian period (704–1192), with numerous handscrolls on the theme having been painted since at least the fifteenth century. The scroll depicts a lively retinue of one-eyed goblins, bird-beak ogres and ugly monsters, reflecting on the one hand a Japanese delight in the grotesque, bizarre and humorous, but on the other a more serious intent of frightening the Buddhist faithful into good behaviour. Many of the goblins are the spirits of particular objects and this 'procession' parodies various religious rituals. The reference to the Kasuga procession in the title of this scroll implies that the goblins are mimicking the participants in the annual festival of the grand Kasuga Shrine in Nara.

Ōtagaki Rengetsu
Japan, 1791–1875
Untitled poem
hanging scroll: ink on paper,
29.4 x 41
Purchased 1994
19.1994

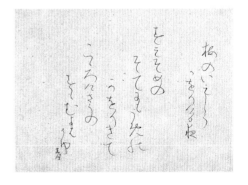

From an early age Rengetsu showed talents for poetry and swordsmanship. She married young, but as her husband died in 1823, and her four children also died at young ages, she entered the Buddhist priesthood and adopted the name Rengetsu, meaning Lotus Moon. She dedicated the rest of her life to writing poetry and making pottery, known as Rengetsu ware. This poem reads:

> *The evening is fragrant with plum blossoms*
> *Oh, this fragrance!*
> *It penetrates the black sleeves of my nun's habit*
> *Even though I have renounced the world,*
> *I enjoy dressing myself in this aromatic midnight scent.*

Kawabata Gyokushō
Japan, 1842–1913
Autumn maples and spring cherry blossoms
pair of two-fold screens: ink, colours and sprinkled gold on paper
each screen 163.2 x 86
David Wilson Bequest Fund 1997
419.1997.1-2

The late nineteenth and early twentieth centuries were an inspired time for artists
in Japan, who sought to infuse their traditions with modernity while retaining
an essential Japanese spirit. At the forefront were artists of the *nihonga* school,
experimenting with new techniques, often inspired by Western perspective and
chiaroscuro. In this brilliant and unusual pair of screens, the sense of the
contemporary is fused with the traditional. The emphatically rich colours of the
autumnal maples, punctuated with deeper moments in red, gold and pale green,
contrast with the quiet and economic aesthetic of spring cherry blossoms. The
white cherry blossom is bunched at the bottom of the screen, against an expanse
of gold-flecked sky and the silver-metallic ovoid shaped moon. The result is a
perfect study in ambiguity: in design and imbalance, space and denseness.
Kawabata Gyokushō was one of the most prominent of the *nihonga* artists at
the turn of the nineteenth century. The son of a *maki-e* lacquer artist, he studied

the Maruyama school
of *nihonga* and oil
painting technique
with Takahashi Yuichi,
Japan's first important
and influential oil
painter.

Taninaka Yasunori
Japan, 1897–1946
Ōkawa bank 1940
from the series 'New one
hundred views of Japan'
colour woodcut: 22.5 x 30
Yasuko Myer Bequest Fund 1997
8.1997.28

Taninaka was one of the most
talented and original print artists in
modern Japan whose work focused
on urban life. Taninaka stands out
among his peers for his originality and uninhibited imagination. In this print
Taninaka depicts Ōkawabata, a part of the Sumida River in Tokyo and a
popular picnic and entertainment destination since the Edo period, disturbingly
deserted. The atmosphere of disquiet would be even more intense and perturbing
for a Japanese viewer for whom Ōkawabata would resonate with pleasurable
associations of crowded days of merriment. This series of landscape prints
involving a number of artists and published by the Japan Print Association from
the late 1930s to early 1940s. As the war in the Pacific progressed, the authorities
stopped the series after thirty-nine prints had been published: they feared that
the Japanese interior might become known to the enemies.

Tsukioka Yoshitoshi
Japan, 1839–1892
*Looking smoky – appearance of the
housewife of the Kyōwa era* 1888
from the series 'Thirty-two aspects
of customs and manners'
colour woodcut, 36.7 x 24
Purchased 1991
368.1991

In terms of the centuries-old *ukiyo-e*
tradition, the period from the mid to
the end of the nineteenth century is
considered the 'decadent period', since
the prints are often characterised by
crude and violent subjects, by harshness
rather than delicacy, and by gaudy
synthetic colours rather than the delicate
vegetable dyes of earlier prints. Although
Yoshitoshi's works fall within the
'decadent' category, he was perhaps the
most creative of his contemporaries and capable of subtle, graceful compositions
as exemplified in this beautiful print which shows a middle-class woman
fanning a fire. The print belongs to the series 'Thirty-two aspects of customs
and manners', which depicts typical moments in the daily lives of women of
different social classes during the previous one hundred years.

Tsuruya Kōkei
Japan, b. 1946
Nakamura Tokizō as Kagaribi c. 1986
from the series 'Six images of
onnagata actors'
colour woodcut with mica, 38.7 x 25
Purchased with funds provided by
Yasuko Myer 1987
353.1987

Born into a family of painters, Kōkei spent
brief years as an office worker before he
began making woodblock prints of kabuki
actors in 1978. He taught himself all the
necessary printmaking skills with the motto
of 'self-learning, self-creating, self-executing'.
The extent of his technical skill is evident in
his use of ultra-sheer *ganpi* paper, which
retains the intensity of the ink but is difficult
to work with. All Kōkei's prints depict kabuki actors and he is the official
artist of a kabuki theatre. Most of his prints employ the traditional format –
okubi-e or 'large head picture' – in which the tension and emotion of the figure
are captured by exaggerated facial expressions and hand gestures.

Kon Michiko
Japan, b. 1955
Boot of shrimps 1995
gelatin silver photograph, 51.1 x 41.3
Purchased 1995
205.1995

Kon is one of the leading contemporary
photographers in Japan, whose
idiosyncratic images combine the
familiar shapes of everyday objects with
the unfamiliar textures of raw food.
The surreal images she thus creates not
only break a taboo (of playing with
food) but take the viewer into a realm
of fantasy. Kon began photography as
part of her training in printmaking at
Tokyo's Sōkei School of Art, from
which she graduated in 1978. By the 1980s she was exhibiting widely in Japan,
Europe and the United States, and was awarded the prestigious Kimura Ihee
Award in 1991. Concerning the 'texture' of her work, Kon recounts an incident
on a train when she saw a properly dressed teenage girl suddenly and quite
naturally begin licking the metal lock on the train window. Kon relates this
bizarre behaviour to her own desire to capture the uncommon, the peculiar
and the disconcerting in her photographs.

Kainoshō Tadaoto
Japan, 1894–1978
Mikaeri bijin
(*Woman looking
back*) c. 1925
hanging scroll: ink,
colour and gilt on
paper, 60.3 x 39.5
Purchased 1991
264.1991

As Japan struggled
to come to terms
with the new worlds
of mechanisation
and industrialisation,
forging closer ties
with the countries of the West in the late nineteenth and early twentieth
centuries, Japanese artists became embroiled in the processes of tumultuous
change. Long established and powerfully entrenched traditions were both
challenged and revitalised. In painting two distinctive attitudes emerged. One,
known as *yōga*, followed Western styles; the other, *nihonga*, extended the
Japanese tradition. In the nationalistic Taishō (1912–26) and early Shōwa
eras (1926–89) *nihonga* was the dominant style. Kainoshō, from Kyoto, was
a leading *nihonga* artist. In this beguiling figure he synthesises the Japanese
aesthetic with qualities of modernity, particularly evidenced in the colours and
graphic fluency. The drawing of the face and modelling of the features also
betrays some Western influence. In a biography of Kainoshō, Isamu Kurita
notes that the artist employed one particular model who, according to his sister,
was 'the only woman whom my brother, who preferred men to women, wanted
to marry'. The woman was Maruoka Tokuko, quite possibly the subject of this
painting. Previously the mistress of a stockbroker, she subsequently married a
doctor, while seemingly remaining Kainoshō's constant muse.

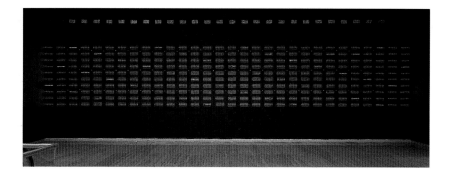

Tatsuo Miyajima
Japan, born 1957
Region No. 126701–127000 1991
installation, 300 LED lights, 190 x 1200
Purchased 1995 with funds from the Mervyn Horton Bequest
32.1995

While the main emphasis for twentieth-century collecting at the Art Gallery of New South Wales has been in Australian and European art, the Contemporary collection also represents Asian artists whose work complements and extends the direction of the collection. Miyajima is one of the most celebrated contemporary artists working in Japan today. The installation is a composition of units of red and green LED counters, the kind that appear everywhere in our daily lives, in watches, calculators, scoreboards, etc. The individual units count from 1 to 9, each with its own rhythm. The various timescales suggested can be seen as metaphors for our everyday existence. Miyajima's Buddhist beliefs are reflected in the work's sense of impermanence and interconnectedness. The artist describes his work as a new humanism based on Buddhism and wishes to bring art back into the realm of ordinary people.

Kushan dynasty
Pakistan (Ancient Gandara), Swat Valley
Seated meditating Bodhisattva stele 3rd century
grey schist, 77 height
Purchased 1997
7.1997

Originating in the north-west regions of present-day Pakistan and Afghanistan, the art of Gandhara represents a unique meeting of East and West. The Gandharan style is characterised by strong Hellenistic influences – a legacy of Alexander the Great's eastward expansions towards the end of the fourth century BC – modified by Persian and Indian elements. From these sources there emerged a remarkable new art that flourished during the first four centuries of the Christian era. This figure of a Bodhisattva is distinguished by its quiet and contemplative attitude, the distinctive face with prominent moustache, the flowing drapery, the ornate pedestal, and the right foot casually raised leaving an empty sandal on the footstool. The right hand lightly touches the head in a pensive gesture, and the left holds a covered casket or alms bowl. It is an image that beautifully and richly embraces its cosmopolitan heritage and lays the foundations for the great traditions of East Asian Buddhist sculpture.

Kushan dynasty

India, Uttar Pradesh, Mathura
Torso of Buddha 1st–2nd century
mottled red sandstone, 47 height
Gift of Alex Biancardi 1998
114.1998

This sandstone figure of a male torso is characteristic of the important Mathura school of art that flourished in Northern India under the rule of the Kushan dynasty which was at its height from the first to the third century CE. There were two major centres of Kushan culture: the region of Gandhara where the art shows the impact of Hellenistic and Roman sculpture; and the city of Mathura where the art displays a traditional Indian aesthetic, as demonstrated in this torso. This figure, carved in the distinctive red-coloured sandstone found around Mathura, wears a transparent robe draped over the left shoulder, with the folds of the robe gathered and carried over the closed fist. The lower garment is clearly decorated with a pattern of flowers. The modelled belly, deep navel and the aureoles of the chest are softly articulated, but the absence of the right hand, which would have been held in a specific *mudra*, precludes accurate identification of the figure.

Chandella dynasty

India, Madhya Pradesh, c. 900–1100
Female torso
carved sandstone, 53 height
Gift of the Margaret Hannah Olley
Art Trust 1990
239.1990

Founded early in the ninth century, the Chandella dynasty, one of thirty-six Rajput clans, was a major regional power by the tenth century. This female figure undoubtedly was part of the luxurious surface decoration typical of the external walls of Chandella religious monuments. The figure may be a *yakshi*, a female nature spirit whose erotic, sensual forms, charged with suggestions of fertility, were lovingly carved by medieval Indian sculptors. It embraces the Indian ideals of feminine beauty: full, perfectly formed breasts set close, a narrow waist, ample hips, elaborate jewellery that accentuates the soft tactility of the flesh, and an ornate headdress and earrings.

Hoysala dynasty
India, c. 1100–1310
The seven mother goddesses 13th century
chloristic schist, 40.5 x 98
Gift of Sir James Plimsoll 1978
6.1978

The powerful sense of rhythm evoked in this relief of Hindu deities suggests an infinity of figures, yet there are just eight principal images. Shiva, the supreme master of music and dance, is depicted on the far left above his vehicle, Nandi the bull. To his right are the seven mother goddesses or *matrikas*, the female counterparts of the most important male Hindu gods. Appearing in sequence from left to right are: Brahmani, the four-headed counterpart of Brahma, the maker of the universe; Maheshvari, the female counterpart of Shiva; Kaumari, the counterpart of Kumara, the warrior son of Shiva and Parvati; Vaishnavi, the counterpart of Vishnu, the principal god of preservation; the boar-headed Varahi, counterpart of Varaha, an incarnation of Vishnu; Indrani, the counterpart of Indra, the war and rain god of the *Vedas*; and finally, on the far right, is Chamunda, the only goddess who is not the counterpart of a male god, but represents a female form of Shiva's power. This beautiful and intricately carved panel is typical of the reliefs found on Hoysala period temples of the Deccan region of central India.

Mughal dynasty
India, 1526–1857
The Emperor Jehangir returning from a hunt c. 1610
gouache and gold leaf on paper, 19.7 x 11.1
Bequest of Miss G. Griffith 1968
EP1.1968

The Emperor Jehangir (reigned 1605–27) was, like his father Akbar, a great
patron of the arts. Under their enlightened and spirited rule Mughal India
embraced the cosmopolitan influence of Persian, European and Indian styles,
all of which are to be seen in this image of Jehangir astride an elephant, surveying
the scene of his hunting triumphs. The narrative is captured in the jewel-like
detail, the bright and engaging colours, the delicate strokes and the delight in
beauty. In the more distant reaches of the painting a leopard savages its prey
amid green rolling hills, with part of the emperor's retinue visible on the right.
The centre is dominated by Jehangir on his elephant, his attention caught by the
attendant holding a pair of geese; and in the foreground two more attendants
carry dead boar. Typical of the Persian influence in Mughal art are the luminous
greens which contrast so richly with the metallic grey of the elephant; the use of
relative scale to convey the significance of the subjects; and the interlocking hills
interspersed with figures that delineate a kind of perspective.

Kota school
India, Rajasthan
Vasant ragini c. 1770
opaque watercolour on paper heightened with gold, 18.2 x 12.2
Purchased 1997
82.1997

The most classic genre of Indian painting is that of the *ragamala*, literally
'garland of ragas', in which paintings are the visual equivalent of specific
musical *ragas* or melodies. There are six main *ragas*, each with a subordinate
raga referred to as a *ragini*. Of the six Indian seasons – summer, monsoon,
autumn, winter, cool season, spring – the *raga* most closely associated with
spring is that of Vasant. Since the major spring festival Holi is a predominantly
Vaishnava festival, the *raga* is also dedicated to the Vaishnava god Krishna.
This exquisite painting, rendered with a gem-cutter's precision, depicts Krishna
dancing to the music of three young women by a lotus-filled lake. Krishna
wears a distinctive layered dancing skirt, each layer a different colour, tasselled
shoes, a jewelled crown, and a long garland of white blossoms, while the body
is covered in pearls and jewels. This folio is from a large set of *ragamala*
pictures credited to Kota, a small Rajput kingdom in south-eastern Rajasthan.

Basohli school
India, Rajasthan
Ragaputra Velavala of Bhairava c. 1710
opaque watercolour with gold on paper, 15.8 x 16 (excluding border)
Margaret Hannah Olley Art Trust 1992
199.1992

The *ragamala* is a linked series of paintings based on the classical Indian musical form of the *raga*. This richly sensual gouache is a classic of the genre, part of an early *ragamala* from a princely state in the Punjab foothills of the Himalayas. The Basohli school, named after the region in which it flourished, specialised in poetic and lyrical subjects such as this: a pair of courtly lovers in a garden setting. Their tryst is set against a stylised and theatrical background of flaming orange, a colour favoured in Basohli practice. The aristocratic musician plays the *vina*, a traditional stringed instrument, while his consort offers him a betel leaf concoction. The sumptuous effect has been heightened with minute fragments of insect wings on the costumes.

Bundi school
India, Rajasthan
Rasalila c. 1850
gouache on paper; 61 x 80
Purchased 1995
216.1995

This exceptionally large and spectacular depiction of the Rasalila, the circular dance Krishna performs with the *gopis* (herd girls) may have been dedicated on the annual festival of the circular dance to a Bundi prince or to a shrine. It depicts Krishna in the centre dancing with Radha. Surrounding the couple is a row of dancing peacocks, each flanked by two excited hens. In the third circle Krishna is shown dancing with *gopis*, watched by a large group of gods, court musicians and admiring devotees. The Rasalila is the ultimate statement of the devotional cult of *bhakti*, a form of religion where the individual devotee achieved an immediate rapport with God and for which the most obvious symbol was Radha's intense longing for Krishna. The *gopis* are the symbol of those who find God by devotion (*bhakti*), without learning. The *gopis* forsake the illusion of family and duty to follow Krishna and dance with him in a ring when each one thinks that Krishna is dancing with her alone.

Jamini Roy
India, 1887–1972
Three men in a boat c. 1942
gouache on board, 27.8 x 40.5
Purchased 1994
20.1994

The robust immediacy, vibrant colours and daring simplicity of form in this painting identify the unique style of India's twentieth-century master Jamini Roy. Born in Bengal, of a typical rural family, Roy graduated from the Government School of Art, Calcutta, and initially produced fashionably 'modern' pictures indistinguishable from the works of many other contemporary Bengali artists. However, he went on to develop a distinctive style independent of the dominant Bengal school of modern Indian painting. In creating his own style, a modernist interpretation of the indigenous folk traditions of Bengal, he was particularly inspired by the dynamic art-form of Kalighat paintings, created in the nineteenth century by anonymous artists as souvenirs for pilgrims to the famous temple to the great goddess Kali. Characteristic of Roy's style is the use of bold black contours to contain strong simplified forms, brightly coloured with the earth and vegetable colours he preferred, imbued with an honest vigour and barely contained by the pictorial format. This painting was acquired directly from the artist in 1942 when he was producing some of his best work and before he succumbed to the pressure of an increasing popularity that forced him to churn out many lesser works.

Bhupen Khakhar
India, born 1934
Bathing ghat 1992
colour lithograph, 37.5 x 53.5
Purchased 1994
356.1994

Bhupen Khakhar is one of India's leading painters. He also works with water-colour and printmaking. He lives an openly gay life in Baroda, an industrial town half-way between Mumbai (Bombay) and New Delhi. Bhupen Khakhar paints everyday, middle-class life in an Indian urban environment. His oil paintings and watercolours, influenced by Indian miniature painting and popular Indian calendar art, take no regard of perspectival accuracy and instead present figures in looming dark and anchorless spaces. One has the sense that his paintings represent stage sets for homosexual dramas. His treatment of the theme is often humorous as well as radical, as his embracing men are depicted in the context of Indian temple life or mythology. The artist draws on the sexual ambiguity in traditional Indian art as the inspiration for his work.

Nalini Malani
India, born 1946
page from 'The Degas Suite' 1992
book, mixed media on paper, 22.8 x 29.3
Purchased 1994
357.1994

Nalini Malani lives in Mumbai (Bombay). She works with watercolour books,
drawings, installations and performance. The Gallery has in its collection two
of her books, the 'Hieroglyph series' and 'The Degas Suite'. A sense of
fragmentation and displacement is at the heart of Nalini Malani's work. Her
parents were from Karachi and the family had to leave in 1947 because of
Partition. Much of Malani's work is also based on the varied and fractured
lifestyles in the district Lohar Chawl (electric market) where the artist's studio is
located. In this area of Mumbai various strata of society live with one another.
In 'The Degas Suite', Nalini Malani has reinterpreted the drawings by the
French Impressionist, Edgar Degas, superimposing other drawings based on the
streets of Mumbai. Malani considers the relationship between Indian
contemporary life and the modernist traditions of Europe.

Angkor period

Cambodia, 802–1431
Elephant-shaped jar 11th–12th century
stoneware with dark brown glaze to lower
body, legs unglazed, 21 height
Purchased 1981
156.1981

This inspired and original interpretation of
a globular-shaped pot bears the instantly
recognisable features of an elephant. Revered
by the Khmer people in their daily lives, the
animal also appears in much Buddhist and
Hindu iconography. This particular example is a stunning marriage of
ornamental impulse and practical need. Ceramics such as this were neither
ceremonial vessels nor ritual objects, but articles of daily use. Because they were
not made for export they remained free of outside influences, retaining their
highly distinctive Khmer character. Made from a light buff coloured low fired
stoneware, and covered with a brittle brown glaze that is prone to flaking, such
wares are the hallmark products of the Khmer ceramic tradition.

Angkor period

Cambodia, 802–1431
*Bas-relief of two dancing
apsaras* 12th century
stone, 57.2 x 47
Florence Turner Blake Bequest
Fund 1967
EV2.1967

Khmer art finds its most memorable and durable expression in
the magnificent stone sculptures
that adorned the palaces and
temples of the god-kings; especially those at Angkor, one of
the most remarkable capitals of
the ancient world. By the end
of the eighth century a state religion had emerged in Cambodia
that combined elements of
Buddhist and Hindu thought into a new theology in which the traditional
Cambodian concept of ancestor worship maintained its central role. It was this
concern that was behind the emergence of the Hindu *devaraja*, literally god-
king, in whom all secular and religious power was vested. Under the patronage
and inspiration of the kings of Angkor, Khmer sculptors produced distinctive and
beautiful monuments such as this relief illustrating a pair of *apsaras* – female
celestial beings – dancing on lotus blossoms, the Buddhist symbol of purity. Both
stylistically and iconographically this panel bears witness to the rich heritage of
Buddhist and Hindu art, while demonstrating a distinctive Khmer character.

Pagan

Burma, late 12th century
Seated Buddha
brass and copper, 12 height
Purchased 1997
83.1997

Early Buddhist images from Burma have
distinctive stylistic qualities that distinguish
them from their South-east Asian counterparts.
The broad forehead, slightly Mongoloid
eyes, tapering face and high *ushnisha* – the
cranial bump that symbolises the Buddha's
wisdom – are all distinctively Burmese features.
In Burmese Buddhism, which followed the
Theravada path, the dominant figure is Akshobhya, represented here. In this
characteristic pose the Buddha is seated with feet upturned, bearing wheel
marks on his soles. A button-like protuberance on his forehead resembles the
urna. The left hand rests face up on the lap in the meditation *mudra*; the right
hangs with the tips of the outstretched fingers touching the ground in the
bhumispara mudra. With this gesture the Buddha invokes the earth to witness
his resistance of the temptations of the spirit of evil, Mara.

Ly dynasty

Vietnam, c. 1420–1787
*Large dish with a
central medallion
depicting a crane with
pine and bamboo*
15th century
porcelain with underglaze
blue decoration
38 diameter
Purchased 1991
7.1991

The ceramic traditions of
Vietnam, which date back
to the first century AD,
were strongly influenced
by those of its omnipresent
northern neighbour, China.
The so-called 'golden age'
of Vietnam – the Ly and Tran dynasties – commenced with Vietnam's independence from China. During a subsequent and short-lived Chinese incursion in
the fifteenth century, the great innovation of blue and white porcelain came to
Vietnam with migrant potters from the north. Characteristic of the Vietnamese
style is the unglazed rim, suggesting that it was fired upside down, and the speckled
grey-blue colour of the painted design. The design – a crane amid bamboo and
pine (traditional symbols of longevity), with scrolling floral motifs – also echoes
the Chinese style.

Rama III period

Thailand, 1824–1851
Phan waen pah
(*Two-tiered receptacle*)
black lacquer with mother-of-pearl inlay, 38 height
Purchased 1993
523.1993

The skill and dedication required to make fine lacquer objects such as this had a natural parallel in Buddhist devotions. For this reason the utensils, furniture and fittings that adorned the more important and wealthy Buddhist temples were usually flamboyant objects that glittered with subtle reflections of mother-of-pearl. Elaborate trays like this were used in Buddhist ceremonies by the monks, who would place their robes on the upper pedestal before an image of the Buddha. A classic and uniquely Thai form, this receptacle is decorated with seated *thepanom* – minor Buddhist deities – and floral-inspired ornamental motifs that echo the Buddhist decorative style. Thailand is renowned for its distinctive *hoi fai*, or flaming mother-of-pearl, made from the shell of the turbo snail that is indigenous to the Gulf of Thailand.

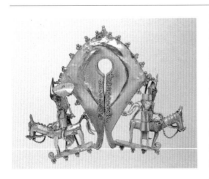

Indonesia, East Sumba

Mamuli 19th–early 20th century
gold, 9 height
Edward and Goldie Sternberg Southeast Asian Art Purchase Fund 1992
265.1992

Ear pendants (*mamuli*) were part of the store of sacred heirlooms, along with old textiles and porcelains, handed down through the noble families of the island of Sumba, at the eastern end of the Indonesian island chain. Secret and ritualistic objects, *mamuli* were brought down from dark attic stores by the *rato*, or priest, and used in ceremonies to make contact with the spirits (*marapu*). It was only for special occasions such as funerals that these spiritually charged objects were released from their dark hiding places, for fear that their great powers would bring havoc and disaster upon those who saw them. With such powers accorded them the *mamuli* were regarded as emblems of the social and political powers of a family and its lineage.

Indonesia, Central Java
Figure of Ganesha 10th century
volcanic grey buff stone, 67 height
Anonymous gift 1985
178.1985

The most common account of how Ganesha obtained his elephant head relates
to the occasion when Ganesha, then a handsome youth created by Parvati
from the slough of her skin, was decapitated by Shiva's hordes (*gana*) when
Ganesha, on Parvati's instructions, barred Shiva from entering her apartment.
To appease Parvati's anger at the loss of her son, Shiva sent out his followers
with instructions to sever the head of the first living creature they encountered
which was an elephant. Ganesha has become one of the most popular of the
Hindu gods. In this image, his corpulent body sits on a double lotus throne
with the soles of his human feet touching. This pose, unknown in India, is
unique to Java and Cambodia. The snake coiled around the sacred thread
across his chest, the elaborate headdress with a crescent moon and a skull, as
well as the vertical third eye in the centre of his forehead, all indicate his close
association with the Hindu god Shiva. Of his four arms, his front right hand
holds his broken tusk; his front left hand (now missing) would have held a
bowl full of rice, sweets or jewels, while his two posterior hands would have
held an axe and a fly whisk.

INDEX